The Enterprise Engineering Series

Enterprise Engineering is an emerging discipline for coping with the challenges (agility, adaptability, etc.) and the opportunities (new markets, new technologies, etc.) faced by contemporary enterprises, including commercial, nonprofit and governmental institutions. It is based on the paradigm that such enterprises are purposefully designed systems, and thus they can be redesigned in a systematic and controlled way. Such enterprise engineering projects typically involve architecture, design, and implementation aspects.

The Enterprise Engineering series thus explores a design-oriented approach that combines the information systems sciences and organization sciences into a new field characterized by rigorous theories and effective practices. Books in this series should critically engage the enterprise engineering paradigm, by providing sound evidence that either underpins it or that challenges its current version. To this end, two branches are distinguished: Foundations, containing theoretical elaborations and their practical applications, and Explorations, covering various approaches and experiences in the field of enterprise engineering. With this unique combination of theory and practice, the books in this series are aimed at both academic students and advanced professionals.

Pedro Sousa • André Vasconcelos

Enterprise Architecture and Cartography

From Practice to Theory;
From Representation to Design

 Springer

Pedro Sousa
Instituto Superior Técnico
University of Lisbon
Lisbon, Portugal

André Vasconcelos
Instituto Superior Técnico
University of Lisbon
Lisbon, Portugal

ISSN 1867-8920   ISSN 1867-8939   (electronic)
The Enterprise Engineering Series
ISBN 978-3-030-96266-1   ISBN 978-3-030-96264-7   (eBook)
https://doi.org/10.1007/978-3-030-96264-7

This Springer imprint is published by the registered company Springer Nature Switzerland AG
The registered company address is: Gewerbestrasse 11, 6330 Cham, Switzerland

To my friends José Tribolet, André Sampaio, and Ricardo Leal, for all the inspiring discussions about these themes.
To my wife Maria and my sons Miguel and Marta.
Pedro Sousa

To my wife, Ana
my children, Leonor, Diana and Helena
and my parents, Fernanda and Fernando.
André Vasconcelos

Foreword

Warning

I bear a very special relationship with the authors of this book, so be aware of the implicit bias this foreword inevitably possesses. The authors are Professors of Information Systems at the Department of Computer Science and Engineering (DEI) of IST, University of Lisbon, where I was Full Professor until my retirement 2 years ago. With Pedro Sousa, I had the privilege to initiate the teaching of Information Systems Architecture two decades ago, in the then novel specialized curriculum of Information Systems of the Computer Science and Engineering Bachelor and Master of Science Degrees. André Vasconcelos has done his Ph.D. thesis under my supervision, and we all have been involved in the establishment and development of Enterprise Engineering, since 2004 to the present day.

All of us have been very active also in research, supervising many M.Sc. and Ph.D. students, while pursuing also professional activities as practicant engineers, in private and public companies and in public administration institutes and departments.

About This Book

This book represents a major milestone in the maturation and the alignment of the fundamental concepts that our Lisbon pole of Enterprise Engineering has focused on after these two decades. The authors present in the book their specialized views, which are naturally distinct from each other given their specific research and professional focus, in an integrated and coherent way, a feat only possible by their vast experience in jointly teaching M.Sc. and Ph.D. courses.

My recommendation to someone with potential interest in enterprise architecture and trying to decide whether this book is worth paying attention to is to read first, slowly and reflexively, Chap. 2—Founding Concepts. Understanding the deep relation between Systems and Architecture, as it concerns the human capability to deal intelligently and purposefully with Enterprises, both individually as collectively, is a solid and sound starting point to benefit in full from the pedagogical exposition of the different subjects presented in the book.

The book addresses the two most relevant dimensions of Enterprise Architecture, representation and design, detailing in the several chapters both theoretical and practical aspects relevant for these purposes.

I choose to emphasize in this foreword the relevance of Enterprise Cartography, as the means for humans to apprehend and comprehend the context, the facts, the actions, the evidences, and the effects that occur with their enterprise context, with a shared semantic and ontological context.

The availability of proper, truthful, real-time Enterprise Cartography, enabling effective and efficient communication among all Enterprise collaborators, maximizes the effects of systemic, timely, and synchronized actions. Today, the advent of 5G and the IoT provides affordable technological means to achieve real-time systemic and global "As Is" representations of an Enterprise, as long as there is sound and solid Enterprise Architecture tools and infrastructures in place, dynamically and constantly updated to track the continuous changes that occur as time goes by.

It is my deep belief that we will be seeing the emergence of the collective awareness of the state and the dynamics associated with any enterprise, continuously construed and reified from the data collected by the sensors and the human actors as they act, enriching the information available to and surrounding each actor and enabling him to make better decisions.

The impressive advances we are witnessing in AI and Deep Learning will further potentiate the capabilities of each human and of the collective of humans that are at any given moment an Enterprise, to act intelligently toward achieving their intended purpose.

In Conclusion

I consider that the contexts of this book represent a major contribution toward the Body of Knowledge of Enterprise Engineering, in the "latu sensu," valuable to those involved in teaching, research, and professional practice.

The existence of systemic and holistic perspectives of Enterprise Architecture, founded on solid enterprise semantics and ontology basis, will constitute "Must Have" requirements adopted by all Enterprise Architects and by all Enterprises. Without it, I fear for the pernicious and uncontrolled usage and effects of AI and ML in the future.

INESC   José Tribolet
Lisboa, Portugal
January 2022

Contents

**Part III   How We Do It: Supporting Methodologies and
             Technologies**

6   Enterprise Architecture Development Framework 159

7   Enterprise Strategy Design 169

Acronyms

ADM	Architecture Development Method
APM	Application Portfolio Management
BMM	Business Motivation Model
BPMN	Business Process Modeling Notation
CEO	Chief Executive Office
CMDB	Configuration Management Database
CRM	Customer Relationship Management
CRUD	Create, Read, Update, Delete
EA	Enterprise Architecture
EC	Enterprise Cartography
EDI	Electronic Data Interchange
ERP	Enterprise Resource Planning
ETL	Extract, Transform, Load
IEEE	Institute of Electrical and Electronics Engineers
ISA	Information Systems Architecture
IT	Information Technology
ITIL	Information Technology Infrastructure Library
KB	Knowledge Base
ODM	Organizational Data Mining
OMG	Object Management Group
PESTEL	Political, Economic, Social, Technological, Environmental, and Legal
SWOT	Strengths, Weaknesses, Opportunities, and Threats
TOGAF	The Open Group Architecture Framework
UML	Unified Modeling Language

Part I
Motivation: Why We Wrote This Book

Chapter 1
Introduction

Pedro Sousa

Abstract This chapter introduces the major motivations behind this book. Enterprise Architecture (EA) expected results and drivers are firstly introduced, along with EA challenges. Then, a separation between enterprise representation and enterprise design is presented, introducing Enterprise Cartography and AS-WAS, AS-IS, and TO-BE models. The need for an Enterprise Cartography approach is next presented. Finally the book contributions and structure are presented.

1.1 Enterprise Architecture: Expectations and Disappointments

In its simplest form, the architecture of a system is merely a listing of its components and how they interact. In a more complex form, it is a formal definition of the structure and the properties of its components, their relationships and behavior, as well as the principles necessary for its analysis, design, and evolution. In this last definition, the architecture has both a descriptive and a prescriptive role—descriptive since it describes the components and their relations and prescriptive because it also restricts the degree of freedom of those designing and implementing the system, by defining what can be freely modified and what remains unchanged. The double role of enterprise architecture has been a point of convergence and widespread agreement among many authors [1].

Enterprises that have succeeded to implement an enterprise architecture initiative have delivered business value mostly in dealing with change. Since enterprises must transform to respond to external pressures, the enterprise architecture provides a clear view of the current and the desired future situation so that it is easier to plan and analyze proper scenarios of enterprise's changes. Enterprise Architecture clarifies:

- How strategic requirements are related to future enterprise state, which shows how the multiple futures enterprise views should look like in order to support the business strategy.

P. Sousa, A. Vasconcelos, *Enterprise Architecture and Cartography*,
The Enterprise Engineering Series, https://doi.org/10.1007/978-3-030-96264-7_1

- What transformation initiatives are required to reach that future state, making explicit the requirements and principles that steer the implementation of transformation initiatives.
- How information systems, information entities, infrastructure, and people are articulated to support business processes and enterprise operations as a whole. This provides the basis for many analyses and what-if scenarios regarding the enterprise artifacts.

The need to maintain explicit knowledge of the architecture of enterprises is an indisputable fact nowadays given their constant need to evolve. Since the Enterprise Architecture provides such explicit knowledge, the expectations on Enterprise Architecture are high. Either for enterprise governance, engineering, compliance, or maintenance, architectural representations are an enterprise asset that must be governed, as stated by many authors. For example, Enterprise Architecture is used to support the implementation of a business strategy [2, 3], to support the governance of the enterprise [1, 4], to support the management of IT, and, more recently, as an instrument for the management and coordination of the digital transformation [5].

In [6], Stefan presents a list of 28 application scenarios of enterprise architecture in enterprises and the corresponding literature sources, making clear the importance of enterprise architecture for enterprise maintenance, planning, and evolution. Opt´Land [7] presents a comprehensive list of the benefits of enterprise architecture for enterprises that are able to implement EA initiatives.

Organizations such as IEEE [8] also present a long list of usages of architecture descriptions for several stakeholders, being the first ones the basis for system developing, for impact analysis, for the evaluation of alternatives, and so on. Finally, the law in several countries also force enterprises to build and maintain their enterprise architecture. Furthermore, several external factors have been imposing to enterprises the need to have an enterprise architecture for specific domains, namely:

- In the USA, the Information Technology Management Reform stated, in the Clingler-Cohen Act of 1996 [9], that all US government agencies must explain how their strategic missions are sustained in their IT, implement capital control processes, and sustain their IT investments on business transformation needs. This was an important stimulus for the development of the discipline of enterprise architecture.
- Also in the USA, the Sarbanes-Oxley Act of 2002 [10] states that management staff is personally responsible for ensuring the effectiveness of financial control mechanism of an organization. This forces companies to develop good governance practices, which include the need to have an "accountability" of each employee's responsibilities and report processes and technologies. This obligation is mandatory for all companies at the US stock exchange.
- In Europe, Basel II e III (2004 e 2010) [11] states that EU financial institutions need to control credit and operational risk. This implies that companies maintain an explicit knowledge of their architecture, leading to the discipline of enterprise architecture.

- In Portugal, the Decree Law 107/2012 states that IT investments from central Government bodies, which accounts over 600 institutions, need to submit an update to the enterprise architecture along with their IT spending´s.

Given such wide range of benefits, one could expect that Enterprise Architecture would be a reality in most enterprises. Furthermore, given the variability and quality of existing enterprise architecture tools and their representation capabilities [12], one could argue that enterprises could easily create and maintain an enterprise architecture repository where all models are kept updated so that core enterprise activities could benefit from such information [6]. In addition to the variety of enterprise architecture tools, one can also find multiple methods and frameworks [13–18] to successfully implement enterprise architecture initiatives, both in white papers from specialized consulting companies and in technical and management textbooks.

Despite such recipes for success, the challenges to achieve an enterprise architecture are many and come from all directions: organizational, managerial, personal, and communications, among many others. The result is that, in many enterprises, Enterprise Architecture seems to be something intangible. This statement is supported not only from our professional experience in numerous enterprises but also from multiple sectors and countries where we have noticed not merely the absence of an enterprise architecture but also the abandonment of such initiatives by the effort that document the organizational artifacts seems to imply. Many unsuccessful cases reported [19–21] also highlight the challenges to achieve an Enterprise Architecture.

One of the major difficulties pointed out in the industry in the adoption of an Enterprise Architecture initiative is the effort it requires to keep representations updated, in particular when enterprises change over time. Given the fact that the rate of enterprises´ change seems to be increasing, maintaining the Enterprise Architecture seems harder to achieve day by day. The effort required to keep Enterprise Architecture models up-to-date becomes a critical one, since commercial enterprises are unlikely to spend resources on more structural initiatives when they lack of resources in more operational activities. We refer to commercial enterprises since in specific industries, such as defense, where effort is not a critical aspect, these enterprises go much further with their architecture frameworks such as *Department of Defense Architecture Framework* (DODAF [22]), *NATO Architecture Framework* (NAF [23]), *British Ministry of Defence Architecture Framework* (MODAF [24]), *Department of National Defence/Canadian Armed Forces Architecture Framework* (DNDAF [25]), or *Atelier de Gestion de l'ArchiTEcture des systmes d'information et de communication* (AGATE [26]).

1.2 Enterprise Design and Representation

Despite the potential benefits from having an Enterprise Architecture repository describing the enterprise's models, enterprises are far from being able to create and maintain an Enterprise Architecture repository updated, given the effort that such endeavor entails. This is a very common perception that enterprise leaders have regarding Enterprise Architecture. There are multiple reasons for such a perception, and we believe that a significant part of such extra effort results from the following organizational aspects:

- The teams involved in the change of the enterprise use multiple "Enterprise Architecture" tools, being office tools the most commonly used ones. Such tools are rarely integrated and do not provide coherent information. For example, when the board of directors of a company, acting as an architect designing the company, decides to create a new department, the board will not use a traditional enterprise architecture tool to express the new company design. The new department will be most likely designed in a board meeting minutes using an office document. In this example, the office document is the tool where the enterprise evolution was designed. If the enterprise structure is modeled in some enterprise architecture tool, effort is required to update it in conformity with this new design. The person that performs such update in the enterprise architecture tool is not designing but updating the model and its architectural representations according to the information in the tool used for enterprise design (the office document with the meeting minutes). The same occurs with many other design changes made by several other people in the enterprises, each using different tools to register the enterprise new design.
- Enterprise evolution is mostly a distributed and asynchronous process using ad hoc information. Enterprise evolution is planned and designed by different units in an asynchronous and distributed process, involving many actors and many concerns without formal mechanisms of communication among the designers. For example, when a director decides to make changes in his or her department, he or she probably will conduct meetings with other departments to check for possible dependencies and impacts. Directors of other departments can do the same for their departments. Despite the number of face-to-face meetings, there is no design process established so that the knowledge gathered in such meetings is consolidated and shared across the enterprise, so that the design actually uses coherent and updated information.

In such context, one can envisage the huge effort required to update the models in the Enterprise Architecture tools used. The faster the enterprise changes, the more effort is required to keep such models updated. When enterprises are already faced with lack of resources for the day-to-day projects, they are not willing to allocate effort to keep enterprise models updated.

Therefore, to abstract and represent enterprise reality, one also needs principles and instruments to deal with the continuous and fast transformation of the enterprise. Without them, enterprises will likely change faster than one can represent them, and representations become obsolete long before they are completed. This is, in fact, the application of the famous Nyquist's sampling theorem [1] applied to Enterprises:

---

[1] https://en.wikipedia.org/wiki/Nyquist_rate.

the sampling rate of sensing events must be high enough to follow the underlying dynamics of changes occurring in the underlying physical environment.

But the problem is actually more complex because enterprise models are also a moving target. In fact enterprises need models that refer to different points in time, namely:

- *AS-WAS* models. These models represent the enterprise's past state, including not only the past architecture but also the plans of transformation initiatives that were considered in the past. These models are most useful for auditing and accountability purposes since they can hold justifications for the decisions taken in the past. For example, the decision taken in the past to acquire development capacities in some technology could be sustained on the plans of a transformation initiative to build new products using that technology, regardless the fact of that planned transformation was actually put forward or dismissed.
- *AS-IS* models. These models represent the current enterprise. *AS-IS* models are required for current operations and for reacting to events. *AS-IS* models include the plans of today's transformation initiates. For example, if the organization intents to create a new department and has done several plans (models) related to the operation of the new department, such as the business processes, the tools, the required competences, and so on, such plans are part of the enterprise *AS-IS*.
- *TO-BE* models. These models represent the future architecture of the enterprise and are necessary for planning and estimating the duration, costs, and risks of the transformation initiatives before they start. For example, to plan a project that will start in 6 months, one needs to know what will be the Enterprise Architecture in 6 months from today. The current architecture has little use since many changes may occur in the meantime. The need to relate project management and Enterprise Architecture has been recognized both by Enterprise Architecture [27–29] and project management [30, 31] communities.

Naturally, *AS-WAS* models are just the old *AS-IS* and do not pose a major challenge. But *AS-IS* and *TO-BE* models are a real challenge, since they must take into consideration the multiple ongoing transformation initiatives and are subject to delays. Furthermore, models that start as a *TO-BE* model will eventually become an *AS-IS* model, even after adjustments, and then become an *AS-WAS* model. So if *TO-BE* and *AS-IS* models are kept apart and considered as different models, effort must be made to later move *TO-BE* to become *AS-IS* models.

The need for updated representations of the enterprise (both *AS-IS* and *TO-BE*) is essential to plan transformation initiatives and, consequently, has an impact on the costs, the time, and the risks to achieve the expected outcomes [27, 31].

Consider the illustrative scenario presented in Fig. 1.1. At the very beginning of the year, a given enterprise approves the three transformation initiatives T_1 to T_3 to move the enterprise from the *AS-IS* situation, on the left-hand side, into the intended *TO-BE* situation, on the right-hand side.

The enterprise has models of the current situation and also of the intended situation. Furthermore, each transformation initiative has also its own *AS-IS* and

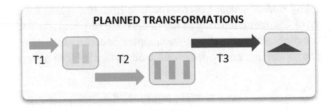

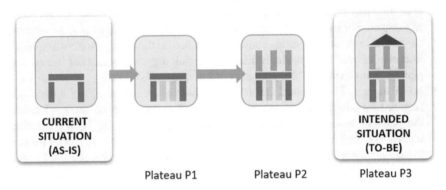

Fig. 1.1 Planning transformation initiatives to move from current (AS-IS) situation to a future (TO-BE) situation

TO-BE models, corresponding to plateaus P_1 to P_3. Each plateau embodies a series of architectural views of the enterprise.

Transformation initiative T_1 starts in January, and if everything goes as planned, when it is completed, the enterprise should be according to plateau P_1. However, in practice, many factors not considered in the plans may introduce new changes to the timings and to the actual plans of the transformation initiatives. If T_1 changes its outputs or timings, the enterprise must update the content of plateau P_1 according to the status of initiative T_1, so that the enterprise could have updated views of the current architecture. It looks simple with three projects. But in enterprises with over a hundred projects changing the architecture annually, each changing its outputs and timings, the effort to keep the Enterprise Architecture views updated is simply too high. Without updated views, enterprises have no longer "current views," because all the models considered at the very beginning of the year are now obsolete. So the transformation teams are working without accurate architectural views during the whole year, from the very first day. Thus, the later in the year, the greater the error.

Keeping Enterprise Architecture views updated is a means to sustain explicit knowledge about enterprise operation and construction. Accurate views of the enterprise are a key asset not only to support day-by-day operations but also to support the planning of transformation initiatives. We argue that keeping such views continuously updated is easier when the roles of architectural design are kept apart from the roles of architectural representation, thus enabling the separation of concerns between architecture and cartography.

1.3 Enterprise Cartography

According to Merriam-Webster dictionary,[2] Cartography is *the science or art of making maps*. It is an old and established discipline of producing representations of an object from its observation and measurement. Traditionally, these maps require not only geographic or spatial referential but also scientific, technical, and even aesthetic ones. Unlike traditional maps, enterprise representations do not have necessarily a geographic or spatial referential. Nevertheless, since the definition of *Cartography* matches our concept, we adopt the term *Enterprise Cartography*, hereafter referred to as *EC*.

We define EC as the process of representing an enterprise observed directly from reality. By reality one means the observed reality. Given that information systems are part of the enterprise reality, gathering information from information sources, such as information systems, is one common manner to observe the enterprise reality.

EC differs from Enterprise Architecture because it focuses on producing representations based on observations. To abstract and represent the enterprise, one requires a full set of familiar concepts from the Enterprise Architecture discipline, such as model, views, viewpoints, representation rules, etc. However, to abstract and represent the enterprise reality, one also needs principles and instruments to deal with the continuous and fast change going on in the enterprise. Without them, enterprises will likely change faster than one can represent them, and representations become obsolete long before they are completed.

Representation is a purely descriptive perspective, since it does not explicitly incorporate the purposed design of the new enterprise artifacts, as one expects in enterprise architecture. Such a difference is also evident in the definitions of the *architect* and *cartographer* roles. According to the IEEE Standard Glossary of Software Engineering Terminology [32], the term *architect* is defined as *"The person, team, or organization responsible for designing systems architecture"*, and in the Merriam-Webster dictionary,[3] the term *cartographer* is defined as the *person who makes maps*. So, an *architect* is essentially a person that designs and shapes intended changes to the architecture of the present enterprise reality, while a *cartographer* is essentially a person that aims at representing reality as it happens, including the changes as they are occurring.

Mapping the changes as they are happening is the most challenging aspect in EC since it implies doing representations of evolving objects. To address this problem,

---

[2] https://www.merriam-webster.com.

[3] https://www.merriam-webster.com.

one must ensure that the practices of abstracting and representing the evolving enterprise occur at a rhythm that is faster than the actual rhythm of enterprise changes. We have been working on this issue over a decade and have come up with a set principles and instruments to enable effective EC in continuously changing enterprises.

Steering enterprises entails not only new processes and systems but also greater integration with existing ones. More and more integrated processes and systems result not only in an increase in enterprise complexity but also in a greater need to know the enterprise current and emerging processes and systems. Unfortunately, these two factors feed each other in a positive feedback loop: the more complex the enterprise is, the more one needs to know, and the harder it gets to know it. Such positive feedback significantly contributes to the increase in costs, risks, and execution time for transformations initiatives, as well as the complexities of systemic enterprise steering and governance.

The problem of keeping a set of accurate representations (i.e., models) of an enterprise is not an easy one for large enterprises, which can have hundreds of transformation initiatives, of different scopes and sizes, each year. The origin of this difficulty is that the planning process originates in many of the enterprise's communities without a consistent, coherent, and complete systemic view of the enterprise to support them, individually and as a whole.

Based on our observations, the design of the enterprise's architecture is a distributed process in most enterprises, performed by architects from different domains (from business to technology), each planning, designing, and deciding based on partial and often conflicting or even incompatible views of the enterprise. This state of affairs is entirely different from the one it is observed in some industries, in particular, those for which real-time systemic integrity is essential to their survival, such as Defense, where all the efforts are made to ensure at all times the enterprise transformations are steered by a centralized and fully controlled design processes [22].

The list of reports on failed *EA* programs in enterprises is large [21]. Nevertheless, in spite of high levels of *EA* program failures, enterprise transformations continue to lack purposeful designs, according to systemically coherent architectures! In fact, most enterprises today are still the result of the "natural evolution" that happened from their original birth configuration. Current transformations keep being designed by enterprise architects according to partial needs and points of view, regardless of the eventual existence of global Enterprise Architecture programs to guarantee the global integrity of the *TO-BE* enterprise.

What Enterprise Architecture programs fail to produce is not the architecture of an enterprise, but the establishment of the processes and tools to provide complete and accurate information that sustain a good architecture design, where alignment between the different elements was taken into consideration and resulted from a conscious design. In other words, they cannot create a single, consolidated view of the enterprise because this requires coordination between different areas, from coherent and non-conflicting goals, rational and implementable use of resources, cost sharing, work methods, languages, tools, etc. [21].

Such a consolidated model can be obtained and sustained by forcing all architects to use and share the same modeling notation, the same level of detail, and probably also the same modeling tool. However, this is very hard to achieve in real enterprises, because enterprise architects are in fact a very heterogeneous group, in what concerns their backgrounds, their knowledge, and needs. In practice, different architects can use different notations, different levels of detail, or even different tools, making harder to support a design process that enables consistent and coherent views of the enterprise architecture.

With the introduction of the concept of Enterprise Cartography, we can decouple the problem of design from the problem of building a consolidated set of representations of the enterprise. Different architects can use their preferred design approach, leaving up to the cartographer the task of consolidating each partial architecture into a single global set of maps representing the enterprise architecture of the *AS-IS* as well as of the *emerging AS-IS*. In the course of this consolidation process, many inconsistencies may arise. However, they should pass on to the Enterprise Architects involved so that any inconsistencies and opposing points of the views can be dealt with the adequate governance mechanisms, which form the essential core of the entire organizational governance. As a matter of fact, enterprises do not have explicit governance mechanisms aimed at maintaining global systemic integrity, while subject to the multitude of changes that are in progress in a distributed fashion throughout the enterprise. To realize such governance mechanisms, they need a systemic, coherent, and complete view of the enterprise as provided by Enterprise Cartography.

Another important aspect is that Enterprise Cartography is less intrusive than Enterprise Architecture and, therefore, easier to implement in real enterprises, considering that defining the shape of the enterprise is naturally perceived as a more relevant role than representing it. Enterprise architects are naturally more willing to cooperate with others when the ownership of the design remains theirs than with other architects with whom they would have to negotiate and share the ownership of the new designs.

Enterprise *AS-IS* and *emerging AS-IS* are used for different purposes. The first is a key asset to operate the enterprise, for example, to analyze the impact of a response to an event, whereas the second is a key asset for the planning of the transformation initiatives. For example, consider that today's date is January and one wants to plan a transformation initiative that is expected to start in April and to conclude in September. Assuming there are other ongoing transformation initiatives, the enterprise might change from January to April, and therefore the *AS-IS* state in January is not sufficient for the planning of the actions that will occur in April. In fact, to do the job properly, one needs to keep estimating as best as possible the enterprise future *TO-BE* states from April to September, based on the best available *AS-IS* at any point in time during the transformation time frame.

Transformation initiatives create, remove, or change artifacts and their interdependencies that might result in changes to the architecture, as stated in the description of their outcomes. In IT, where transformations initiatives are typically called projects, such descriptions are either stated in natural language or models such as BPMN [33], ArchiMate [34], and UML among others. The conciliation of all these descriptions in an integrated and consolidated vision is a task that entails a massive human effort and is therefore far beyond the reach of the vast majority of enterprises. Thus, the key motivation for Enterprise Cartography is to provide architectural maps of the enterprise *current AS-IS* and *emerging AS-IS* with the necessary architectural information to those planning and executing the changes. We claim that Enterprise Cartography allows us to provide a generic and systemic approach, where only a minimum effort is necessary to create and maintain *current AS-IS* and *emerging AS-IS* architectural maps.

1.3.1 Approaches to Enterprise Cartography

The idea of creating maps from observation of the enterprise reality is not new, in particular if one considers data extracted from systems in an efficient manner to observe the enterprise reality.

At the business and organizational layers, many cartography techniques have been presented in the domain of Organization Design and Engineering [35–38] and Organizational Data Miming (ODM) [36]

At the business process layer, cartography techniques are found within the discipline of business process management, especially in process mining. These techniques make use of event logs to discover process activities, control, and data flows and also to assess the conformance of existing processes against constraints. Mined processes correspond to the actual instances of processes, not to the designed or modeled processes. Another example of Enterprise Cartography is the inference of inter-organizational processes based on EDI event logs.

Business intelligence techniques that collect data from enterprise systems to produce reports and dashboards may be considered yet as another example of cartography, even though it is mostly concerned with the analytic aspects rather than with architectural (relational) aspects of the enterprise. However, we can still envisage many analytical views within an architecture, and therefore we may also consider business intelligence techniques as another example of cartography and the traditional ETL (Extract Transformation and Loading) process as a cartographic one.

At the infrastructure level, Configuration Management Databases (CMDB) as defined by ITIL [39] represent the configurations and relationships of the IT infrastructure components. Such information can be used to produce architectural maps of the enterprise infrastructure. For example, some solutions provide auto-discovery techniques that detect nodes, virtual machines, and network devices to create infrastructure architectural views. Auto-discovery is a cartographic process and requires that the type of the concepts to be discovered be known in advance. The resulting Configuration Management Database (CMDB) instance is a partial model of the enterprise's infrastructure. This model can be communicated through different visualization mechanisms, such as textual reports or graphical views that require a symbolic notation and design rules.

As any other discovery process, infrastructure discovery requires that the type of the concepts to be discovered be known in advance. So, one must ensure the meta-model has the concepts one will find during discovery. For example, discover processes cannot distinguish between system software from an application component, because it only finds installed binaries. Furthermore, if an application has a front-office server and a back-office server, it cannot identify those servers belonging to the same application.

One may say that Enterprise Cartography has been a reality in many specific domains, concerning specific variables and hard-coded with limited and predefined meta-models and concepts. Most commonly, referred techniques aim at producing *current AS-IS* views of the enterprise. Even though not so common, some also address the *emerging AS-IS* views of the enterprise, especially the analytical approaches.

We aim at a generic and systemic approach, where the effort to produce and maintain such *current AS-IS* and *emerging AS-IS* enterprise architectural views is kept to a minimum.

1.4   Book Structure and Contributions

This book aims at providing guidance to practitioners of Enterprise Architecture both to develop and to maintain enterprise models. Rather than providing yet another list of Enterprise Architecture notations and frameworks from A to Z, we focus on methods to perform such task.

The problem of Enterprise Architecture maintenance is an important aspect addressed in this book, because Enterprise Architecture is a never-ending initiative within enterprises. One thing is one person develop some models of some artefacts of the enterprise. A much harder achievement is for several persons to develop a set of coherent models, and an even harder thing is to sustain that along the time, where enterprise models must be maintained.

This entails dealing with issues such as lack of consensus among enterprise staff, for example, about the structure of a business process or information systems. We also address the difficulties that one has about things that are commonly taken as granted and are much harder in real enterprises. For example, finding the limits of an information system—where it starts and ends—may be hard to reach consensus. This may explain why notable references, such as TOGAF [16] and ArchiMate [40], do not consider the application concept but rather the application component concept.

The long-time perspective also entails the evolution of architectural frameworks and notations, something that does not occur when developing new models. So, we present a catalogue of patterns, principles, and methods to develop and maintain enterprises's architectural models and views.

1.4.1 Book Contributions

This book helps beginners and professionals to create and maintain enterprise architectures in changing enterprises.

Briefly, we present the following contributions:

- The selection of a reduced set of concepts in each architectural layer, not only because they are the most frequently used, but also because they are sufficient for the application of the patterns, principles and methods to create and maintain enterprise architectures.
- A compilation of a comprehensive set of principles and patterns expressed in terms of the selected concepts. In this way, it not only guides those who are learning the rules for using the selected concepts, but also helps professionals about the rules applicable to each concept.
- The presentation of useful methods to guide the construction of models in each architectural layer. Methods are fundamental for the construction and maintenance of architectures. Regardless of the degree of individual creativity, the design of an architecture implies the clarification of methods for teamwork, since they simplify the transfer of work between people. Methods also simplify the traceability between assumptions and the produced architectural artifacts, thus reducing the effort to review the work done when any of the assumptions change.
- Finally, we present a model and method for Enterprise Cartography, aiming at simplifying and reducing the effort of maintaining enterprise architectures in general and, in particular, in generating views of the emerging architecture of the organization - something absolutely essential for the planning of new development initiatives.

1.4.2 Book Structure

After presenting ground concepts in Chap. 2, we present in Chap. 3 the set of Enterprise Architecture concepts one needs, and, in Chap. 4, the patterns and principles. In Chap. 5, Enterprise Cartography concepts and principles are described.

Afterward, in Part III of the book, we present the techniques and methodologies. Thus, in Chap. 6, we summarize TOGAF ADM for EA development. In Chap. 7, an enterprise strategy design approach is proposed. In Chap. 8, a business process design methodology is described. Information architecture design approach is next presented. Information systems architecture design is described in Chap. 10, including information systems architecture planning and application portfolio management. Chapter 11 describes a method for EC design.

Finally, several case studies on EA and EC are proposed in the last chapter.

1.5 Exercises

Exercise 1.1

Look up for common arguments organizations use to justify the lack of enterprise architecture initiatives.

Exercise 1.2

Identify situations where the architecture designer will not likely use an enterprise architecture tool to design the organization.

Exercise 1.3

Identify in one organization you know situations where the architecture designer will not likely use an enterprise architecture tool to design the organization.

Exercise 1.4

Describe one scenario where the enterprise architect that plays the role "designer" is not the one responsible for maintaining the organization representations.

References

1. J. Hoogervorst, *Enterprise Governance and Enterprise Engineering* (Springer Nature, Switzerland AG, 2012)
2. J. Ross, P. Weill, D. Robertson, *Enterprise Architecture as Strategy. Creating a Foundation for Business Execution* (Harvard Business School Press, 2006)
3. F. Radeke, C. Legner, *Strategic Enterprise Architecture Management: Challenges, Best Practices, and Future Developments*, chapter Embedding EAMS into Strategic Planning (Springer, 2012)
4. G. Hobbs, F. Ahlemann, E. Stettiner, M. Messerschmidt, C. Legner, *Strategic Enterprise Architecture Management: Challenges, Best Practices, and Future Developments*, chapter EAM Governance and Organization. (Springer, 2012)
5. H. Proper, R. Winter, S. Aier, S. De Kinderen, *Architectural Coordination of Enterprise Transformation* (2017)
6. S Bischoff, *The Need for a Use Perspective on Architectural Coordination* (Springer, 2017), pp. 87–98
7. M. Op't Land, E. Proper, M. Waage, J. Cloo, *Enterprise Architecture Creating Value by Informed Governance* (Springer, Steghuis, C, 2009)
8. IEEE Computer Society, The IEEE standard 1471-2000 systems and software engineering - architecture description (2000). Superseded by ISO/IEC/IEEE 42010:2011
9. US Government, Us 104th congress public law 104-106–feb. 10, 1996. U.S. Government Printing Office (1996)
10. US Government, Us 107th congress public law 204. U.S. Government Printing Office (2002)
11. Basel Committee on Banking Supervision, Basel ii and basel iii (2002)

12. S. Bibitemeavt Roth, M. Zec, F. Matthes, Enterprise architecture visualization tool survey 2014 technical report. Technical report, Technische Universit at Munchen., Sebis (2014)
13. J. Zachman, A framework for information systems architecture. IBM Syst. J. **26**(3), G321–5298 (1987)
14. United States Government Federal Enterprise Architecture Program Management Office, Fea consolidated reference model document, version 2.3
15. P. Hagan, Eabok - guide to the (evolving) enterprise architecture body ofknowledge. McLean Virginia: The Mitre Corporation (2004)
16. The Open Group, Togaf version 9.1 (2011)
17. Gartner, Gartner enterprise architecture framework (geaf) (2005)
18. Capgemeni, Integrated architecture framework (iaf) (1993)
19. Gartner, Gartner identifies ten enterprise architecture pitfalls (2009)
20. I. Kabai, 8 reasons enterprise architecture programs fail, in *Information Week*, number online, 8 (2018)
21. S. Roeleven, Why two thirds of enterprise architecture projects fail. An explanation for the limited success of architecture projects (2010)
22. Deputy Chief Information Officer, The dodaf architecture frameworkversion 2.02. U.S. Department of Defense, 8 (2010)
23. Noth Atlantic Treaty Organization, Nato architecture framework, version 4 (nafv4) (2018)
24. UK Ministry of Defence, Mod architecture framework v1.2 (2010)
25. Government of Canada, The dnd/cf architecture framework (can) (2007)
26. French government agency, Atelier de gestion de l´architecture, version 3 (2005)
27. K. Ugwu, Understanding the complementary relationship between enterprise architecture & project management, in *Architecture & Governance Magazine (online version*, 5 (2017)
28. N. Labusch, *Architectural Coordination of Enterprise Transformation*, chapter Information Requirements for Enterprise Transformation (Springer, 2017), pp. 111–117
29. J. Tribolet, P. Sousa, A. Caetano, The role of enterprise governance and cartography in enterprise engineering. Enterprise modelling and information systems architectures (2014)
30. K. Schomburg, T. Barker, Integrating the it pmo with enterprise architecture for better government, in *Proceedings of PMI®Global Congress 2011-North America* (Project Management Institute, Dallas, TX, Newtown Square, PA, 2011)
31. M. Bernardo, P. Sousa, Portfolio management enabling a dynamic organization is representation, in *22nd International Congress on Project Management and Engineering*, Madrid, Spain (2018)
32. IEEE, *Systems and Software Engineering – Vocabulary in ISO/IEC/IEEE 24765:2010(E)*, pp. 1–418 12 (2010)
33. OMG, *Business Process Modeling Notation (BPMN) Specification 2.0* (2010)
34. The Open Group, *ArchiMate®2.1 Specification* (Van Haren Publishing, Zaltbommel, 2015)
35. R. Winter, Organisational design and engineering: proposal of a conceptual framework and comparison of business engineering with other approaches. Int. J. Organ. Des. Eng. **1**(2), 126–147 (2010)
36. H.R. Nemati, C.D. Barko, Organizational data mining: Leveraging enterprise data resources for optimal performance (2004)
37. D. Olgun-Olgun, A. Pentland, Sensor-based organisational design and engineering. Int. J. Organ. Des. Eng. **1**(1/2), 1 (2010)
38. J. Tribolet, P. Sousa, R. Magalhaes, The role of business processes and enterprise architectures in the development of organizational self-awareness. Polytech. Stud. Rev. **VI**(9) (2008)
39. K. Tambralli, Configuration management database (cmdb) (2021)
40. M. Lankhorst, Enterprise architecture at work: Modelling, communication and analysis (2009)

Part II
Theory: The Theories Behind

Chapter 2
Founding Concepts

Pedro Sousa and André Vasconcelos

Abstract The founding concepts that support this book are introduced in this chapter. Firstly, the concepts of system and enterprise are presented, including system composition, environment, structure, and production. Next the concepts of architecture and enterprise are discussed. In Sect. 2.3, the purposes of representation and design are introduced. Finally, the concepts of views, viewpoints, model, stakeholder, and domain are presented.

2.1 Systems and Enterprises

2.1.1 Systems

The concept of a system is core for the topics addressed in this book since it is present in Enterprises, Information Systems, and many other Enterprise artifacts.

The notion of a system simply as a set or interacting components such that system components could be broken down into components that in turn be analyzed as an independent entities comes from a long time. An essential step was proposed in the General Systems Theory [1], where the interaction of systems components is characterized by the interactions of its components and the nonlinearity of those interactions, both between themselves and with the external environment. Maier and Rechtin [2] add to the system definition that the functions performed by the system cannot be performed by any of its individual components.

The notion of a System as a set of components that perform a set of functions to the environment that no component can perform individually, by interacting with themselves and the environment, is characterized in [3] by a Composition, Structure, Environment, and Production. Considering the dark circles in Fig. 2.1 as components of a given system S, one can define:

- System Composition: $C = 8, 9, 10, 11$. The list of the System Components.
- System Environment: $E = 1, 3, 5, 12, 18$. The list of the external Components/systems that interact with the System Components.

© The Author(s), under exclusive license to Springer Nature Switzerland AG 2022
P. Sousa, A. Vasconcelos, *Enterprise Architecture and Cartography*,
The Enterprise Engineering Series, https://doi.org/10.1007/978-3-030-96264-7_2

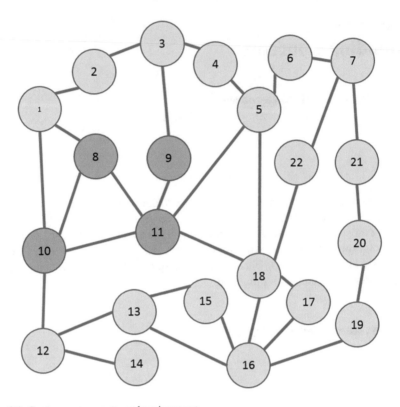

Fig. 2.1 System, components, and environment

- System Structure: $S = (8, 10); (8, 11); (10, 11); (9, 11)$. The System components and their inter-dependencies
- System Structure: P. What the system delivers to the Environment. This is not defined in the figure, but it could be any of the environment elements, for example, the 1. In this case 1 does not belong to the environment set.

But one still lacks purpose for a system. As Hoogervorst [4] discusses, the purpose is a fundamental notion in a system, because the components purpose can only be understood regarding the purpose of the whole. If one does not consider the purposefulness as a requirement, in practice, any set of components might become a system, since there is always some kind of interaction among the components, for example, the gravity for physical components.

The requirement that systems have a purpose has major implications, since purposefulness is something that only designed systems have. Thus, only systems created by living organisms are indeed systems. For example, a bird nest made of small interleaved small branches and sticks is a system, which has the purpose of hosting the specie reproduction. However, a bundle of interwoven branches resulting from a strong wind is no longer considered a system, for the lack of purpose. This also means that since the Solar System has no purpose, it is not a System at all.

In what concerns with enterprises they clearly are systems, as they are purpose-fully designed as a set of interacting parts. Moreover, most, if not all, enterprise components are also systems. In fact each component (also called enterprise artifact) was purposefully designed to play a role in the enterprise, and each component also includes a set of interacting components both between them and with other components of the enterprise.

In general speaking, Enterprise Architecture presents the types of components and the types of dependencies one should use to model the enterprise as a set of systems, each with a Composition, an Environment, a Structure, and a Production, as any system does.

To conclude this section on Systems, our proposal of Systems also exceeds the one proposed by the ISO/IEC 15288:2008, as "concerns those systems that are man-made and may be configured with one or more of the following: hardware, software, data, humans, processes (e.g., processes for providing service to users), procedures (e.g., operator instructions), facilities, materials and naturally occurring entities" [5], since it include all kinds of designed enterprises.

2.1.2 Enterprises

So far we have been using the term enterprise as a buzz word to refer to institutions, organizations, and any other kind of social purposeful designed forms of social organization.

The usage of the term *enterprise* instead of *organization* or *institution* has always been an issue in public entities, since the term *enterprise* is often understood as much more close to a profit focused company than the terms *organization* or *institution*, which are equally applied to public and private entities.

We refer to *enterprises* and not to *organizations* since the first term has a wider scope according to the Open Group definition *enterprise is any set of organizations that have a common set of goals* [6]. An example of an enterprise is the *Portuguese National Health System*,[1] that includes more than 100 health organizations. Both the notions of enterprise architecture and enterprise cartography apply equally to enterprises and organizations. However, since the concept of enterprise is broader than organization or institution, we will use the first whose meaning includes the others.

We also consider a distinction between enterprise transformation and enterprise evolution, the difference being that the former is mostly related with top-level restructure and the later is related with the optimization of current state of affairs [7]. Despite the differences, they both require Enterprise Architecture's input data, and

---

[1] Serviço Nacional de Saúde: https://www.sns.gov.pt.

they both cause changes in the enterprise, thus likely inducing changes in the Enterprise Architecture. Although the adoption of the term "change initiatives" would be probably more consistent with the previous statements, in this book we will use the term "transformation initiatives" in the broadest sense, also including changes derived from the current state optimization. Since transformation initiatives are temporary, unique, and a purposeful activity, they correspond to the concept of projects as defined in the project community [8].

2.2 Architecture and Enterprise Architecture

According to the Merriam Webster dictionary,[2] the meaning of the word architecture is as quoted next in verbatim:

1. *the art or science of building*;
2. *a formation or construction resulting from or as if from a conscious act*;
3. *a unifying or coherent form or structure*;
4. *architectural product or work*;
5. *a method or style of building*;
6. *the manner in which the components of a computer or computer system are organized and integrated different program architectures*;

While the first and fifth are related with ways of acting, the remaining ones are related with the structure of the artifact. This duality has been debated by many authors over the years [4, 9–11]. Maier and Rechtin [9] dedicate a full Annex to the presentation of different meanings of the term Architecture proposed by multiple authors. Among the different aspects, the prescriptive and descriptive role of the architecture are highly relevant for this book.

In the descriptive perspective, an architecture expresses the models of a system, which ultimately shows how the system is structure and organized into components and their relations (the C, E, S, and P referred earlier). In the prescriptive perspective, an architecture expresses the principles, guidelines, or rules that should be used to design the systems, not the actual system's organization and structure.

In a pure descriptive perspective, the Architecture is knowledge about the system construction. In other words, architecture is a model of the system. The concept of a model is also subject to several discussions, but we adopt the notion of a model as presented in [3] after [12] presented in verbatim and quoted below:

> Any subject using a system A that is neither directly nor indirectly interaction with system B, to obtain information about the system B, is using A as a model of B.

In a pure prescriptive perspective, the architecture is a set of Architecture Principles [4], which reduce the degree of freedom in the design of the systems.

---

[2] https://www.merriam-webster.com.

Hopefully, good Architectural Principles should reduce the freedom to produce bad designs. However, in a pure prescriptive perspective, the architecture is not a model of the system. One may argue against this last statement, given that knowing the design and constructing principles and rules used to build a system is already knowing something about the system. However, following such an argumentation, then the architecture of all systems built under the same set of rules would have the same architecture. So this knowledge is not about a particular system but a family of systems. This can be true if one sees architecture as a high-level knowledge of the systems, as stated in [4].

Upon these two perspectives of architecture, descriptive and prescriptive, one may add functional or usage domain perspectives that provide additional classifications. Greefhorst and Proper [11] consider three perspectives for architecture, regulation-oriented, design-oriented, and knowledge-oriented, where the first corresponds to the prescriptive perspective, the third corresponds to the descriptive perspective, and the second (the design-oriented) corresponds to the high-level design decisions of the system.

Smolander [13] presents an empirical study that shows the four most common meaning for architecture as follows:

- *Architecture as blueprint*: architecture is the structure of the system to be implemented.
- *Architecture as language*: architecture is the language for achieving common conception about the system.
- *Architecture as literature*: architecture resides at the documentation and reference architectures for future readers.
- *Architecture as decision*: architecture is the decision and basis for decisions about the system to be implemented.

The first three are clearly under a descriptive perspective of the architecture, and the last one might be more close to the prescriptive perspective. Despite such (more) practical notions of architecture might be more easy to work with, they are far more difficult to define. So, in this book, we adopt the IEEE concept of Architecture. The IEEE defines Architecture as [14]:

> The fundamental concepts or properties of a system in its environment embodied
> in its elements, relationships, and in the principles of its design and evolution.

Such definition is also in concordance of the TOGAF [6] concept of architecture, which proposes two definitions: the IEEE definition presented above and a second one described as "The structure of components, their inter-relationships, and the principles and guidelines governing their design and evolution over time" [6]. Thus, both IEEE and TOGAF propose a mixed notion of Architecture, with both a descriptive and prescriptive perspectives, but in a clear and explicit manner.

2.3 Design and Representation

The differentiation between *Design* and *Representation* has a structuring role in the
Enterprise Architecture approach.

Design can be both a noun and a verb. As a noun, according to the Merriam-
Webster dictionary [3], it means "a method worked out in advance for achieving some
objective" or "the way in which the elements of something (as a work of art) are
arranged." As a verb, it means "the way something has been made: the way the parts
of something (such as a building, machine, book, etc.) are formed and arranged for
a particular use, effect, etc."

According to these definitions, the design (verb) of a system is the action to
produce the design (noun) of a system. As a noun, design is similar to architecture,
even though such similarity is not revealed in Merriam-Webster thesaurus.

Architecture is the art and the science of building a system through the specification and organization of its components. An architecture is a formal description of a
system that defines the structure and properties of its components, their relationships
and behavior of components, as well as the principles necessary for its analysis,
design, and evolution. Note that the definition of architecture includes the design
(blueprint) and principles. Architecture can also be defined as the art and the science
of designing complex structures. Architecture is a means of putting restrictions, that
is, to define what can be freely modify and what remains unchanged.

Notice that architecture is different from implementation. An implementation
is a practical solution that meets one or more functions. It is an application or
implementation of a plan, idea, model, design, standard, algorithm, or policy.
Architecture is also different from a framework. A framework defines how to
organize the structure, artifacts, and views of an architecture.

In engineering disciplines (e.g., civil, aviation, mechanical, naval, electronics,
chemistry, physics, etc.), the formal representation of concepts is essential. In
management disciplines, written representations are more rare, but there are also a
few, for example, organizational charts, value chain, Fishbone diagrams, Timelines,
ISO 9000 flow charts, or TQM Process Flows. Nevertheless, without representation:
(i) knowledge sharing is limited; (ii) it is not possible to define an architecture or to
engineer products; (iii) and it is very complex to align concepts.

The representation of the Architecture of a system is an exercise of instantiation
of concepts, in which each instance has the graphics of the corresponding concept,
and has a name that distinguishes it from the other instances. The meaning of the
element is in the graphic symbol and not in the words used in its name. Perhaps
the most common error of architectural representations is precisely in assuming that
words also define concepts (have meaning). For example, it is not by giving the
name "Flying Car" to an element whose symbol is a "Car" that one represents a
flying car.

A good example of a "bad" diagram is presented in Fig. 2.2 since all the meaning
relies solely on words.

---

[3] https://www.merriam-webster.com.

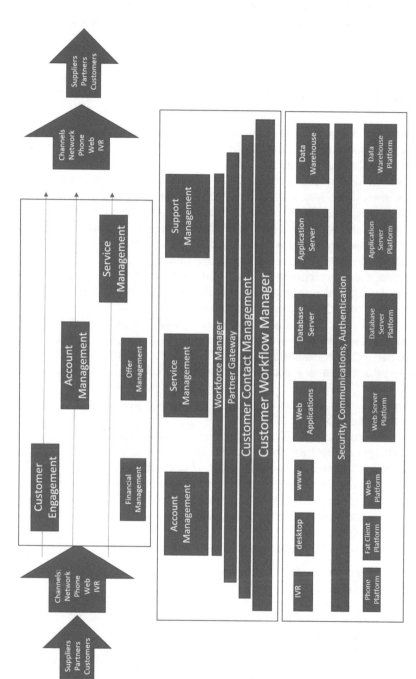

Fig. 2.2 An example of an enterprise architecture diagram with no semantics

Therefore having a common modeling notation that supports the representation of enterprise artifacts is central for understanding and managing the enterprise assets.

2.4 Architecture Views and Viewpoints

EA comprise a diverse and large number of models and descriptions. EA is used to describe the whole enterprise and usually have many architectural views that have to be perceived by the stakeholders.

The way to deal with this complexity is to have a composition approach that distinguishes between system components and relationship among the components. For example, to describe how a car works, we first describe the parts of the car (e.g., wheels, engine, and brakes) and then the relationship among the parts. Similarly, the enterprise information is seen as a set of systems and their relationships.

As presented before, architecture is the fundamental organization of the system components, their relationships to each other and to the environment, and the principles guiding its design and evolution. An architectural description is a collection of products to document an architecture.

A **stakeholder** is an individual, a team, or an organization (or class) with interests in, or concerns relative to, a system. An architecture is perceived by every party (stakeholder), but its communication always involves a description. This description is always associated with a concern, a viewpoint, a notation, and a model for a domain.

A **domain** is a set of elements (concepts) that result from a given conception (e.g., systematization) in a given universe.

A **model** is an abstraction (unambiguous) of the concepts in a domain.

The **viewpoints** describe the concepts, models, visualizations, and analysis techniques that are used to construct views of a description of an architecture. The viewpoints are a specification of the conventions to build and use the views. Viewpoints are like a pattern or template from which individual views are developed through the establishment of the purposes, audiences, and the techniques for views creation and analysis.

Through the book, we present several viewpoints organized in:

- Strategy viewpoints.
- Business viewpoints.
- Information viewpoints.
- Information systems viewpoints.
- Technological viewpoints.

Views are (part of) a system from the perspective of a number of concerns (derived from stakeholders). The same view can have multiple visualizations.

As presented in Fig. 2.3, the enterprise architect manages the whole EA model and, according to the stakeholder profile and concerns (e.g., business analyst, CTO,

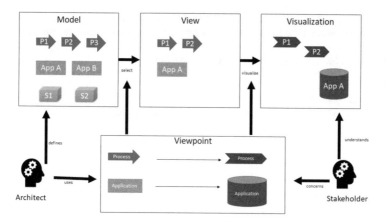

Fig. 2.3 Viewpoint, model, view, and visualization relations

CEO, developer), selects a viewpoint, producing a view that may have one or several visualizations (e.g., present the business processes as a rectangle or as an arrow or in a domain specific notation).

Notice that views imply **symbols**. However, symbols alone have no semantics! The vast majority of graphical notations do not define the semantics of each symbol. The vast majority of graphical notations leaves the semantics in the words (e.g., descriptions, tags, notes). A **symbolic model** expresses properties of architectures of systems by means of symbols that refer to the reality. A **semantic model** is an interpretation of a symbolic model, expressing the meaning of the symbols in that model.

References

1. L. Von Bertalanffy, G. Braziller, General system theory. Foundations, development, applications (1968)
2. M. Maier, E. Rechtin, *The Art of Systems Architecting* (3rd edn.) (CRC Press, 2009)
3. J. Dietz, *Enterprise Ontology - Theory and Methodology* (1st edn.) (Springer, Berlin, Heidelberg, 2006)
4. J. Hoogervorst, Enterprise governance and enterprise engineering (2012)
5. IEEE, *IEEE 15288-2015 - ISO/IEC/IEEE International Standard - Systems and Software Engineering – System Life Cycle Processes*, p. E15288 (2015)
6. The Open Group, Togaf version 9.1 (2011)
7. H. Proper, R. Winter, S. Aier, S. De Kinderen, Architectural coordination of enterprise transformation (2017)
8. Project Management Institute, *A Guide to the Project Management Body of Knowledge* (6th edn.) (Newtown Square, Pa, 2017)
9. M. Maier, E. Rechtin, *The Art of Systems Architecting* (2nd edn.) (CRC Press, 2002)
10. M. Op't Land, E. Proper, M. Waage, J. Cloo, *Enterprise Architecture - Creating Value by Informed Governance* (Springer, Berlin, 2009)

11. D. Greefhorst, E. Proper, *Architecture Principles. Theory and Practice* (Springer, 2010)
12. L. Apostel, Towards the formal study of models in the non-formal sciences. Synthese **12**(2-3), 125–161 (1960)
13. K. Smolander, Four metaphors of architecture in software organizations: Finding out the meaning of architecture in practice, in *Proceedings of the International Symposium on Empirical Software Engineering (ISESE02)* (2002)
14. IEEE Computer Society, The ieee standard 1471-2000 systems and software engineering - architecture description (2000). Superseded by ISO/IEC/IEEE 42010:2011

Chapter 3
Enterprise Architecture

André Vasconcelos and Pedro Sousa

Abstract This chapter introduces Enterprise Architecture (EA) foundations. After introducing the major motivations that drive the EA, the layers used to describe the EA are presented. The remaining of the chapter is organized around each EA layer, describing the business, information, application, technology, and service architectures, including its concepts and dependencies. Finally, several exercises are proposed.

3.1 Introduction

Enterprise Architecture may be driven by several motivations, including understanding and communication, development of systems, products and services according to business goals, optimization of operations and organizational resources (including people), and supporting the alignment among Enterprise Architecture layers.

Each Enterprise Architecture layer has a different pace. Usually, the business needs to adapt and change in short cycles, while strategy has longer cycles. Applications and infrastructure also change at different paces. Therefore, the Enterprise Architecture allows the specification of the different paces in order to ensure that change is enabled in the enterprise (see Fig. 3.1).

Having a common set of concepts is central for understanding and managing the enterprise assets that have different changing paces.

3.2 Enterprise Architecture Domains and Frameworks

The artefacts of the architecture of an enterprise may be organized in different layers, which in turn are structured in Frameworks. We start by presenting Zachmam Framework, a notable framework, and, the two currently most used from Open-Group, TOGAF and ArchiMate.

© The Author(s), under exclusive license to Springer Nature Switzerland AG 2022
P. Sousa, A. Vasconcelos, *Enterprise Architecture and Cartography*,
The Enterprise Engineering Series, https://doi.org/10.1007/978-3-030-96264-7_3

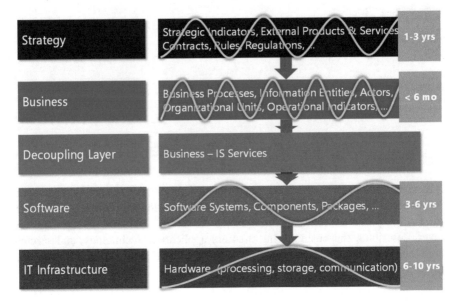

Fig. 3.1 Strategy, business, IS, and IT dynamics

3.2.1 The Zachman Framework

The Zachman Framework (www.zifa.com) was formally published in 1987; its aim was described as an architecture that represents the information systems' artifacts, providing a means of ensuring that standards for creating the information environment exist and are appropriately integrated. It proposes a logical structure for classifying and organizing the descriptive representations of an enterprise, in different dimensions, and each dimension can be perceived in different perspectives. The Zachman Framework was developed taking into consideration all the participants involved in the planning, conception, building, using, and maintaining activities of the Enterprise Information Systems [1].

The Zachman Framework helps govern the architectural process and manage change. In this framework, the architecture is described across two independent aspects: i) the rows represent the different perspectives which may be used to view a business, a situation, an opportunity, or a system, and ii) the columns represent the different dimensions which apply to each perspective of the business, situation, opportunity, or system.

- Perspectives
  Regarding the perspectives, they mimic the old Greek knowledge of the stages required to transform some idea into something real: *Identification, Definition, Representation, Specification, Configuration, and Instantiation*[1]

---

[1] https://www.zachman.com.

- Scope (Identification—planner's perspective): the planner is concerned with positioning the product in the context of its environment, including specifying its scope.
- Enterprise Model (Definition—owner's perspective): the owner is interested in the business deliverable and how it will be used.
- System Model (Representation—designer's perspective): the designer works with the specifications for the product to ensure that it will, in fact, fulfill the owner's expectations.
- Technology Model (Specification—builder's perspective): the builder manages the process of assembling and fabricating the components in the production of the product.
- Detailed Representations (Configuration—subcontractor's perspective): the subcontractor fabricates out-of-context components which meet the builder's specifications.
- The actual Enterprise (Instantiation—employee's perspective). This is the actual Enterprise.

• Dimensions
While the rows in the Zachman Framework describe the participant's views, the columns provide a description on each dimension and independently of the other dimensions. To describe each perspective, Zachman proposes the use of the primitive interrogatives of communication to fully describe a fact: the what, the who, the when, the why, and the how.[2]

The information in each column is modeled as a *thing relates to a thing* meta-model. At each dimension, the *thing* and the *relates to* are instantiated to different concepts, as presented below.

- Data (What?)—Each of the rows in this column address the understanding of, and dealing with, any enterprise's data. The description of enterprise data can be done using by the Entity (as a specialization of a *thing*) and the Relationship (as a specialization *of relates to*).
- Function (How?)—The rows in the function column describe the process of translating the mission of the enterprise into successively more detailed definitions of its operations.
  The function description of enterprise can be done using a sequence of *input-transform-input-transform-...*, where input is a specialization *of relates to* and transform is a specialization of a *thing*.
- Network (Where?)—This column is concerned with the spatial distribution of the enterprise's artefacts.
  The organization networks can be described using sequences of *connection-node-connection-node-...*, where *connection* is a specialization of *relates to* and *node* a specialization of a *thing*.

---

[2] Originated in Aristotle's work on ethics (https://en.wikipedia.org/wiki/Five_Ws).

– People (Who?)—The fourth column describes who is involved in the business and in the introduction of new technology.

The Who should be described using pairs of *Role-Work*, where *Role* is a specialization of *relates to* and Work is a specialization of a *thing*.

– Time (When?)—The fifth column describes what happens at each time on the enterprise.

Time is modeled as a *cycle* and at a *moment*, where *Cycle* is a specialization of *thing* and *moment* is a specialization of *relates to*.

– Motivation (Why?)—This domain is concerned with the translation of business goals and strategies into specific ends and means.

Motivation is modeled as a *ends* and *means*, where *ends* is a specialization of *thing* and *means* is a specialization of *relates to*.

Given its structure, the Zachman Framework can be applied to almost every artefact per se, to products of enterprises, and to enterprises. As a matter of fact, the framework was initially presented as an Architecture Framework for Information Systems, then as a framework for Enterprise Architecture, and more recently as a Classification Framework.

Using an airplane as an example, in the planner's perspective, one must describe the purpose using the six primitive interrogatives of communication: it is a bomber that must fly at given altitude, for a given duration, carrying a given weight, by a given crew, and to fulfill a set of goals. In the owner's perspective, one must describe how to operate the airplane, from flying to maintenance. Again this description should be presented in the six primitive interrogatives of communication. In the designer view, one describes each system of the airplane, for example, the engine system, the breaking system, and the communication systems, among many others. The next perspective, the builder's view, is to describe the technology used to build each system. Finally, the subcontractor view describes the parts each subcontractor must provide so the builder can build the airplane.

The Zackman framework provides no architecture language nor explains how the models at each column relates with the other columns. Zachman argues the columns are all equally important, given no hints for the best way to establish the relations between the columns. Establishing a relation between every possible pairs of columns would be too redundant in many situations and would take too much effort. The opposite approach, having a single column (named as anchor column) at each layer that relates with all the other columns, is a very practical approach [2].

In our experience we found out that the fact is that the anchor column depends on the enterprise business, as presented next.

• In process-based industry, as chemical, mining, manufacturing, or services enterprises, the how column would likely be the anchor column because it describes the key processes. The remaining columns are used to characterize each process.

• In knowledge-based enterprises, as lawyers, universities, research, health, and many others, the who column would likely be the anchor column. The persons are the key asset.

- The where column would likely be the anchor column in logistics industry.
- In event-based enterprises, as police, fireman, emergency, and so on, the when column is most likely the anchor column since it establishes the key events, and the remaining ones are used to characterize the response to that event.
- In finance and other data intensive industries, the what column would likely be the anchor column, given they are information-based industries.
- The why-based enterprises are not so obvious, but religion's enterprises are likely to be among the ones to have the why as the anchor column.

3.2.2 The Open Group Architecture Framework

The Open Group Architecture Framework (TOGAF) describes the Enterprise Architecture along four domains [3]:

- Business architecture
- Data architecture
- Application architecture
- Technology architecture

The business architecture addresses topics as the goals and drivers, organization roles, actors, and functions, business processes, and events.

In the TOGAF meta-model (see Fig. 3.2), the data and the application architectures are framed into the Information Systems Architecture. The data architecture includes the data concepts (including at logical and physical level). The application architecture, according to TOGAF meta-model, includes the information systems (including the concept of application at logical and physical level).

Finally, according to the TOGAF meta-model, the technology architecture identifies the platform services and the logical and physical components. TOGAF has many other key elements, as the ADM presented in Sect. 6.2.

3.2.3 ArchiMate

ArchiMate, an open and independent EA standard, defines three core layers (see Fig. 3.3) that are further expanded in the full framework (see Fig. 3.4).

Thus ArchiMate core layers are [4]:

- Business layer: It offers services (through products) to customers. The services are realized by business processes that use the information entities of the organization and are run by business actors.
- Application layer: It supports the business level with application services realized in application components.

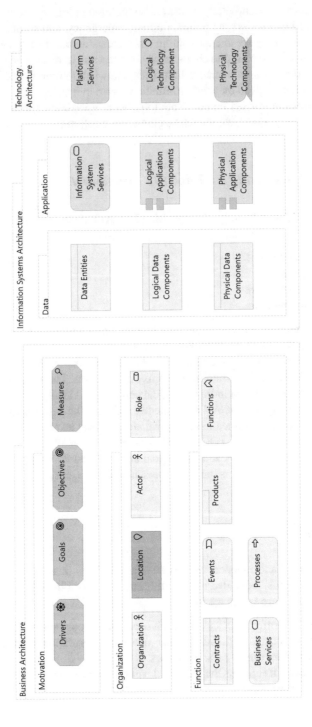

Fig. 3.2 TOGAF meta-model concepts (based on [3])

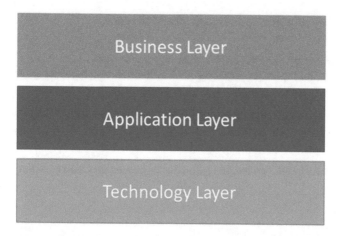

Fig. 3.3 ArchiMate core layers (based on [4])

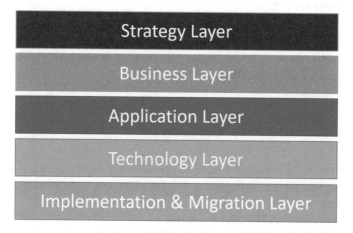

Fig. 3.4 ArchiMate full framework (based on [4])

- Technological layer: Provides infrastructure services (e.g., processing, storage, and communication) to the application layer. The services are realized by machines, computer devices, and software.

ArchiMate 3.0 adds two extra layers in the full framework [4]:

- Strategy layer, which identifies the capabilities and resources needed to achieve the goals of the organization.
- Implementation and migration layer, which supports the description of the initiatives that change the architecture.

3.2.4 Commonly used Architecture Layers

In this book we consider the layers most commonly used in the establishment of an EA. Besides the layers proposed by ArchiMate, we also consider information and service layers, both existing as subsets in other ArchiMate's layers.

- The Information layer defines the major data subjects used by business.
- The Service layer identifies and characterizes the services supported by the organization IT Application Architecture.

Thus, in this book, we use the following layers to structure and describe the EA concepts:

- Strategy
- Business
- Information
- Information systems
- Technology
- Service

In Table 3.1, we map the architecture layers used in this book, with Zachman, ArchiMate, and TOGAF domains.

3.3 The Architecture of the Enterprise

In order to manage the enterprise architecture and use the approaches and techniques described in this book, it is important to have a common understanding of the EA core concepts.

Thus, next, we use the strategy, business, information, information systems, technology, and service layers to describe the EA concepts.

In this chapter, and throughout the book, we use ArchiMate, BPMN, and UML notations to model the EA concepts, and, exceptionally, ad hoc diagrams to introduce some concepts.

3.3.1 Strategy Architecture Layer

The word strategy comes from the Greek word "strategos," which strictly means "General in command of an army." Therefore, the term strategy has mostly been developed in a military context [5]. Sun Tzu, for example, refers to it as the basis of military success: "All men can see the tactics whereby I conquer, but what none can see is the strategy out of which victory is evolved" [6].

Table 3.1 Architecture Layers adopted in this book and corresponding elements in other frameworks

Layers considered in the book	Zachman dimensions and perspectives	Layer in ArchiMate	TOGAF dimensions
Strategy layer	Motivation (Why?) dimension	Strategy	Business Architecture
Business layer	Function (How?) and People (Who?) dimensions	Business	Business Architecture
Information layer	Data (What?) dimension	Described as passive structure elements at the business, application, and technology layers	Data architecture (part of the Information Systems Architecture)
Information Systems layer	System model (designers' perspective)	Application	Application architecture (part of the Information Systems Architecture)
Technology layer	Technology model (builder's perspective), including Network dimension (Where?)	Technology	Technology architecture
Service layer	Does not exist explicitly	The business layer use services provided by the Application Layer	The lower layers provide services to the upper layers

One of the famous examples of strategy in ancient times is the Trojan Hour; according to the legend, in order to find a way to enter the gates of Troy, the Greek soldiers planned a ploy that involved creating a giant wooden horse, hiding the soldiers inside it, and offering the horse to the Trojans as a gift. The Trojans were tricked and brought the horse inside the city; at night, the hidden Greek soldiers opened the gates for their army leading to the Greek victory.

The previous example uses strategy as a plan, particularly it uses strategy as a ploy, i.e., just a specific maneuver intended to outwit an opponent or competitor [7].

The first modern writers to relate the concept of strategy to business were von Neumann and Morgenstern [8], in their book *Theory of Games and Economic Behavior*. They define strategy as a plan which specifies what choices a player will make in every possible situation, for every possible actual information which he or she may possess at that moment in conformity with the pattern of information which the rules of the game provide to him or her for that case. Thus, strategy is a series of actions that are decided on according to the particular situation. Strategy cannot be viewed as a simplistic, mechanistic process. According to Mintzberg and

Lampel [9], there are different views about the source of strategy; business strategy is an enormous domain in which little consensus exists. Different views include that strategy is about defining a set of goals and objectives and the steps to achieve them and the way to measure them.

Bernard Boar in his book *The Art of Strategic Planning for Information Technology* [10] states that strategy is one of the most abused words in the business lexicon. He reinforces the importance of getting a clear strategy definition and presents a definition that he is comfortable with: "The eternal struggle of business is the struggle for advantage. The one with more advantage wins; the one with fewer advantages loses. Strategy is the ceaseless pursuit of advantage." This definition also states that strategy needs to take in consideration the way of achieving the expected results.

Michael Porter in his Harvard Business Review article [11] argues that "competitive strategy is about being different." He adds that "it means deliberately choosing a different set of activities to deliver a unique mix of value," choosing to perform different activities from the rivals or similar activities in different ways. In his earlier book *Competitive Strategy: Techniques for Analyzing Industries and Competitors* [12], he defines competitive strategy as "a combination of ends (goals) for which the firm is striving and the means (policies) by which it is seeking out there." It is important to notice that he sees strategy as both a plan and a position. Henry Mintzberg states that we need more than a single definition of strategy, because it has been used implicitly in different ways even if it has conventionally been defined formally in only one. People use the word strategy in several different ways, the most common being the following [7]:

- Strategy is a plan, a guideline (or a set of guidelines) to deal with a situation. According to this definition, strategies have two essential characteristics: they are made in advance of the actions to which they apply, and they are developed on purpose. It is relevant to notice that as a plan, strategy can be a ploy too. In the example of the Trojan Horse given previously, the real strategy as a plan was to open the troy gates for the Greek army, and the ploy was make the Trojans think that the wooden horse was a gift;
- Strategy is a pattern, specifically a pattern in a stream of actions over time. In other words, strategy is consistency in behavior, whether or not intended. Mintzberg labels the first definition as intended strategy and the second one as realized strategy. Deliberate strategies are those where intentions existed previously, and emergent strategies are those where patterns were developed in the absence of intentions;
- Strategy is a position, specifically where we locate an organization in an environment, i.e., between the internal and external context. This definition can be compatible with the previous ones, a position can be aspired through a plan (or a ploy) and can be reached, perhaps found, through a pattern;
- Strategy is a perspective, if we look inside the organization, inside the heads of the person responsible to develop a strategy, that person has a way of perceiving the world. Some organizations favor marketing, others engineering, and others operational efficiency, depending on the way organization perceives the world.

3.3.1.1   Top Layers of the Enterprise Architecture

There are different approaches to address EA top layers. Nevertheless, it is commonly recognized that the EA strategy is something that must be considered since it drives and justifies most of the business architecture options.

For example, according to [13], strategy strongly influences the structure, the human resources management, the reward system, and the business processes.

Robert Winter also considers in Institute for Information Management of the University of St. Gallen (IWI-HSG) framework that strategy drives other EA domains (including organization and application layers)—see Fig. 3.5.

At a pure management level, strategy is defined at a corporate and business level, as a consequence of the vision, the mission, and the objectives. The strategy is then used to define the tactics that will implement it [15].

In management disciplines, the corporate strategy is formulated by six major blocks: (i) Mission, Objectives, and strategy; (ii) Products-Markets; (iii) Vertical Integration; (iv) Organizational development; (v) Internationalization; and (vi) Diversification—see Fig. 3.6.

Fig. 3.5   Strategy in the context of EA (based on [14])

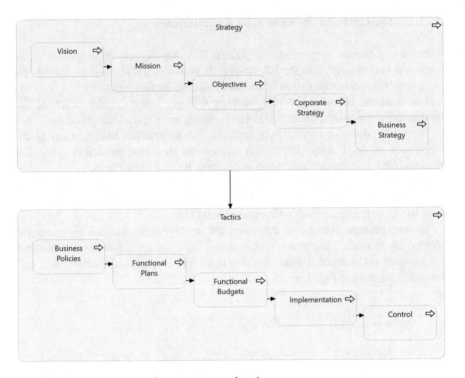

Fig. 3.6 Management perspective on strategy and tactics

3.3.1.2 Business Motivation Concepts

Organizations do not act randomly. Activities performed within enterprises, either as a business process or simply applying a business rule, should know:

- why the business wants to do something?
- what do you want to achieve?
- how do you plan to get there?
- how to measure the achievement?

If an enterprise establishes a certain approach to its work, it should be able to explain "why, " that is, the result(s) the approach aims to achieve, what motivates the Business Plan, what are the elements of a **business plan**, and how does the "motivation" and "actions" relate?

We will use OMG Business Motivation Model (BMM) [16] to frame the concepts most commonly used when describing the motivation elements of the EA. The Business Motivation Model provides a scheme for developing, communicating, and managing business plans in an organized manner by:

- Identifying factors that motivate the establishing of the business plans.
- Identifying and defining the elements of the business plans.
- Indicating how all these factors and elements are interrelated.

BMM does not address business processes, workflows, business vocabulary, etc. The major goal is to develop a business model that supports the identification of the principles, requirements, and constraints for the business and system design.

3.3.1.2.1   BMM Overview

The main areas of the BMM are the Ends, the Means, and the Influencers. BMM established the dependencies among the concepts of these areas, including the identification of the means to achieve the enterprise goals.

Each BMM element is presented in Fig. 3.7.

Ends define what the organization wants to be (not considering the "how").
Means establish the "how" the organization plans to achieve its ends.
Directives establish the rules and policies for the use of the available means.
Influencers are the sources of change that can impact the organization, including the application of means or the implementation of its ends.
Assessment represents the assessment that an Influencer (relevant to the enterprise) does on the enterprise ends and the means used.

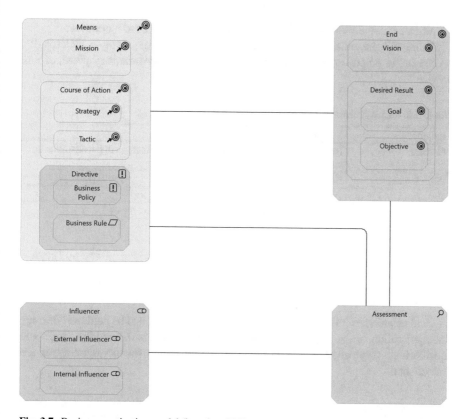

Fig. 3.7 Business motivation model (based on [16])

3.3.1.2.2 Ends

Ends define the organization vision and goals. The ends are not concerned about how the vision or the goals will be achieved. Ends are expected to focus on the position and goals of the organization (including changing or maintaining its current market position). Ends are specialized in **Vision** and **Desired Results**, and Desired Results in Goals and Objectives.

3.3.1.2.2.1 Vision

A Vision represents the highest level of what the enterprise wants to be. It is the "dream" it pursuits every day. A Vision describes the future state of the enterprise, not considering how it will be achieved. In defining the Vision, a desired end state is established. This final state may not be attainable. Typically, the vision is not focused on a single aspect of the business, but on a composition. The vision is categorized by:

- Being unambiguous.
- Being clear.
- Harmonizing organization's culture and values.

Vision statements should be shorter so that they are easier to memorize.

Table 3.2 presents examples of vision statements. For example, Microsoft's vision is "to empower people through great software, any time, any place, or any device."

Table 3.2 Vision statements examples

Enterprise	Vision
Eu-Rent	Be the cart rental brand of choice for business users in the countries in which we operate
Pizza Rapida	Be the city's favorite pizza place
Technical University	Be the number 1 engineer school in the country
Retail Things	Sell merchandise and services at everyday low prices

A Vision is supported or made operative by Missions. It is amplified by Goals.

3.3.1.2.2.2 Goal

A Goal establishes a future state of the enterprise (which must be achieved through the application of the appropriate "means"). Thus, a goal is defined long term and qualitatively (typically). Based on the goal, the objectives for the organization are established.

3.3.1.2.2.3   Objectives

A goal is divided into different objectives. Each objective must have an explicit completion date and criteria. By consolidating the achievement of objectives, it is possible to assess whether the goals are (or not) being achieved (Table 3.3).

Table 3.3 Objective statement examples

Enterprise	Objective
Retail Things	By the end of the current year, be rated in the top 3 retail companies operating in the city
Pizza Rapida	By January 1, 2023, 99% on-time pizza delivery
Technical University	Be rated as the TOP research school in the country

3.3.1.2.3   Means

The means define what an enterprise has decided to do to become what it has decided to be. Thus, a means is some "device, capacity, technique, instrument or method that can be invoked, activated, or imposed to achieve Ends." The means are specialized in mission, courses of action, and directives.

3.3.1.2.3.1   Mission

The organization's operational activity is explained through the mission. The mission must be broad enough to include the various operational areas of the organization. The mission describes the day to day of the organization, making the mission a reality. Mission planning is done through strategies (Table 3.4).

Table 3.4 Mission statement examples

Enterprise	Mission
Pizza Rapida	Provide pizza to customers city-wide
Technical University	Provide knowledge to people
Retail Things	Provide merchandise to the retail market

A mission must be doable and achievable. Thus, it must be possible to achieve the mission in the organization's operation. Additionally, the mission must be inspiring for the organization's customers, managers, and employees. For example, Microsoft's mission is to "help people and businesses throughout the world to realize their full potential." Walmart's mission is "to give ordinary folk the chance to buy the same thing as rich people."

3.3.1.2.3.2 Course of Action: Strategy

What the organization has decided to do is defined as Courses of Action. Performance measures for courses of action are set out in Objectives. In turn, Courses of Action are categorized as Strategies and Tactics—which represent courses of action with less or more level of detail.

Strategies are typically defined long term and broad in scope. Thus, each strategy is implemented through tactics (whose scope and execution time are more focused). Each tactic can contribute to the implementation of more than one Strategy (Table 3.5).

Table 3.5 Strategy statement examples

Enterprise	Strategy
Retail Things	Operate nationwide, focusing on major cities, competing with other national retail companies
Pizza Rapida	Deliver pizzas to the location of the customer's choice
Technical University	Hire the best teachers

It is common to make a correspondence between Course of Action and Desired Results. Generally, the Strategies are defined considering the goals and the Tactics considering the Objectives of the organization.

3.3.1.2.3.3 Course of Action: Tactic

Strategies are carried out by tactics, which tend to be shorter and narrower in scope. A Tactic can contribute to the implementation of more than one Strategy (Table 3.6).

Table 3.6 Tactic statement examples

Enterprise	Tactic
Pizza Rapida	Hire drivers with their own vehicles to deliver pizzas
Technical University	Increase teachers wages by 20%
Consulting Company	Call first-time customers personally
Retail Things	Ship products for free

3.3.1.2.3.4 Directives: Business Policies

Directives are specialized in business rules and business policies (Table 3.7). Different levels of enforcement can be defined by organizations for each directive (such as strictly enforced, deferred enforcement, override with explanation, and guideline, among others).

Table 3.7 Enforcement Levels of Directives examples

Enterprise	Directive	Enforcement Level
Technical University	Students are always first	Strictly enforced
Pizza Rapida	A cooker who delivers pizzas more than 30 min after costumer request will be counseled to additional training	Pre-authorized override
Retail Things	An article rated negative by more than ten other customers is never more sell in the store	Override with explanation

Business policies are organization principles that are used for guiding courses of action. Policies define what can be done and what must not be done and set limits on how it should be done. A Business Rule tends do be less formal than a Business Policy. Business rules are actionable directives (Table 3.8).

Table 3.8 Business Policy statement examples

Source	Business Policy
Technical University	Cheating is not allowed
Pizza Rapida	Hot Pizzas ensure frequent customers
Retail Things	The Store Director will contact each customer who makes a complaint

3.3.1.2.3.5   Directives: Business Rule

Business Rules are derived from Business Policies (Table 3.9).

Table 3.9 Business Rule statement examples

Source	Business rule
Technical University	If a student is caught cheating, that student will be suspended between 1 and 5 days
Pizza Rapida	Pizzas must be delivered hot
Retail Things	Credit sale is not allowed

3.3.1.2.4   Influencers

An Influencer is some actor that affects the way the organization uses its Means in pursuing its Ends (Table 3.10). There are internal (from within the organization) and external influencers (from outside the organization—as competitor, customer, environment, partner, regulation, supplier, technology) (Table 3.11).

Table 3.10 External influencer examples

Enterprise	External influencer	Category
Technical University	Two smaller competitors have merged, and the joint university is now bigger than the Technical University	Competitor
Pizza Rapida	Pizza Rapida's primary target is Z generation, but it recognizes the need to appeal to the Y generation	Customer
Retail Things	VAT increase next year is expected to have a negative impact on sales	Regulation

Table 3.11 Internal influencer examples

Enterprise	Internal Influencer	Category
Technical University	Research impact must increase each year	Assumption
Technical University	Junior researchers are generally hired within Technical University Master Students	Habit
Pizza Rapida	Fast cooks may have longer work breaks	Habit
Pizza Rapida	Pizza Rapida is environment-friendly. All products used are environment-friendly and 100% biodegradable	Explicit Corporate Value
Retail Things	Warehouses are clustered next to major cities	Infrastructure
Retail Things	Availability of market-leading brand products and white label products	Issue

3.3.1.2.5 Assessments

An Assessment judges the organization's ability to use its Means to achieve its Ends. This analysis can be performed using different techniques (but it is beyond the scope of this book and of enterprise architecture)—see an assessment example in Fig. 3.8.

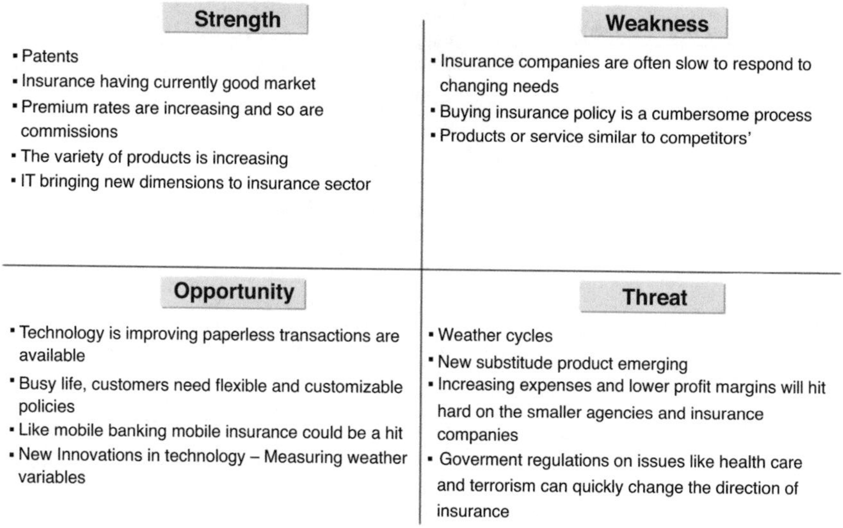

Strength	Weakness
• Patents • Insurance having currently good market • Premium rates are increasing and so are commissions • The variety of products is increasing • IT bringing new dimensions to insurance sector	• Insurance companies are often slow to respond to changing needs • Buying insurance policy is a cumbersome process • Products or service similar to competitors'
Opportunity	**Threat**
• Technology is improving paperless transactions are available • Busy life, customers need flexible and customizable policies • Like mobile banking mobile insurance could be a hit • New Innovations in technology – Measuring weather variables	• Weather cycles • New substitude product emerging • Increasing expenses and lower profit margins will hit hard on the smaller agencies and insurance companies • Goverment regulations on issues like health care and terrorism can quickly change the direction of insurance

Fig. 3.8 SWOT analysis example

3.3.1.3 Motivation Modeling

In order to model what triggers the EA, we will adopt ArchiMate Motivation Aspect Model Extension [4]. Motivational concepts are used to model the motivations or reasons that underlie the development or modification of any enterprise architecture. These motivations can influence, guide, and constrain the design (Fig. 3.9).

It is important to understand the factors, often referred to as drivers, which influence the motivational elements. They may be triggered from inside or outside the enterprise. Internal drivers, also called concerns, are associated with stakeholders, which can be any individual human being or a group of human beings, as a project team, company, or society. Examples of such drivers are customer satisfaction, accordance to the law, or profitability. It is common for companies to undertake an assessment of drivers, for example, using a SWOT analysis. The real motivations are represented by goals, principles, requirements, and restrictions.

Goals represent some desired outcome—or end—that stakeholders want to achieve, such as "increase customer satisfaction by 10%."

Requirements and **Principles** represent the desired properties of the solutions.

Principles are regulatory guidelines that guide the design of all possible solutions in a given context. For example, the principle of "data should be stored only once" is a means to achieve the goal of "data consistency" and applies to all possible architectural projects of the organization.

Requirements represent formal statements of a need expressed by stakeholders that must be met by the architecture or solutions. For further details on modeling Enterprise motivation with ArchiMate, please see [17] and [4].

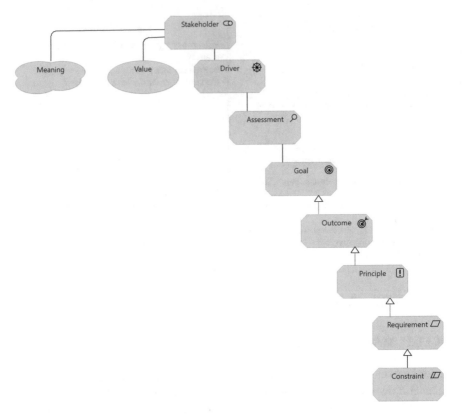

Fig. 3.9 ArchiMate motivation modeling—based on [17]

3.3.2 Business Architecture Layer

3.3.2.1 System Context

According to ISO/IEC/IEEE 42010:2011: "a system inhabits an environment. A system's environment can influence that system. The environment, or context, determines the setting of developmental, operational, political, and other circumstances of the system. The environment can include other systems that interact with the system of interest, either directly via interfaces or indirectly in other ways. The environment determines the boundaries that define the scope of the system of interest relative to other systems" [18].

Therefore, a system context model represents the direct environment of the system and gives initial information about the communication flowing from and to the system. The "system" is the object of concern, which is the enterprise (or company, or business unit). The system context model represents the direct environment of the system, comprising all its relevant stakeholders and their respective concerns. Figure 3.10 presents the context of a university.

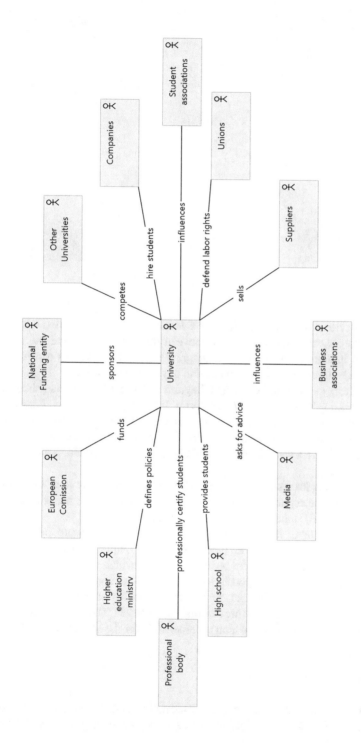

Fig. 3.10 University context example

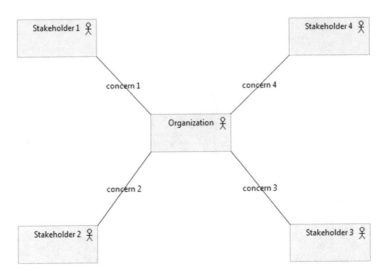

Fig. 3.11 Context diagram (black-box)

In the previous diagram, all the flows toward the organization (University) represent the concerns and interaction between the organization and the outside world. Each interaction in the context diagram should be linked to a process. It should not exist interactions not connected to any specific process.

Thus, we can summarize the context diagram as a functional vision (black box) of the organization's relations with its exterior. It represents all the relations (input and output) between the organization and the elements interested in the organization (stakeholders). It represents at least the relationship between the organization's customers (which are a specific class of stakeholders) and the products and services of the organization.

The business context is usually done in two steps. First, there is a "black-box" approach, where the organization is considered as a whole. The focus is only on identifying (external) stakeholders and their concerns (Fig. 3.11).

In the second stage, it is important to relate each relationship between the organization and a stakeholder to an input event and/or output. Each event should be forwarded to a business process (or business service), which will have to be able to interpret the received event. Responses to the event have to conform to the outputs of the process. Another viewpoint that can be drawn from the context diagram are the business units involved in supporting external stakeholders. Thus, each event should be forwarded to a business unit, which is responsible for the event management.

3.3.2.2 Business Process

A business process is a sequence of interrelated activities that transforms inputs into outputs and that has the goal of producing a service or product for a customer or a

Fig. 3.12 Business process classic IPO paradigm (input "Process" output)

particular market. The inputs and outputs can be material goods or information (i.e., physical or logical elements)—Fig. 3.12.

Some business process definitions are just focused on transforming inputs into outputs (mostly on the engineer/production side), while others are focused on the process added value. For example, the ISO 9000 defines a process as "a set of interrelated and cooperative activities that transform inputs into outputs," not considering the value creation of the business process. Hammer and Champy [19] define a process as "a collection of activities that takes one or more kinds of input and creates an output that is of value to the customer." Johanson [20] considers a process "as set of linked activities that take an input and transform it to create an output. Ideally, the transformation that occurs in the process should add value to the input and create an output that is more useful and effective to the recipient either upstream or downstream." Thus, the definitions from the engineering context tend to focus on the processing procedure and the finished product, while the management definitions tend to focus on the achieving of value.

A business process usually starts at the organizational boundaries and crosses the all enterprise (Fig. 3.13). Business processes are "virtual," that is, each one sees "his/her business process" (see Sect. 8.1 for further information on identifying the "right" business processes). Business processes usually model only activities associated with people, stating what has to be done at the operational level. A business process may or may not state: who, how, where, when, importance, or the risks involved.

Therefore, a business process can be defined according to Fig. 3.14. A business process should comply with a set of rules, including:

- Any process has at least one input.
- Any process has at least one exit point (i.e., a product or service business).
- The outputs of a process are different from the inputs.
- Any process must have at least one client (internal or external).

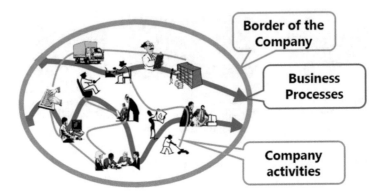

Fig. 3.13 Company business processes (Reprinted with permission from Linkconsulting)

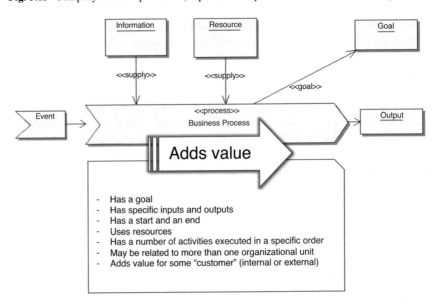

Fig. 3.14 Business process definition

3.3.2.2.1   Business Process Orientation

Nowadays, several enterprises still have a vertical orientation, having several levels of business units, departments, divisions, teams, etc. organized around functions or competencies (engineering, marketing, warehouse, finance, etc.)—Fig. 3.15.

Business workflows are horizontal, crossing different business units. Consequently, the vertical management of organizations leads to gaps and overlaps (because some tasks are "shared" among units, not being clear where the "responsibility" lays). The "island" effect tends to reduce the process performance, since there is an optimization of the functions (leading to a sub-optimization of the whole

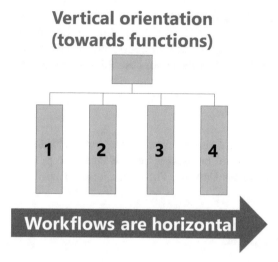

Fig. 3.15 Traditional view of enterprises

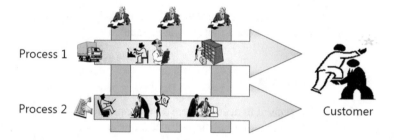

Fig. 3.16 Business process-oriented organization (Reprinted with permission from Link Consulting, SA)

horizontal process). The management of cross-functional "blank" spaces is usually unclear. The traditional view of organizations does not show how the value is added. Functions become more important than customers, but responsibilities are lost at the interfaces between functions. In business process-oriented organizations, there is a horizontal management by processes crossing organizational functions and focusing on customers (Fig. 3.16).

In a nutshell: a business process is a set of interrelated activities that transform inputs into outputs and that create value for a customer. Business process is used as a method to model value creation, regardless of the organizational structure, allowing the explanation of operations, analyses, and optimizations.

Therefore, we may conclude that all the work performed in organizations is part of a process. Consequently, all organization's products and services are result of a process. A process is the result of cooperative articulation of actors and resources. A process approach is a structured way of managing workflows.

3.3.2.3   Business Layer Concepts

Most of the business concepts next presented are based in [4, 17, 21], including TOGAF, and ArchiMate meta-model for describing the business layer.

3.3.2.3.1   Business Actor

A business actor is an active entity that performs behavior (i.e., the "subject" of behavior). Examples of business actors are Person (e.g., employee, customer), Department, or Business Unit [4]. The designations of business actors should be nouns.

3.3.2.3.2   Business Role

A business role has the responsibility for performing specific behavior, to which an actor can be assigned [4].

The same actor can play multiple roles, and the same role can be played by multiple actors. Business roles are a more stable element than actors.

3.3.2.3.3   Business Interface

A business interface is a point of access where a business service is made available to the environment. It exposes the functionality of a business service (provided by an interface) or requires business services. It is used to set the "channel" in which a service is provided (e.g., telephone, web, face to face) [4].

A business interface may be part of a business role through a composition relationship, and a business interface may be used by a business role.

A business interface may be assigned to one or more business services, which means that these services are exposed by the interface. The name of a business interface should preferably be a noun.

3.3.2.3.4   Location

Location is a conceptual point or extent in space. It is used to distribute structural element physical or conceptually. Location models the distribution of structural elements such as business actors, application components, and devices. Indirectly, a location can also be assigned to a behavior element, to indicate where the behavior is performed [4].

The model in Fig. 3.17 shows the departments of a company distributed over different locations. The Engineer and the Production departments are located in the factory, and the finance and the human resource departments are in the regional office.

Fig. 3.17 Location example

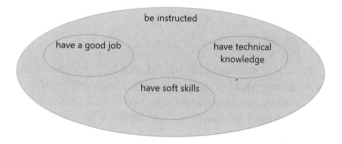

Fig. 3.18 Value example

3.3.2.3.5   Business Object

Business Object is a passive element that has relevance from a business perspective (handled by behavior). Business Objects represent "informational" or "conceptual" business elements. Generally, a business object is used to model an object type (like a UML class), of which several instances may exist within the organization. A wide variety of types of business objects can be defined. Business objects are passive in the sense that they do not trigger or perform processes [4].

3.3.2.3.6   Value

Value is the relative worth, utility, or importance of a business service or product. Value is often expressed in money and may be associated with business services.

In the example of Fig. 3.18, the value "Be Insured" is the highest-level expression of what the service "Provide Insurance" enables the client to do; three "sub-values" are identified that are part of what "Be Insured" includes [4].

3.3.2.3.7   Product

A Product is a coherent collection of services, accompanied by a contract/set of agreements, which is offered as a whole to (internal or external) customers. Products can be based on services or information. A product consists of a set of services. The product name is the name used to communicate with the outside (e.g., customers) [4].

3.3.2.3.8   Contract

A Contract is a formal or informal specification of an agreement that specifies the rights and obligations associated with a product. It can be used to model a formal contract, as an informal agreement on a product. It may contain Service Level Agreements (SLAs). It is a business object specialization [4].

3.3.2.3.9   Business Service

A business service is a coherent piece of functionality that offers added value to the environment, independent of the way this functionality is realized internally. A service may be internal or external, and it is associated with a value. A service is realized through business behavior, including activities, processes, or functions [4].

3.3.2.3.10   Business Process

As presented before, business process stands for a behavior element that groups behavior based on an ordering of activities. It is intended to produce a defined set of products or business services. It describes the internal behavior performed by a business role that is required to produce a set of products and services [4].

3.3.2.3.11   Business Function

The business function is a behavior element that groups behavior based on a chosen set of criteria (usually required business resources and/or competences). Business processes are generally defined based on products or services offered by the organization, while the business functions are the basis for allocating resources to support tasks. The name should be a verb in the gerund.

3.3.2.3.12   Business Event

A business event is something that happens and may influence behavior—business processes, functions, or interactions. It is something instantaneous (no duration). It can be generated externally (e.g., a client) or internally in the enterprise [4].

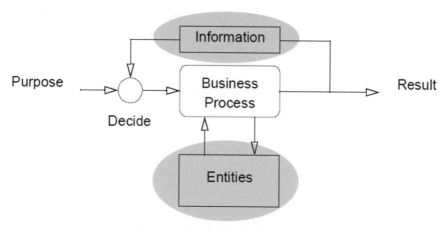

Fig. 3.19 Information in the business context

3.3.3   Information Architecture Layer

The Information Architecture (IA) specifies the key concepts to understand and operate the business (Fig. 3.19).

The IA specifies the life cycle associated with the entities (tangible and intangible) of the enterprise. It makes communication easy among people who manage the business and the technology. IA makes possible to manage information independently of the business processes and the information systems.

The IA defines (i.e., restricts) what information exists and how it is related. The IA provides assurance of consistency to the organization's data. It ensures that the data is properly named, defined, structured, and documented.

IA provides stability in the dynamic business environments. Business processes often change. A stable resource, as information, ensures that data is available to answer information needs. Therefore, IA sets the life cycle of information entities independently of the business processes and IS.

3.3.3.1   Concepts

The IA (aka Data Architecture) defines the major types of data used by the business processes of the enterprise; these data types are known as information entities.

An **information entity** represents any concept that has meaning for the operation of the business and on which is relevant (and possible) to keep information; for example, a person, a place, an idea, a thing or an event that is relevant to the organization's business processes and on which it is necessary to store information.

Data flows define how the main types of data are used by business processes. Depending on the authors information entities come up with different names, including (information) entity, business object, business information, and (business) resource, among others.

An information entity is characterized by:

- a name (noun);
- a unique identifier, by which their occurrences (instances) are uniquely recognized in the enterprise;
- its attributes;
- a description;
- its structural relationships with other entities (and the derived relations with processes and applications).

Examples of information entities are Course, Classroom, Student, Customer, Supplier, Train, etc.

Information entities instances must be clearly and unambiguously identified. The unique identifier of the entity must be a function of its attributes! Therefore, (numerical) identifiers not known in the business context (e.g., GUID) are usually inadequate identifiers.

3.3.3.2 Information Classification

According to Inmon [22], data can be classified into three dimensions:

- Primitive vs. Derived
- Historical vs. Projected
- Public vs. Private

Each information attribute is classified in each of these three dimensions. The dimensions determine the requirements to access the data that the information systems manage.

3.3.3.2.1 Primitive vs. Derived

Primitive information specifies a single fact or occurrence. Examples of primitive data are record of the date, value associated with an invoice, participants in a transaction, and amount of material ordered.

Derived data is calculated data aggregated or summarized. It is based on one or more primitive data or other derived data. Examples of derived data are average hours worked per day or training cost in the first quarter.

3.3.3.2.2 Historical vs. Projected

Historical data records unambiguous and irrefutable facts. The values recorded are accurate, and there is an agreement about the means to obtain or calculate them.

On the other side, projected data are estimates, predictions, or inferences from facts that might happen. The concept of "correction" does not apply to projections. There may be a probabilistic degree of confidence about the projection. There may not be unanimity about the means to obtain or calculate them.

The safety training that an employee had in October 12, 2021, is an example of historical data. And the training needs in "Advanced Security" is a projected data example.

3.3.3.2.3 Public vs. Private

Public data is data that have multiple stakeholders and may be visible outside the enterprise. Its integrity is maintained by the enterprise.

Private data is owned by a single individual or group of individuals. It reflects specific needs and may not be relevant or may not make sense out of a limited context. Its integrity is managed locally.

Usually, public information belongs to the enterprise, while private information belongs to the individual (e.g., password from a user).

3.3.3.2.4 Information Classification Impacts

For each information entity, its attributes may be classified in the previous three dimensions (Fig. 3.20).

Usually, primitive data has different characteristics from derived data (Fig. 3.21).

The characteristics of the data have a strong relationship with the systems where it can be found. Usually, operational systems deal with more primitive, historical, public data. Operational data is detailed day by day, with high probability of access, and application oriented.

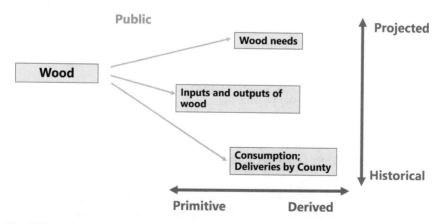

Fig. 3.20 Wood information entity and its attribute classification

Fig. 3.21 Information entity attribute classification

Characteristic	Primitive	Derived
Detail level	High	Low
Performance	High	Low
Usage Pattern	High	Low
Availability	High	low
Users	Various	concentrated
Update requirements	Real time	Periodic
Definition	Static	dynamics
Quantity of Access	Many / short	Few /long
Modification rate	High	Low

On the other hand, derived, projected data is mostly useful at strategic management layers, using datamarts, while unit managers are more focused on data type from the different vectors. Data warehouses put together derived and aggregated data by subject and are used at unit management layers.

3.3.3.3 IA Modeling

IA modeling specifies the information entities and their relationships. It is suggested using an object-oriented approach (similar to UML). It involves identifying:

- The key/identifier of each entity.
- The properties/attributes of each individual entity.
- The structural relationships between entities.
- Types of relationships (composition or aggregation and specialization).

Notice that since behavioral relationships change more often than information, they are not represented in the IA.

3.3.4 Information Systems Architecture Layer

Information System is a system that manages business information and has as inputs or outputs information used by business processes. An information systems

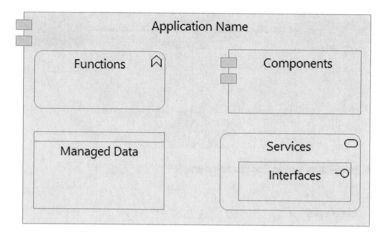

Fig. 3.22 Information system elements

may be:

- an Excel spreadsheet with a list of customers of an organization;
- a machine that produces computer tomography images for analysis;
- an ERP that is being used to support business processes;
- a file of paper with the suppliers of an organization and its accounting information.

An **Application** is defined as an information system that uses digital technology to store and process information. In this definition, we exclude analogue systems.

An information system is described through (Fig. 3.22):

- the name (i.e., identification) of the system;
- The behavior of the application, where we can include the purpose (from a high-level perspective) and the functions it performs (from a detailed perspective).
- The information that the application maintains and manages
- Dependencies with other systems, which can include services and interfaces, both realized and consumed

Therefore, the **Information System Architecture** (ISA) is the identification of the information systems of an organization and their inter-dependencies (Fig. 3.23).

The ISA provides an answer to the question: "What ISs an organization should have?" It helps decide how to evolve the current infrastructure for the future, in order to improve business support, and reduce costs associated with IT.

The ISA provides justification for a set of IS (and not other) based on the business processes and the information managed. It provides traceability among decisions taken in the design of the ISA, processes, and information. The ISA is less dependent on subjective factors and therefore more deterministic than ad hoc approaches regarding the analysis of IS.

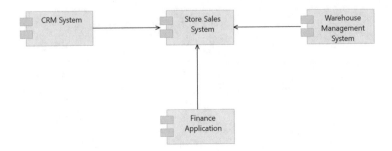

Fig. 3.23 Information System Architecture example

3.3.4.1   Concepts

The main concepts defined at the application level are discussed below.

3.3.4.1.1   Application Component

An application component is a self-contained part of a system that encapsulates its contents and exposes its functionality through a set of interfaces [4].

3.3.4.1.2   Application Interface

An application interface defines the set of operations and events that are provided by the component or those that are required from the environment [4].

3.3.4.1.3   Data Object

A data object is a coherent, self-contained piece of information suitable for automated processing.

3.3.4.1.4   Application Service

Application service is an externally visible unit of functionality, provided by one or more components, exposed through well-defined interfaces, and meaningful to the environment [4]. Application services may be further specialized. Please see "Service Architecture" section for further details.

3.3.4.1.5 Application Function

The internal behavior of a component needed to realize one or more application services [4]

3.3.5 Technology Architecture Layer

The aim of the Technology Architecture is to define the types of technology that will be used to support the Information Architecture, the Application Architecture, and, hence, the business processes.

The main results expected from a technology architecture are the definition of (i) the principles of the technology of the enterprise and (ii) the technology initiatives.

Therefore, the technology architecture defines the technologies that implement applications (identified in the application architecture) and describes the technological environment available to these applications. This architecture identifies technology concepts—such as networks, communication, distributed computing, etc.

The technology architecture addresses a high variety of concepts due, on the one hand, to the fast technological evolution and, on the other hand, to the need for specialized views of the technological components—such as security, hardware views, communication views, and development views, among others. Thus, depending on the stakeholder concern, different concepts may be important to model in the technological architecture, such as application, system, platform, software, repository, middleware, application components, specific products, services, interfaces, devices, development/production environments, and software infrastructure (DBMS, operating system, etc.).

3.3.5.1 Concepts

3.3.5.1.1 Node

A node is a computational resource upon which artifacts may be deployed for execution. Nodes are active processing elements that execute and process artifacts. Nodes are often a combination of hardware devices and system software. Nodes can be interconnected by communication paths. Artifacts are deployed in nodes. Nodes are active elements that perform processes and artifacts (such as software components and data objects) used to model application servers and database servers [4].

3.3.5.1.2   Device

Device is a hardware resource upon which artifacts may be stored or deployed for execution. It is a specialization of a node that represents a physical resource with processing capability. It models hardware systems such as mainframes, PCs, or routers. A device may be part of a node (in conjunction with system software) and may be constituted by wrapping other devices. Software artifacts can be deployed on devices. The name should have the kind of hardware it refers to (e.g., MyHome server, business mainframe, etc.) [4].

3.3.5.1.3   System Software

A system software is a software environment for specific types of components and objects that are deployed on it in the form of artifacts. In ArchiMate, System Software is a specialization of a node. It is used to model the software environment in which artifacts run [4].

It stands for the software environment in which software artifacts are deployed. A system software is a software defined and implemented by third parties and used unchanged by the enterprise. Operating system, DBMS, and workflow systems are examples of a system software [4].

A system software may contain other system software. The name should refer to the execution environment (e.g., J2EE Server).

3.3.5.1.4   Infrastructure Interface

An Infrastructure Interface is a point of access where infrastructure services offered by a node can be accessed by other nodes and application components. It specifies how the infrastructure services of a node can be accessed by other nodes (provided interface), or which functionality the node requires from its environment (required interface). It exposes an infrastructure service to the environment. The same service may be exposed through different interfaces. In a sense, an infrastructure interface specifies a kind of contract that a component realizing this interface must fulfill. This may include, for example, parameters, protocols used, pre- and post conditions, and data formats [4].

3.3.5.1.5   Network

A network is a communication medium between two or more devices. It represents the physical communication infrastructure. It may comprise one or more fixed or wireless network links. It is the physical realization of a "communication path," i.e., a means of physical communication between two or more devices. It can be wired or wireless, satellite, etc., and it has to be a physical mechanism (e.g., air, laser, fiber, etc.) that connects the two devices. The "Network" performs the "communication paths" [4].

3.3.5.1.6 Communication Path

A communication path is a link between two or more nodes, through which these nodes can exchange data. It is a logical communication relation among nodes. It is realized by one or more "networks" (that represents the physical communication infrastructure) [4].

3.3.5.1.7 Artifact

Artifact is a physical piece of data that is used or produced in a software development process, or by deployment and operation of a system. It represents a tangible element in the physical world. It is used to model software products such as source files, executables, scripts, database tables, messages, documents, specifications, and model files. Two typical ways to use the artifact concept are as an execution component and as a data file [4].

3.3.5.1.8 Infrastructure Function

Infrastructure function groups infrastructural behavior that can be performed by a node. It may describe the internal behavior of a node. This function is invisible for the user of a node that performs an infrastructure function. It may also realize infrastructure services. If behavior is externally visible, it is through infrastructure services. An infrastructure service may need to have access to artifacts to implement its behavior (e.g., tables, database, code, etc.). The infrastructure function name should be in the gerund form ("ing") [4].

3.3.5.1.9 Infrastructure Service

Infrastructure service is an externally visible unit of functionality, provided by one or more nodes, exposed through well-defined interfaces, and meaningful to the environment [4].

It exposes the functionality of a node to its environment. The functionality is accessed through one or more infra-structure interfaces (e.g., messaging, storage, naming, and directory services) [4].

3.3.6   Service Architecture Layer

As mentioned in Sect. 3.3, the services layer contains the services performed by applications. The architecture of application services is often known as Service Oriented Architecture (SOA), and stands for the architectural principles for building applications based on the composition of features of other applications. SOA arises from the consolidation of areas, such as Application Integration, Workflow, Interoperability between organizations, etc. SOA has the "Services" as a structuring element. The most important outcome that SOA is expected to deliver is the definition of new services by the composition of other services (through orchestration or choreography). As presented in Fig. 3.24, services are provided by one or several applications (provider) and are composed and used in application processes of the consumer applications.

The services must have a set of characteristics that can be used for the definition of other services. The first architectural question that arises is how to define or

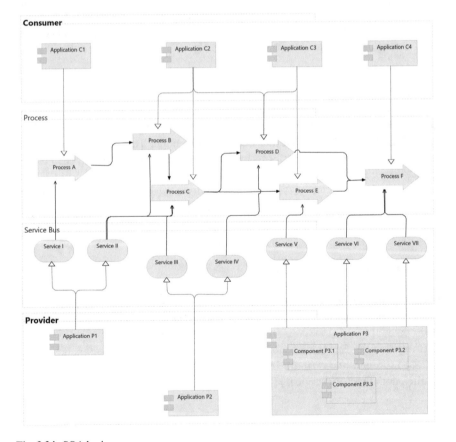

Fig. 3.24 SOA basis

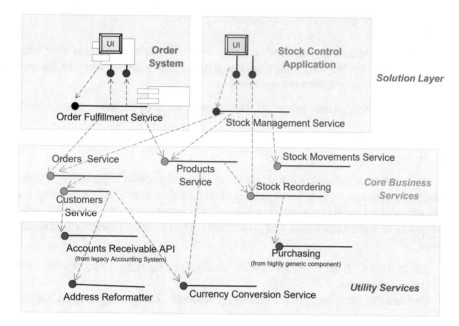

Fig. 3.25 Service-Oriented Architecture Layers (reprinted with permission from Link Consulting)

identify the most appropriate services—see Sect. 10.3 for further service design methods.

3.3.6.1 Concepts

Application Services, introduced in the Information System Architecture, may be further specialized.

Services are structured in layers according to their potential for reuse and complexity (see Fig. 3.25).

At the solution layer, services implement processes with human interaction. In the Core Business Services Layer, services implement automatic sequences of activities with a high degree of reuse (e.g., service products). Utility services are highly reusable services, but do not perform the core business activities.

3.3.6.1.1 Solution Layer

The services defined in the Solution Layer implement processes with human interaction (UI). Each interface is seen with a specific service, which is called by the execution engine (e.g., workflow). Their reuse is limited and is very dependent on the reuse of the interfaces.

3.3.6.1.2   Core Business Services Layer

The services defined in the Core Business Services Layer implement automatic sequences of activities with a high degree of reuse. These services may be focused on processes or information management:

- Processes services are "processes fragments" formed by sequence of automated operations.
- Information services are sequence of activities needed for information entities management.

A Core Business Service is a sequence of interactions with information systems that is repeated in various processes. It aims to factor activities, simplifying the definition of business processes. The Information Services encompass the activities necessary to ensure consistency of information. They have two fundamental objectives:

- Ensure that such activities are actually carried out, ensuring the proper information management.
- Remove this complexity of the remaining processes, simplifying its specification.

3.3.6.1.3   Utility Services

Utility services are highly reusable services. They may arise from business services or information services decomposition.

3.4   Exercises

Exercise 3.1

Pizza Rapida, managing partners in order to increase customer satisfaction and profitability, and after finding out that many of the pizzas were delivered to the customer more than 1 hour after ordering and cold, having as a result customers' complaints and loss of market share, defined as goals:

- Reduce Pizza delivery time
- Deliver the pizzas hot
- Reduce complaints by 50% until the end of the year

For this purpose, they decided that all deliveries must be made in less than 1 hour and that the customer satisfaction level should be always recorded.

It was also decided to buy thermal containers to transport the pizzas and to hire two more employees for the deliveries.

1. Model the motivation elements in ArchiMate including the stakeholders, drivers, assessments, goals, principles, and requirements.

Exercise 3.2

Consider the following description of the Lisbon Institute of Technology (LIT) strategy.

LIT is a fresh private Portuguese University (created 5 years ago) that is focused in providing Information Technology courses for speakers of the Portuguese language. The Sales director (CSO) is defining LIT business strategy for the next 3 years which is driven by the internationalization of the business, student satisfaction, and online courses.

LIT strategy must also consider the Financial Director (CFO) main driver, "Operational Efficiency," along with the Chief Research Officer (CRO) main driver "Innovation."

The following issues have been identified:

- Course Management functions are very centralized, and the different courses don't have any autonomy for specific adaptations
- Students' complaints have been increasing in the last 3 years
- Broadband is available in all Portuguese-speaking countries
- Online courses have been doubling sales in the last 3 years
- Online courses have autonomous business processes (not sharing any activities with traditional courses)
- Average course costs are 10% higher than competitors
- Researchers' publications have a low impact rate

The following goals have been established:

- Empower course management functions
- Increase student satisfaction (including reducing in 10% of student complaints each year)
- Reduce operational costs (including human resources costs)
- Reduce course costs to industry average
- Be the n.1 online University in Angola, Mozambique, Cabo Verde, and Brazil
- Increase average research impact rate by 25%, by 2030.

The following principles were established:

- Business units are autonomous
- Customers have a single point of contact
- Channel-specific components are separated from channel-independent components
- Management layers are minimized
- Common components are centralized (as the HR management process, or the course platforms)

- Messages with all internal and external systems are exchanged through LIT Enterprise Service Bus (ESB)

It was also decided to:

- Reengineer the course management process
- Implement an ESB (which must be in open source technology)
- Hire local professors in each country where LIT is operating
- Increase online target advertising budget by 30%.
- Increase by 20% R&D yearly budget

1. Taking into consideration the statement above, model the LIT stakeholders, drivers, assessments, goals, principles, requirements, and constraints.
2. Are there any motivation elements that are negatively influencing others? Model these relationships in ArchiMate.

Exercise 3.3

Consider the following description of the SIMPLEX program. SIMPLEX is a government program for legislative and administrative simplification and the modernization of the public services. SIMPLEX is managed by the Secretary of State of Administrative Modernization (SSAM) who has defined as main drivers for the program the citizen satisfaction and the economic growth. The Minister of Finance sets the operational efficiency of the public administration as a driver of the program. However, from the Prime Minister's perspective, the main driver for SIMPLEX is to implement a "paper free public administration."

SSAM team, before proposing the SIMPLEX program, assessed the following issues:

- The average time to create a business in Portugal is 5 weeks, which is 2.5 times higher than EU average
- Citizen complaints have been increasing in the last 3 years
- Broadband is available to citizens in more than 95% of the country (which is above EU average)
- There are no mechanisms available to the general population for electronic authentication and signing of documents
- Most of the communications within the public administration are supported in paper
- The administrative cost of the public administration increased by 23% in the last decade.

The following goals have been established:

- Empower regional and local government functions
- Increase citizen satisfaction (including reducing in 10% the citizen complaints each year and increasing average online citizen ratings to 95%)
- Reduce operational costs by 3% per year (including human resources costs and external supplies costs)

- Reduce paper usage by 40% in 2 years
- Reduce public administration costs by 3% per year

The following principles were established:

- Citizens have a single point of contact
- Channel-specific components are separated from channel-independent components
- Management layers are minimized
- Common components are centralized (as the financial systems, or the email service)

It was also decided to:

- Reengineer the change of address process
- Reengineer the business creation process
- Create a mobile authentication and signature app
- Define guidelines for interoperability among workflow systems within the public administration
- Implement a centralize printing service in each public agency (in order to reduce printing and printing costs)
- Implement a CRM (Citizen Relationship Management) system where all interactions between citizens and the public administration must be recorded

1. Taking into consideration the statement above, model the SIMPLEX stakeholders, drivers, assessments, goals, principles, requirements, and constraints (and the relationships among them) in ArchiMate.

Exercise 3.4

Consider the following Expense Reimbursement Process.

After the Expense Report is received, a new expense account must be created, if the employee does not have one. The report is then analyzed for automatic approval, considering that:

- Values below 100 Euro are automatically approved
- Values greater than or equal to 100 Euro require the approval of the supervisor

In case of rejection, the employee must receive a rejection notice by email. The refund is credited directly to the employee's bank account. If no action happens in 7 days, then the employee should receive an email indicating that the analysis is in progress. If the refund request is not completed within 30 days, then the process is stopped, and the employee receives notice of cancellation by email and must re-submit the expense report.

1. Using a BPMN Process diagram, model the Expense Reimbursement Process.

Exercise 3.5

Pizza Rapida is a pizzeria located in an area of high competition (especially with McDonald's and Pizza Hut, less than 500 meters away).

Pizza Rapida has a partnership with the local gas pump, offering discount to gas pump customers.

The pizzas can be purchased online, by telephone, or in the store (face to face).

Ingredients suppliers of the pizza (flour, salt, fresh products, etc.) and complementary products (drinks, desserts, cakes, bread) deliver products daily.

Suppliers of water, electricity, phone/Internet, gas, and firewood ensure such needs of Pizza Rapida.

Regulators (e.g., City Hall) and inspectors can change the law and/or audit Pizza Rapida compliance.

The personnel, including the manager, cooker, cashiers, and office employees, ensure the daily activities of the pizzeria.

A pizza delivery within 5 km is done by employees of Pizza Rapida, while for distances over 5km, the delivery is subcontracted to LogiPro Company. Pizza Rapida is part of the "FastFood Corp Group."

1. Model the context of Pizza Rapida (black-box)

Exercise 3.6

Consider the process held between a client and "Pizza Rapida" restaurant:

- After feeling like eating pizza, the customer selects the pizza and proceeds with the order.
- The bartender receives the client request and, if all ingredients exist, transmits it to the chef.
- The chef after cooking the pizza places it at the disposal of "the delivery boy" that delivers it to the customer.
- The customer pays the pizza (the payment is received by the "delivery boy").
- The customer eats pizza and the hunger is satisfied.
- As any restaurant, there are general rules and a complain book.

1. Identify and model in ArchiMate Pizza Rapida products and services.
2. Using ArchiMate, structurally decompose the Request for pizza process into its subprocesses.

Exercise 3.7

Consider the process held between a client and "Pizza Rapida" restaurant described in exercise 3.6.

1. Model the informational entities and their relationships in a class diagram
   (UML). Indicate the relevant attributes for each information entity. Select the
   identifier(s) for each information entity

Exercise 3.8

In the context of the Navy Information Architecture, provide three (or more) examples of possible Ship attributes, and classify them according to Inmon taxonomy
(Table 3.12).

Table 3.12 Ship attributes

Attribute name	Primitive	Derived	Historical	Projected	Public	Private	Justification
Ship attribute example	X			X	X		Here goes the explanation. Example line, ignore please

1. Each line must have 3 "X" (in Inmon classification columns). For the table, each
   Inmon classification column (Primitive, Derived, Historical, Projected, Public,
   Private) must have at least one "X." Explain and justify your options.
2. Which set of attributes would you recommend to be used as identifier of the ship
   information entity? Justify your answer.

Exercise 3.9

Considering the Pizza Ordering business process for Pizza Rapida (including
the activities of Request, Cook, Deliver, and Pay), the following were identified
application services:

- Search for Pizza (I, FC)
- Place the Order (I, FC)
- Schedule Pizza execution (FC)
- Update Pizza execution status (FC)
- Create invoice (FC)
- Create Customer (FC)
- Update Customer Data (FC)
- Get Customer Data (I, FC, WS)
- Update Order (FC)
- Receive payment (FC)

Between parentheses are indicated the interfaces in which services are available: Internet (I), Fat Client (FC), Web service (WS). The following applications are used:

- Customer Management System
- Catalog and order Management system
- Financial system, with an accounting module and a treasury module

Present the Information System Architecture and the Business and System dependencies for Pizza Rapida considering:

1. The processes and the application services
2. The application components in which the services are realized (identifying the relevant services and interfaces)

Exercise 3.10

Consider the CRUD Matrix in Fig. 3.26. The rows of the matrix represent different Processes, while the columns represent different Information entities. The rectangles are the resulting information systems (for further information on this technique, please see Sect. 7.3 of the book).

1. Model the structure of the applications and their relationships with the Information entities using ArchiMate "Application Structure" viewpoint.
2. Model the relations among applications using ArchiMate "Application Cooperation" viewpoint—not modeling, for now, the application services.
3. Detail the relationships among applications, identifying the application services and interfaces provided and consumed among them, and redraw the "Application Cooperation" view—including the services and interfaces among applications—considering:

   - Each application provides an application service (for integration with other applications) for each information entity that it manages (E1 to E7).

		Information Entity					
		E4+E7	E5	E2	E3	E1	E6
	P5	CRUD	RU				
	P6		RU	R		R	
	P7		CRUD	RU			
	P1			CRUD	CRUD	CRUD	
Process	P3	R		R	CRUD		
	P2			R	RU		
	P9+P10		R				CRUD
	P4				R		
	P8		R	R		R	R

Fig. 3.26 CRUD matrix

- The application responsible for managing the entities E1, E2, and E3 provides services to other applications using webservices.
- The remaining applications provide integration services with other applications by exchanging files (ftp).

4. Now detail the relationships between applications and business processes, identifying the application services available to business (viewpoint "Application Usage") considering that:

  - Each process (P1 to P10) uses an Application service (AS1 to AS10) which, in turn, is held in the respective application (which supports the business process identified in the CRUD Matrix) except for processes unsupported by information systems.

Exercise 3.11

Model in ArchiMate a Oracle 11G database executed in a RHELsrv, a X86 based server with 8 cores running the Red Hat Enterprise Linux 8 Operating System. Its installation file is rdmms1. It provides database services for general applications, implemented by Oracle DB 11G functionalities. It also uses Linux services that are realized by Red Hat Enterprise Linux 8 functionalities.

Exercise 3.12

In order to expand business to other cities, Pizza Rapida is implementing a new Customer Management System that is made of the following components: Process Management, telephone, Face-to-face, and the Internet. The Process Management Component is responsible for the provision of data and processes among the remaining components (which consumes data through a Java interface).

The Customer Management System is supported by four databases: customer data, guidelines for customer care, IVR configuration data, and content and configuration portal data (all supported in an Oracle Database 12c). The DBMS is implemented in two high availability servers (active-active) that share the same Netapp storage through a SAN (Storage Area Network).

The Process management component is implemented on jBoss AS7 platform (in Java).

Software components for automatic Voice Recognition (IVR) are integrated with a legacy PBX Alcatel Omni Vista. IVR components are implemented in a Java application running on the same JBoss application server.

The Internet services are implemented in LifeRay on another JBoss server instance including the following components:

- Content Management Portal
- Online Users Management
- Forms Management
- Customer Management System

Consider that:

- The CRM System is integrated with the Financial System, using web services provided by SAP.
- The Financial System is a SAP module (implemented in an SAP application server and supported in a 5th database on the same Oracle DBMS).

Also consider that Platforms Jboss, Jboss/LifeRay, and SAP are implemented in virtual servers (on a VMWare virtualization platform), supported on two physical redundant servers. All servers are implemented on a Red Hat Linux 8.0 Operating System (except the PBX, which is supported on a physical Windows 2016 Server server) and connected to a firewall.

Model in ArchiMate:

1. The application structure viewpoint, indicating the components and the interfaces among them.
2. The infrastructure viewpoint (including technology platforms, servers, and client computers, among others).
3. The implementation and deployment viewpoint:

   a. Relationship between the logical level and the implemented technological artifacts.
   b. Just the technological concepts.

References

1. J. Zachman, A framework for information systems architecture. IBM Syst. J. **26**(3), G321–5298 (1987)
2. P. Sousa, C. Pereira, *Enterprise Architecture: Business and IT Alignment* (Santa Fe, New Mexico, USA, 2005)
3. The Open Group, *The TOGAF Standard version 9.2* (Number 2)
4. The Open Group, Archimate 3.0.1 specification (2017)
5. R. Evered, *So What Is Strategy?* (vol. 16) (1983), pp. 57–72
6. S. Sun-Tzu, S.B. Griffith, The art of war (1964)
7. H. Mintzberg, *Five Ps for Strategy, in The Strategy Process* (Prentice-Hall International Editions, Englewood Cliffs, NJ, 1992), pp. 12–19
8. H.W. Kuhn, J. Von Neumann, O. Morgenstern, A. Rubinstein, Theory of games and economic behavior (60th anniversary commemorative edition) (1944)
9. H. Mintzberg, J. Lampel, Reflecting on the strategy process. Sloan Manag. Rev. **40** (1998)
10. B.H. Boar, The art of strategic planning for information technology: Crafting strategy for the 90s (1993)
11. M. Porter, What is strategy? Harv. Bus. Rev. **74**(6), 61–78 (1996)
12. M. Porter, *Competitive Strategy: Techniques for Analyzing Industries and Competitors* (Free Press, New York, 1980)
13. J. Galbraith, Designing organizations: An executive briefing on strategy, structure, and process (1995)
14. R. Winter, R. Fischer, *Essential Layers, Artifacts, and Dependencies of Enterprise Architecture*, Hong Kong (2006)
15. A. Freire, Strategic management course, handouts of the lisbon mba (2014)

16. Object Management Group, Business motivation model, version 1.3 (2015)
17. The Open Group, Archimate 2.1 specification (2013)
18. *ISO/IEC/IEEE 42010 Systems and software engineering – Architecture description* (2011)
19. M. Hammer, J. Champy, Reengineering the corporation: A manifesto for business revolution (1993)
20. H.J. Johansson, P. McHugh, A. John Pendlebury, W.A. Wheeler, *Business Process Reengineering: Breakpoint Strategies for Market Dominance* (Wiley, 1994)
21. A. Vasconcelos, P. Sousa, J. Tribolet, Enterprise architecture analysis: An information system evaluation approach. Int. J. Enterp. Modell. Inf. Syst. Archit. **3**(2), 31–53 (2008)
22. W. Inmon, Data architecture: the information paradigm (1993)

Chapter 4
Enterprise Architecture Patterns and Principles

André Vasconcelos and Pedro Sousa

Abstract This chapter describes Enterprise Architecture solutions to common problems. Principles are organized by architecture domain and quality attributes addressed. Firstly, sixteen cross-domain principles are described; next, three business layer principles are introduced, followed by five information principles, four application principles, and seven technological principles. Section 4.8 describes IT patterns, including multi-layer IT architectures and IT architectures for high availability. Finally, IT integration patterns are discussed. At the end of the chapter, exercises are proposed.

4.1 Introduction

According to TOGAF [1], principles are general rules and guidelines. In the context of Enterprise Architecture, the definition of principles is expected to support enterprises in fulfilling their mission.

More specifically, Enterprise Architecture principles support organizations in the process of defining an enterprise architecture that fulfils organizational strategic goals, from values through actions and results [2].

Each architectural principle may address one or several EA layers; for instance, an EA principle may be focused on the business layer (e.g., regarding business process or organizational aspects), or a principle might be relevant to different EA layers. In a similar way, a principle may have a direct impact in an architectural or system quality (security) or in several qualities (efficiency, maintainability, and portability).

4.1.1 Principles Description

In order to describe the EA principles, we will address the following topics (based on [1–4]):

- Name. The name of the principle is expected to be easy to remember and without ambiguities. The name selected should make clear what the principle is.
- Architecture domains. The Enterprise architecture layers where the principle is applicable may include business, information, application, and technology layers.
- Quality attributes. The quality characteristics that the principles address (such as security, performance, or usability) are also an important characteristic of the principle. ISO 9126 [5] and [3] provide 32 quality attributes clustered into six main characteristics—see Fig. 4.1.
- Explanation. For each principle, we provide a short justification on the reasons that support it. The principle explanation ensures that the Enterprise Architect applying it understands its rationale and the principle intentions in order to ensure the principle accurate interpretation.
- Implications. The principle implications, including the derived requirements, are also presented, including its business application or technological impacts.
- Example. For each principle, a brief example of its application, as well as an example that does not comply with the principle, are presented in order to better support its comprehension.

4.1.2 Principles Summary

Tables 4.1 and 4.2 summarize the principles next described, regarding the architecture domains and the quality attributes impacted.

Regarding the architecture domains, most principles are applicable at multiple layers. Maintainability and efficiency qualities are addressed in more than half of the principles described, followed by portability and alignment qualities (addressed in 20% of the principles).

4.2 Cross-Layer Principles

4.2.1 Components Are Centralized

Components are centralized principle is relevant for business, information, application, and technology layers. It is concerned about efficiency and maintainability qualities.

The rationale for the principle is supported in the fact that components in one location are easier to manage (since all efforts are performed in one location). Additionally, consolidation and standardization are easier in central components. Finally, economies of scale are applicable to central components (that are tougher in decentralized environments).

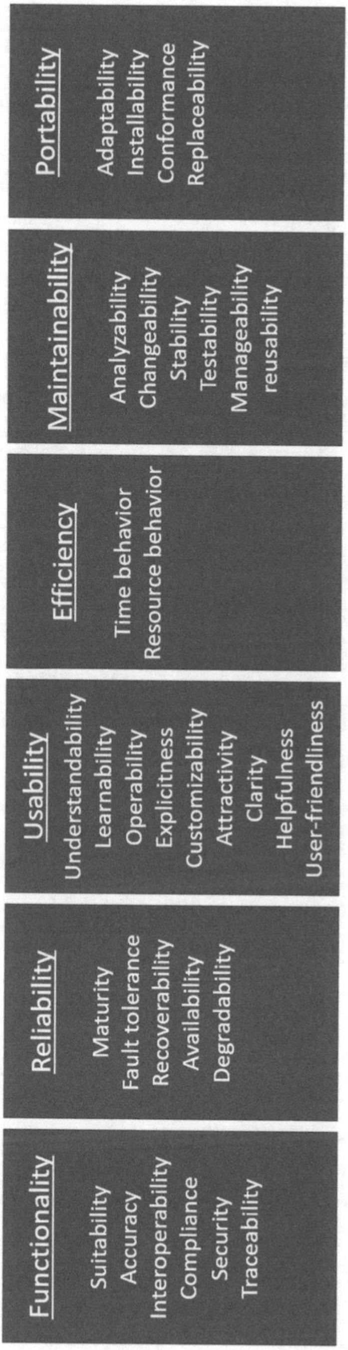

Fig. 4.1 Quality attributes

Table 4.1 Principles summary (part I)

Principle	Architecture domain	Quality attributes
Components are centralized	Business, information, application, technology	Efficiency, maintainability
Front-office processes are separated from back-office processes	Business, information, application	Efficiency, maintainability
Channel-specific is separated from channel-independent	Business, information, application	Reliability, efficiency, maintainability, portability
Data is provided by the source	Information, application	Reliability, efficiency
Data is maintained in the source application	Information, application	Reliability, efficiency, maintainability
Data is captured once	Information, application	Usability, efficiency
IT systems communicate through services	Information, application, technology	Efficiency, maintainability, and portability
Business and information architectures are aligned	Business, information	Efficiency, maintainability, alignment
Business and application architectures are aligned	Business, application	Efficiency, maintainability, alignment
Information and application architectures are aligned	Information, application	Efficiency, maintainability, alignment
Required application services are available	Business, application	Functionality, suitability, alignment
Services have different interfaces	Business, application, technology	Interoperability, maintainability
Applications manage information with the same security level	Business, information, and application	Security, reliability
Critical processes are executed in specific systems	Business, application	Security, alignment
Each information entity is managed by a single application	Information, application	Alignment
Primitive and derived data are managed by different IT components	Information, technology	Alignment
Business units are autonomous	Business	Maintainability, portability
Customers have a single point of contact	Business	Usability and efficiency
Management layers are minimized	Business	Reliability, usability, efficiency, maintainability

Table 4.2 Principles summary (part II)

Principle	Architecture domain	Quality attributes
Information management is everybody's business	Information	Efficiency, maintainability
Common vocabulary and data definitions	Information	Efficiency, maintainability
Content and presentation are separated	Information	Usability, maintainability
Data that is exchanged adhere to a canonical data model	Information	Reliability, maintainability
The number of implementations of the same information entity is minimized	Information	Interoperability, maintainability
Common use applications	Application	Efficiency, maintainability
Presentation logic, process logic, and business logic are separated	Application	Maintainability
Business logic and presentation components do not keep the state	Application	Efficiency
Minimize the number of dependencies and applications per service	Application	Maintainability
Technology independence	Technology	Portability, maintainability
Interoperability	Business, information, and application	Portability, efficiency, maintainability
IT systems are scalable	Application, technology	Efficiency
IT systems adhere to open standards	Information, application, technology	Maintainability, portability
IT systems are preferably open source	Application, technology	Efficiency, maintainability
All messages are exchanged through the enterprise service bus	Information, application, and technology	Maintainability, portability

The major implication that this principle brings is that components should be centralized, unless business, application, or technological requirements require a decentralized approach [2].

Figure 4.2 presents an application architecture that supports the principle components are centralized.

In this example, the company applications (email, finance, human resources, and intranet) are centralized in the headquarters.

On the other hand, Fig. 4.3 presents another application architecture that has several applications replicated through the company offices (e.g., email, finance, human resource applications)—not supporting this principle.

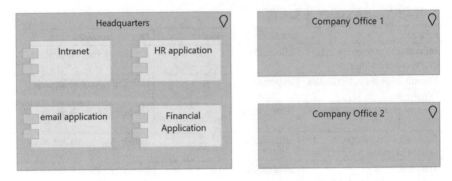

Fig. 4.2 Example of architecture applying the principle components are centralized

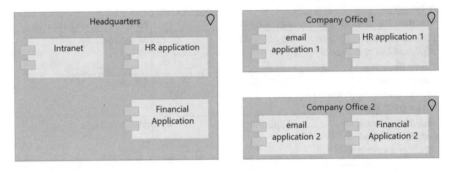

Fig. 4.3 Example of architecture that does not apply the principle components are centralized

4.2.2 Front-Office Processes Are Separated from Back-Office Processes

Front-office processes are separated from back-office processes principle is relevant for business, information, and application layers. This principle addresses the architecture maintainability.

This principle is supported in the fact that the focus of front-office and back-office processes is different. Usually, front-office processes are focused on customer intimacy and back-office processes on operational excellence.

Additionally, the knowledge and skills required for front-office processes (as persuasive speaking skills, empathy, communication, and patience, among others) are different skills and knowledge than back-office processes.

Finally, from an efficiency perspective, separating back-office processes from front-office processes makes easier to reuse back-office processes.

The most significant implications of this principle are at the business architecture, since it is recommended to have a disengagement between front-office and back-office processes, having dedicated processes to the front office and back-office.

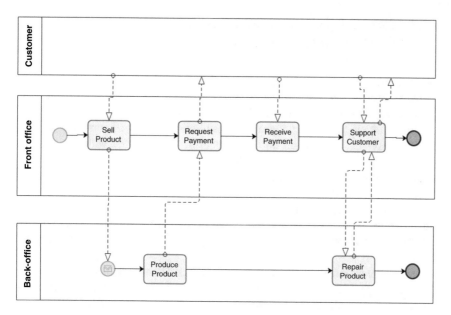

Fig. 4.4 Example of architecture applying the principle front-office processes are separated from back-office processes

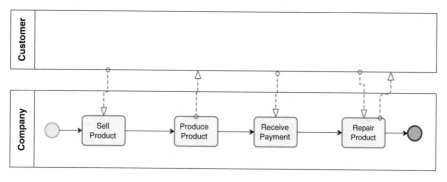

Fig. 4.5 Example of architecture that does not use the principle front-office processes are separated from back-office processes

Consequently, in the application and information architecture, front-office applications shouldn't contain back-office logic or data [2].

Figure 4.4 presents a BPMN diagram of the processes that support the selling, producing, and supporting activities of a company. In this example, there is a full separation of the front-office and the back-office processes.

On the other hand, in Fig. 4.5, back-office and front-office activities are in the same business process (making it difficult to reuse back-office activities or ensuring the right skills to deal with the costumer).

4.2.3   Channel-Specific Is Separated from Channel-Independent

Channel-specific is separated from channel-independent principle is relevant for business, information, and application layers. This principle addresses the reliability, efficiency, maintainability, and portability qualities.

This principle is built on top of the assumption that an important part of the business tasks do not depend on the channel used to interact with the customer (telephone, mail, Internet, office). Thus, in order to allow the business to be developed through multiple channels, the data must be managed in channel-independent processes.

According to [2], the implementation of this principle may be achieved by implementing channel-specific activities at the borders of an end-to-end business process and communicating with the other activities in a channel-independent format.

At the application architecture, it is recommended to have dedicated components for channel-specific processing and others that are channel-independent, where the business logic and the data are managed. An interface among channel-specific and channel-independent components must be implemented.

Figure 4.6 presents a view of an online and a face to face selling processes, where the activities that are specific of the channel (Internet or face to face) communicate with channel-independent activities (issue invoice and produce product).

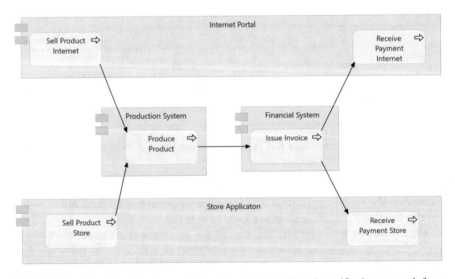

Fig. 4.6 Example of architecture applying the principle channel-specific is separated from channel-independent

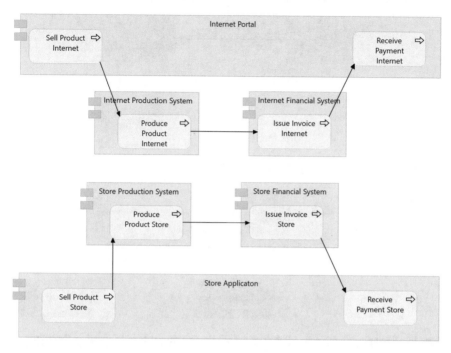

Fig. 4.7 Example of architecture that does not use the principle channel-specific is separated from channel-independent

Figure 4.7 presents an architecture where the channel independent activities and applications are replicated in both channels.

4.2.4   Data Is Provided by the Source

The principle data is provided by the source has impact in the information and application architectures, addressing reliability, performance, and efficiency qualities.

This principle increases efficiency and reliability by removing unnecessary intermediate redirection components, ensuring that the application responsible for managing the data is the one that will also provide it.

Additionally, since the data is provided directly by the source application, without having overhead processing costs or other errors (from other components), the performance and reliability are also expected to increase.

In order to implement this principle, organizations should request customers to insert the data in online forms (avoiding potential intermediary errors), and applications should get the data from the source application [2].

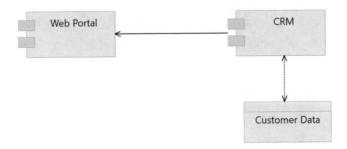

Fig. 4.8 Example of architecture applying the principle data is provided by the source

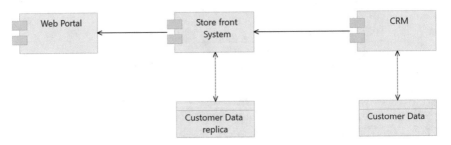

Fig. 4.9 Example of architecture that does not use the principle data is provided by the source

Figure 4.8 presents an application architecture where the customer data is obtained (by the website) directly from the source application (the CRM application).

On the other hand, Fig. 4.9 presents a similar architecture where the data is obtained in an intermediary application (a store front application) that keeps a replica of the customer data.

4.2.5 Data Is Maintained in the Source Application

The data is maintained in the source application principle has several similarities to the data is provided by the source principle. It has impact in the information and application architectures, addressing reliability, efficiency, and maintainability qualities.

Since managing (creating, updating, or deleting) similar data in multiple places introduces inconsistencies and is inefficient, in order to comply with this principle, organizations are expected to [2]:

- Have a clear identification of the source application responsible for managing (create, update, and delete) each data type.
- The data is always obtained from the source application (not from replicas).

- Replicas of data shouldn't be updated (unless synchronization mechanisms are available).
- The data shouldn't be copied before it is finalized.

Figures 4.8 and 4.9 present two application architectures where this principle is followed and not followed, respectively.

4.2.6 Data Is Captured Once

The principle data is captured once has impact in the information and application architectures, addressing usability and efficiency qualities.

This principle is supported by the fact that requesting similar data more than once is inefficient.

In order to comply with this principle, applications should first verify if the data is already available (through services exposed to access it). When the data is already available, it should be used in pre-filling forms [2].

Figure 4.10 presents an application architecture where the CRM application exposes services to access customer data. These services are used by the webPortal and the store front applications (not requesting the user to enter information already available).

On the contrary, Fig. 4.11 presents an application architecture that does request similar data, from the user, depending on the system used.

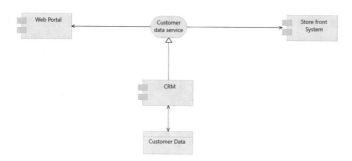

Fig. 4.10 Example of architecture applying the principle data is captured once

Fig. 4.11 Example of architecture that does not use the principle data is captured once

4.2.7   Systems Communicate Through Services

This principle is expected to have an impact in the information, application, and technology layers. Ensuring that systems communicate through services addresses efficiency, maintainability, and portability qualities.

By reusing services, less (new) services are needed, improving efficiency and maintainability. Additionally, reusing services contributes to faster implementation of new applications (that may reuse existing functionalities), reducing new applications implementation effort and duration [2].

In order to implement this principle, organizations must have extra caution in the service definition, in order to ensure services are reusable, hiding implementation details and adopting open standards in its interfaces. It is also recommended to publish services in a service directory [2].

Figure 4.12 presents a CRM application that provides a service that is reusable by three other applications.

In Fig. 4.13, a similar CRM application is integrated with three similar applications, but the services are specific (not reusable).

4.2.8   Business and Information Architectures Are Aligned

The business and information architectures are aligned principle, as expected, addresses the business and the application architectures. This principle is concerned about efficiency, maintainability, and alignment.

The focus is on structuring the information necessary to conduct business, both in operations and in management of information. If information and business

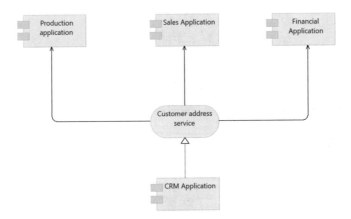

Fig. 4.12 Example of architecture applying the principle systems communicate through services

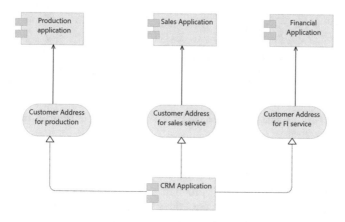

Fig. 4.13 Example of architecture that does not use the principle systems communicate through services

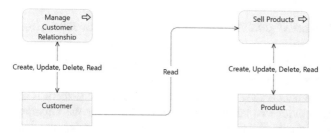

Fig. 4.14 Example of architecture applying the principle business and information architectures are aligned

architectures are aligned, business will have the expected information when needed without wasting unnecessary resources.

In order to implement this principle, organizations should ensure that in its enterprise architecture [4]:

- Information entities contain all information necessary for the activities of processes (automatic or manual).
- All processes that share information entities agree with the concepts behind it.
- The processes that create information entities manage the entire life cycle of those entities.
- All processes create or update at least one information entity.
- Each information entity is read by at least one process.

In Fig. 4.14, each process is responsible for managing (create, update, and delete) its information entity (customer and product). Notice that the sell products process only reads customer information entity (but the create, update, and delete actions are only performed by the manage customer relationship process).

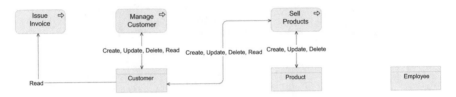

Fig. 4.15 Example of architecture that does not use the principle business and information architectures are aligned

On the other hand, in Fig. 4.15, the customer information entity is managed by two business processes (sell products and manage customer relationship); additionally, the issue invoice process does not create or update any information entity, and the employee information entity is not read by any process.

4.2.9 Business and Application Architectures Are Aligned

This principle addresses the business and application architectures, contributing for efficiency, maintainability, and alignment qualities.

In the alignment between business and applications, the focus is on the automation of the activities of business processes. The larger the alignment, the lower the effort in mechanized operations. It aims to optimize the ratio (operating costs)/(investment) for a given level of service [4].

In order to ensure business and application architectures are aligned [4]:

- All atomic activities of a process are supported by a single system or application.
- The functionalities of the systems are not redundant: support exclusively some activity.
- The characteristics of the activities are in accordance with the features of the systems that support them (e.g., scalability, availability).

In Fig. 4.16, the sell product process is supported by a single application.

In Fig. 4.17, the sell product process is supported by three applications. Assuming that the sell product process is atomic or is performed by the same person, this view presents a misalignment between the business and application architectures.

4.2.10 Information and Application Architectures Are Aligned

This principle is focused on the information and application architectures, addressing efficiency, maintainability, and alignment qualities.

The alignment between information and applications is based on the effectiveness of information systems in business information management. The existence of

Fig. 4.16 Example of architecture applying the principle business and application architectures are aligned

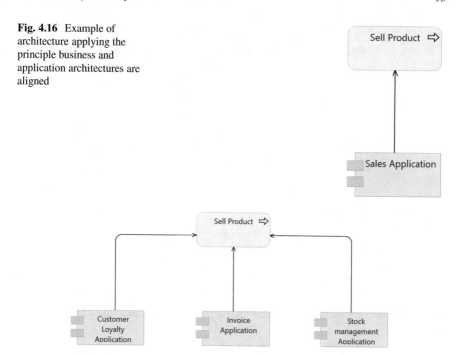

Fig. 4.17 Example of architecture that does not use the principle business and application architectures are aligned

multiple replicas of the same information in different systems is a problem because each replica has structure, syntax, and semantics usually different in different systems, making it difficult to integrate [4].

The following are implications of this principle:

- Each information entity is managed by a single system. Managing means creating and identifying.
- Each attribute of an entity should not be updated by more than one system (different attributes of the same entity may be updated by different systems).
- A system must access information from the system that manages that information, in order to preserve its computational independence.
- Systems must be computationally independent.
- The information characteristics must comply with the characteristics of the system that manages it.
- Distributed transactions should be avoided, and a transaction must involve only one system.

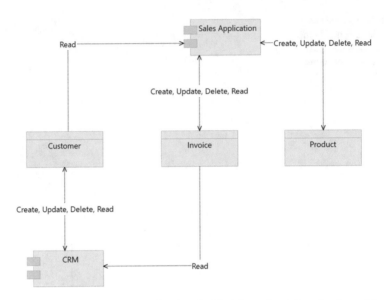

Fig. 4.18 Example of architecture applying the principle information and application architectures are aligned

Figure 4.18 presents three information entities. Each information is managed by one system—product is managed by the Sales application, Invoice is also managed by the Sales application, and Customer is managed by the CRM application.

In Fig. 4.19, the Customer information entity is managed by both applications (Sales and CRM), and the Product information entity is not managed by any application.

4.2.11 Required Application Services Are Available

The required application services are available principle addresses the business and application architectures and the functionality, namely, suitability, and alignment qualities.

In order to ensure that systems functionality is aligned with the business layer, the services required by processes must be supported by application services.

Thus, there should not exist application services required by businesses that are not available in the application architecture [3, 6].

Figure 4.20 presents an online sell process that is supported in two application services (browse products and payment services).

In Fig. 4.21, one application service is missing (Payment service).

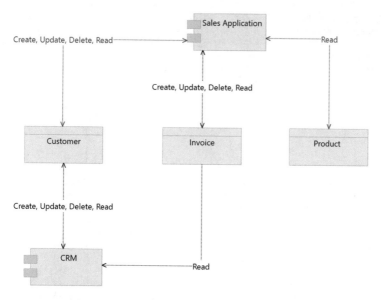

Fig. 4.19 Example of architecture that does not use the principle information and application architectures are aligned

Fig. 4.20 Example of architecture applying the principle required application services are available

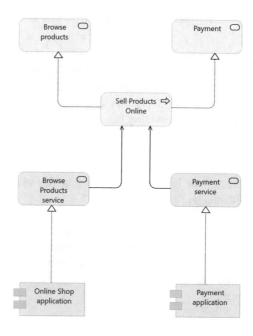

Fig. 4.21 Example of architecture that does not use the principle required application services are available

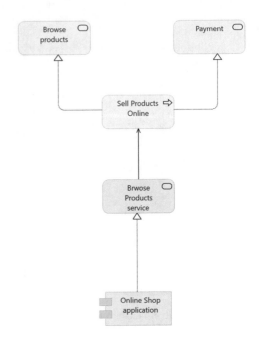

4.2.12   Services Have Different Interfaces

The services have different interfaces principle should be applied at the business, application, and technology layers of the enterprise architecture. It is concerned about interoperability and maintainability qualities.

According to [7] and [3], the technical interoperability of an architecture increases by providing the same services at different interfaces, including different technologies, and business channels.

In order to support this principle, organizations, whenever possible, should provide services using different interfaces, and no new services should be created because of the need of providing the same service through a new channel or technology [3, 7].

Figure 4.22 presents an invoice application service that is made available in three different interfaces (FTP, webservice, and online form).

In Fig. 4.23, the same service is replicated into three different ones, considering the interface required. This approach increases maintenance and implementation costs and reduces the major benefits of implementing a service-oriented architecture.

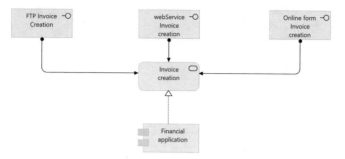

Fig. 4.22 Example of architecture applying the principle services have different interfaces

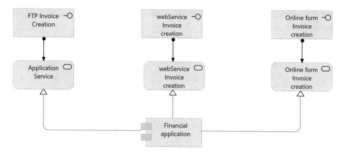

Fig. 4.23 Example of architecture that does not use the principle services have different interfaces

4.2.13 Applications Manage Information with the Same Security Level

The applications manage information with the same security level principle has impact in the information and application architectures. This principle is concerned about security and reliability.

Applications should manage information entities of the same security level, in order not to over- or under-spend resources [3, 4].

In order to implement this principle, information entities with different security requirements should be managed by different systems [3, 4].

In Fig. 4.24, two information entities with different security requirements (customer payment information and a company online catalogue of products) are managed by two different applications (that should be implemented considering the different security requirements of the data managed).

On the other hand, in Fig. 4.25, only one application is managing the two data entities (that have different security requirements)—leading to a mismatch between the application and the information architectures.

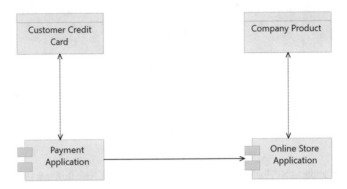

Fig. 4.24 Example of architecture applying the principle applications manage information with the same security level

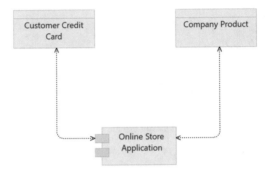

Fig. 4.25 Example of architecture that does not use the principle applications manage information with the same security level

4.2.14   Critical Process Are Executed in Specific Systems

This principle is relevant for the application and business architectures. It is concerned about security and alignment qualities.

As described in [4], the critical business processes should be supported by different applications than non-critical business processes.

Thus, the same application should not manage critical and non-critical business processes [3, 4].

Figure 4.26 presents two business processes. The sales process is considered critical for the company, while the partner management is not (according to the organization business context). Thus, the application architecture has two different applications supporting each process.

In Fig. 4.27, only one application is serving both critical and non-critical business processes.

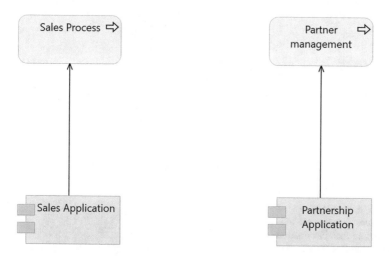

Fig. 4.26 Example of architecture applying the principle critical process are executed in specific systems

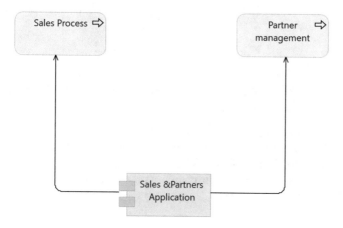

Fig. 4.27 Example of architecture that does not use the principle critical process are executed in specific systems

4.2.15 Each Information Entity Is Managed by a Single Application

This principle has implications for the information and the application architectures and is concerned about alignment quality.

According to [4], each information entity should be managed by a single application. Therefore, the main implications of this principle are [3, 4]:

- Each information entity is created, updated, or deleted by one system.

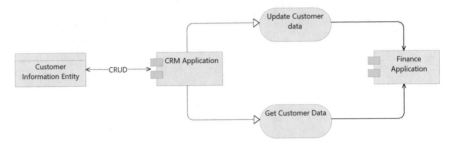

Fig. 4.28 Example of architecture applying the principle each information entity is managed by a single application

Fig. 4.29 Example of architecture that does not use the principle each information entity is managed by a single application

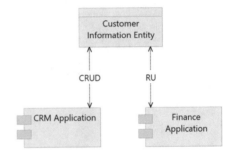

- The application that manages the information entity must provide services on the information entity to other applications.

In Fig. 4.28, the customer information entity is fully managed (created, updated, and deleted) by the CRM application that provides application services to other applications (as the Finance application).

In Fig. 4.29, the Customer information entity is updated by two applications (CRM and finance applications).

4.2.16   *Primitive and Derived Data Are Managed by Different IT Components*

The primitive and derived data are managed by different IT components is an information-technology principle. This principle is concerned about alignment.

According to Inmon, the primitive and derived data present important differences on performance, accessing patterns, and availability, among other issues [8]. Thus, it is considered a "good architectural practice" to use different technology components to support primitive and derived data.

In order to comply with this principle, organizations should ensure that [3, 4]:

- Derived data is not managed in operational IT components.

Fig. 4.30 Example of
architecture applying the
principle primitive and
derived data are managed by
different IT components

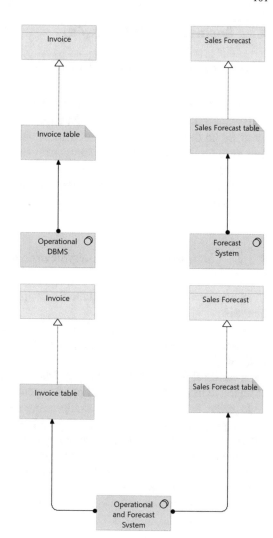

Fig. 4.31 Example of
architecture that does not use
the principle primitive and
derived data are managed by
different IT components

- There are separated hardware and software components to manage primitive and derived data.

In Fig. 4.30, the invoice (primitive and operational data) and the sales forecast (derived data) data are managed by different technological components.

In Fig. 4.31, the same system software is used to realize derived and primitive data.

4.3 Business Layer Principles

4.3.1 Business Units Are Autonomous

This principle is concerned about maintainability and portability qualities.

Having autonomous business units ensures a fast adaptation to change, since there are no dependencies to other business units. Additionally, autonomous business units can be easily separated (supporting organizational restructuring) [2].

In order to implement this principle, organizations should ensure that each business unit has a profit and loss center that is used for its evaluation. Additionally, each business unit is responsible for its investments and decisions [2].

4.3.2 Customers Have a Single Point of Contact

Customers have a single point of contact principle addresses usability and efficiency qualities.

According to this principle, it is better for customers to have a single point of contact, instead of contacting several company employees. It is expected that a single point of contact ensures consistence of the information provided. Additionally, from an operational point of view, having dedicated employees to manage customers is expected to increase efficiency and reduce operational activity interruptions [2].

In order to implement this principle, organizations should provide a single access point to customers (e.g., a contact-center, dedicated person, etc.) that detaches the customer from the internal organization. This access point must have enough information to handle customer requests. Only in exceptional situations, the customer interacts directly with the internal organization [2].

In Fig. 4.32, all the interaction between the customer and the company is managed by the Customer Relationship Department.

On the other hand, in Fig. 4.33, the customer interacts directly with three different organization departments.

4.3.3 Management Layers Are Minimized

The management layers are minimized principle is expected to improve business reliability, usability, efficiency, and maintainability qualities.

This principle is supported in the fact that the nonproductive costs are reduced by minimizing management layers. Another important side effect of minimizing management layers is that operational employees tend to take more responsibility for their work [2].

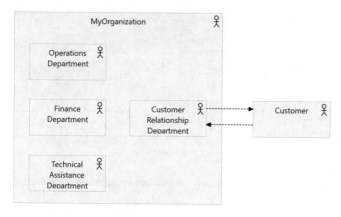

Fig. 4.32 Example of architecture applying the principle customers have a single point of contact

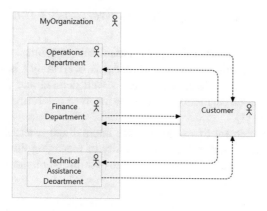

Fig. 4.33 Example of architecture that does not use the principle customers have a single point of contact

From an organizational point of view, this principle imposes a reduction to the minimum of the management layers. In an ideal world, according to this principle, people responsible to perform the actual work would be self-managed in a management layer free organization [2].

Figure 4.34 presents an organization where the management layers are minimized. The production and sales employees are empowered and report directly to the Director.

Figure 4.35 presents an organization with several management layers, where the lower layers report to one or more managers, who report to one or more management layers.

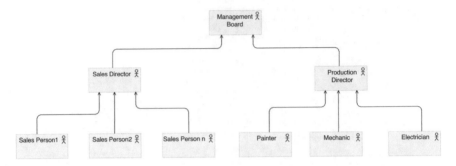

Fig. 4.34 Example of architecture applying the principle management layers are minimized

4.4   Information Layer Principles

4.4.1   Information Management Is Everybody's Business

This principle addresses efficiency and maintainability qualities.

According to the information management is everybody's business principle, information management decision-making is well defined and supports business goals. All organization business units must be involved in information management, working as a team [1].

In order to implement this principle, the internal and external stakeholders of the organization must accept the responsibility of managing the information. The organization must ensure the proper resources to information management [1].

4.4.2   Common Vocabulary and Data Definitions

The common vocabulary and data definitions principle addresses efficiency and maintainability qualities. According to this principle, the enterprise data must be defined and available to everybody in the organization. This data architecture must be used when developing applications [1]. Applications should provide services to exchange data, according to the enterprise common data definitions. From an organizational point of view, data administration responsibilities must be assigned [1].

Figure 4.36 presents an enterprise data architecture, where the data is commonly defined, data management responsibilities are well defined, and applications provide services to access data.

On the other hand, Fig. 4.37 presents an information architecture with data entities dependent on the applications, leading to replicated data and data management conflicts among applications.

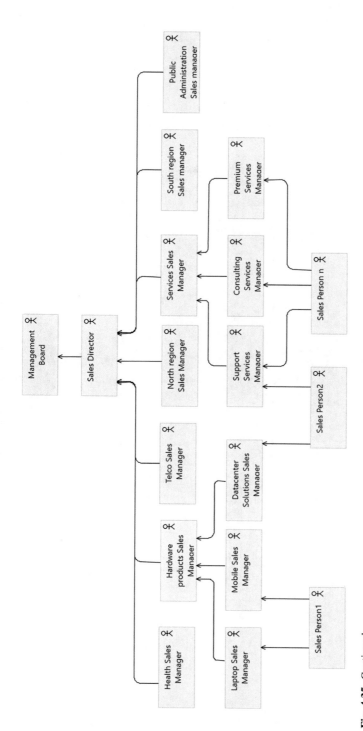

Fig. 4.35 Continued

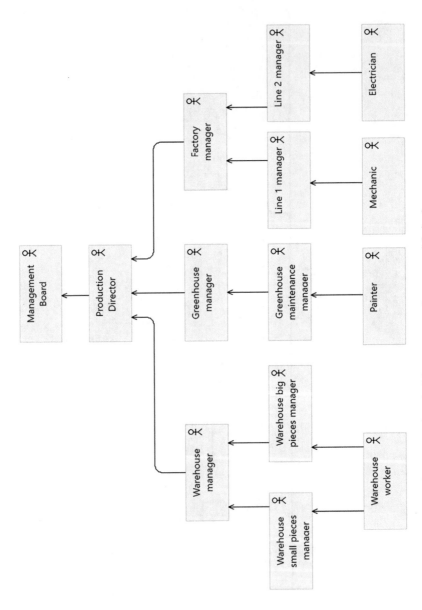

Fig. 4.35 Example of architecture that does not use the principle management layers are minimized

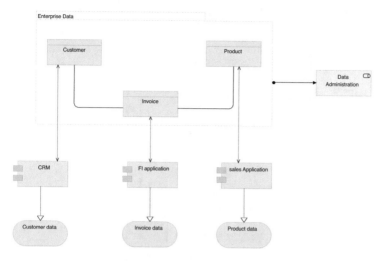

Fig. 4.36 Example of architecture applying the principle common vocabulary and data definitions

4.4.3   Content and Presentation Are Separated

The content and presentation are separated principle main impacts are at the information architecture, ensuring that the content may be reused in multiple channels. By separating content and presentation, each can be managed independently [2].

In order to comply with this principle, organizations should translate data acquired to a format that is independent of the presentation channel. Additionally, there should be specific software components that add to the content the presentation-specific data [2].

Figure 4.38 presents an architecture, where the data of the product information entity is separated between data independent and dependent of the channel (online and physical).

In Fig. 4.39, there is a replication of the product data that is dependent of the channel and the content that is not dependent of the channel.

4.4.4   Data That Is Exchanged Adhere to a Canonical Data Model

According to [2], the adoption of a common definition to the data minimizes the need for translations when applications exchange data, increasing the reliability and the maintainability qualities.

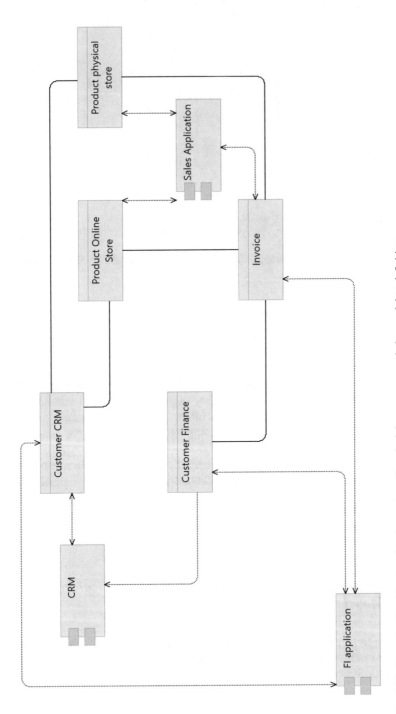

Fig. 4.37 Example of architecture that does not use the principle common vocabulary and data definitions

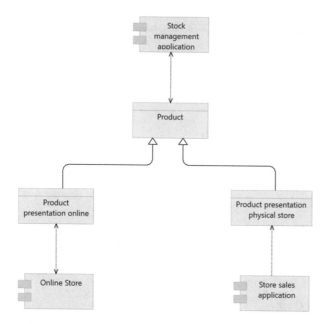

Fig. 4.38 Example of architecture applying the principle content and presentation are separated

Fig. 4.39 Example of architecture that does not use the principle content and presentation are separated

In order to implement this principle, organizations should manage centrally the canonical data model. The canonical data model shall be used when applications exchange information (either directly by the applications involved in the data exchange or by using a integration software for performing the translation from the application-specific data model to the canonical data model) [2].

In Fig. 4.40, the exchange of the customer data among the three applications is supported in a common definition of the customer data.

In Fig. 4.41, there are different definitions of the customer data (in the sales and in the finance applications).

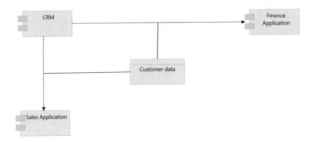

Fig. 4.40 Example of architecture applying the principle data that is exchanged adhere to a canonical data model

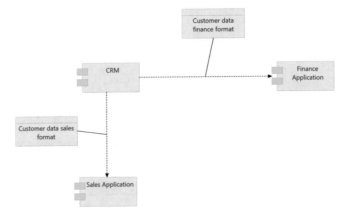

Fig. 4.41 Example of architecture that does not use the principle data that is exchanged adhere to a canonical data model

4.4.5 The Number of Implementations of the Same Information Entity Is Minimized

In order to increase interoperability and maintainability qualities, the number of implementations of the same information entity shall be minimized.

The existence of different implementations of an information entity points to semantic problems for that information entity (e.g., by using different formats or attributes in the implementation of an information entity). Therefore, the realizations of the same information entity in the technology architecture are minimized [3].

Figure 4.42 presents the implementation of the customer and the product information entities in the technology layer. Each data object is realized in a single artifact.

In Fig. 4.43, there are several implementations of each data object—the customer has two different implementations and the product three.

Fig. 4.42 Example of architecture applying the principle data that is exchanged adhere to a canonical data model

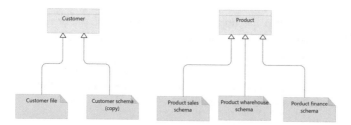

Fig. 4.43 Example of architecture that does not use the principle data that is exchanged adhere to a canonical data model

4.5 Applications Layer Principles

4.5.1 Common Use Applications

The common use of applications principle is concerned about efficiency and maintainability qualities. This principle argues that organizations should avoid the development of multiple similar applications that address a common need. The development of duplicate applications is expensive to implement and maintain and leads to data replication [1].

Thus, business units shall use applications that support the entire enterprise not developing applications for their own needs (for similar enterprise-wide applications) [1].

This principle is a specialization of the components are centralized principle (see Sect. 4.2.1), applied at the application architecture. Figure 4.2 presents an application architecture where the Intranet, email, HR, and Financial applications are used across the organization. In Fig. 4.3, the email, HR, and Financial applications are replicated.

4.5.2   Presentation Logic, Process Logic, and Business Logic Are Separated

This principle is concerned about maintainability quality. According to [2], since the presentation, process, and business logic functionalities are different if they are implemented in different software components, it is expected that its reuse will increase.

In order to comply with this principle, application components must have a layered approach separating presentation logic, process logic, and business logic. Additionally, the access to data is only implemented in business logic components [2].

Figure 4.44 presents the implementation of the online store and the face-to-face sales applications using a layered approach (where the process logic and the business logic are shared among the applications).

On the other hand, in Fig. 4.45, a monolithic approach is selected, where each application is implemented in a single software component (replicating common process and business logic functionalities).

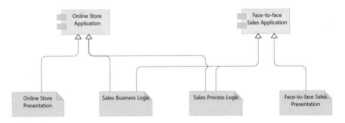

Fig. 4.44 Example of architecture applying the principle presentation logic, process logic, and business logic are separated

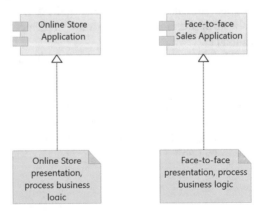

Fig. 4.45 Example of architecture that does not use the principle presentation logic, process logic, and business logic are separated

4.5.3 Business Logic and Presentation Components Do Not Keep the State

This principle is concerned about efficiency quality.

The scalability of an application is increased if business and presentation components do not keep the state (since it will be easier for implementing new parallel instances of these components) [9].

The scalability of an application tends to grow if the presentation and the logic application components do not preserve the application state (stateless). The state of the application should be managed by specific data components.

In order to implement this principle, the application architecture should ensure that [3]:

- Data is not recorded at the business or presentation levels.
- The state of the application in record by data components (e.g., Database Management Systems).

4.5.4 Minimize the Number of Dependencies and Applications per Service

This principle is concerned about maintainability quality.

According to [10], in the software engineering area, the higher the number of paths in a program, the higher its control flow complexity probably will be. The same occurs in the implementation of application services; they tend to be more complex if they depend on more applications [3]. Thus, in order to reduce complexity, each application service should be realized by the least number of applications [3].

In Fig. 4.46, the update customer address is realized by a single application (CRM Application).

On the other hand, in Fig. 4.47, the same application service is realized in four different applications, increasing its implementation and maintenance complexity.

Fig. 4.46 Example of architecture applying the principle minimize the number of dependencies and applications per service

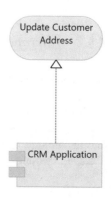

Fig. 4.47 Example of architecture that does not use the principle minimize the number of dependencies and applications per service

4.6   Infrastructure Layer Principles

4.6.1   Technology Independence

This principle argues that applications should not depend on the specific technologies or platforms, following common standards contributing for portability and maintainability qualities.

According to [1], applications that are not technology independent tend not to be developed and operated in a cost-effective way. Thus, the application software used or developed should not be dependent on specific hardware, operating systems, or systems software.

In order to comply with this principle, applications should select standards that support portability, and legacy applications must have Application Program Interfaces (APIs) that enable them to interoperate with the remaining applications. If needed, integration software (middleware, enterprise service bus) may be used to reduce the dependencies on specific technologies [1].

In Fig. 4.48, the SAP application provides a web service interface (independent of the technology).

On the other hand, in Fig. 4.49, the same SAP application only provides SAP Remote Functional Call interface (that is not independent of the SAP technology).

4.6.2   Interoperability

The interoperability principle addresses portability, efficiency, and maintainability qualities.

TOGAF interoperability principle states that software and hardware should conform to defined standards that promote interoperability for data, applications, and technology, in order to maximize return on investment and reduce costs [1]. Thus, it is recommended to comply to standards and to establish internal processes

Fig. 4.48 Example of
architecture applying the
principle technology
independence

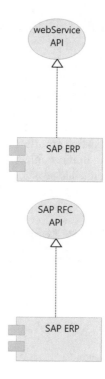

Fig. 4.49 Example of
architecture that does not use
the principle technology
independence

for the definition and revision of the standards accepted in enterprise applications. Technology interoperability is expected to reduce vendor lock-in and increase competition among application vendors.

In order to implement this principle, organizations should use interoperability standards when available [1].

4.6.3   IT Systems Are Scalable

It is important to ensure that IT systems are scalable, since new market opportunities must be supported, even if not anticipated. Since acquiring systems with all the maximum future needs is expensive, considering that the cost of technology tends to be lower over time, it is important to ensure that the technology components are scalable [2].

In order to ensure that IT systems are scalable, IT components must scale horizontally (by adding further nodes performing the same tasks) or vertically (by increasing resources available of existing nodes). Additionally, IT systems should be sized at the current volumes and must be monitored periodically [2].

4.6.4   IT Systems Adhere to Open Standards

IT systems adhere to open standards principle argues that the usage of open standards prevents vendor lock-in and eases the integration of IT systems, increasing maintainability and portability qualities [2].

When selecting standards to adopt, organizations should consider the standard maturity and relevance. Whenever possible, open standards should be selected, and existing proprietary interfaces must be wrapped into open standard interfaces [2].

In Fig. 4.50, the Finance and the HR application follow oAuth open standard to authenticate among both applications.

On the other hand, in Fig. 4.51, the applications use proprietary Interfaces.

Fig. 4.50 Example of architecture applying the principle IT systems adhere to open standards

Fig. 4.51 Example of architecture that does not use the principle IT systems adhere to open standards

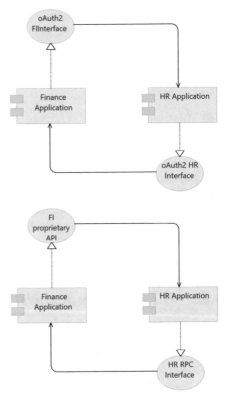

4.6.5 IT Systems Are Preferably Open Source

According to [2], open-source software prevents vendor lock-in and has lower acquisition costs than commercial software. This principle is expected to have a positive impact in efficiency and maintainability.

To implement this principle, when a functionally equivalent open-source software is available, the open source should be selected rather than the commercial version [2].

4.6.6 All Messages Are Exchanged Through the Enterprise Service Bus

In order to increase maintainability and portability, this principles states that and enterprise service bus (ESB) should be used to exchange messages among systems [2].

Having an ESB ensures that changes in a system won't have impact in other systems, since the ESB hides semantic (e.g., data model) or technology changes (e.g., integration or communication protocols used). Additionally, an ESB may increase the quality of the message exchange since the ESB provides specific tools for its persistence and management. Finally, having an ESB contributes for reuse of services among applications [2].

In order to implement this principle, instead of applications which exchange messages directly to other applications, all messages go through the ESB [2].

In Fig. 4.52, there is an ESB that handles the specificity of the integration with four different applications.

Fig. 4.52 Example of architecture applying the principle all messages are exchanged through the enterprise service bus

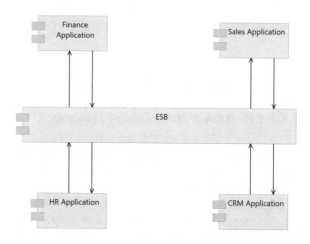

Fig. 4.53 Example of architecture that does not use the principle all messages are exchanged through the enterprise service bus

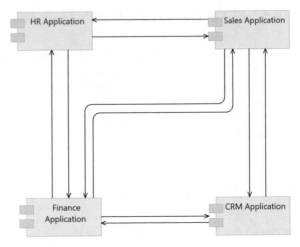

In Fig. 4.53, the integration is done directly point-to-point among applications, imposing that each application is able to deal with the integration technology and the data model of two or three other applications.

4.6.7   Software Components Are Multi-platform

This principle is concerned about the portability quality. The portability and technical interoperability increase with the number of possible platforms where components are able to operate. In order to implement this principle [3]:

- Components should run in multiple operating systems.
- Components that can run on various software and hardware platforms are preferred.

4.7   IT Architecture Patterns and Practices

4.7.1   IT Architecture Layers Patterns

Almost all applications have three structural components: presentation, logic, and data. The differences begin with the introduction of network sections between the components (see Figs. 4.54 and 4.55).

Regarding distributed presentation, "X Window System," dummy 3270 terminals, and pure HTML web pages (no JavaScript) are examples where calculations for the presentation are mostly done on the server side.

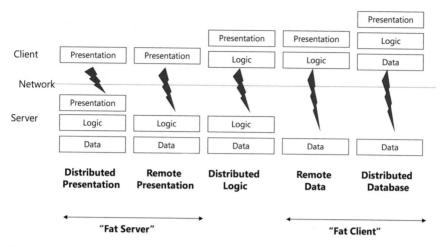

Fig. 4.54 Architectures with one network section's component distribution

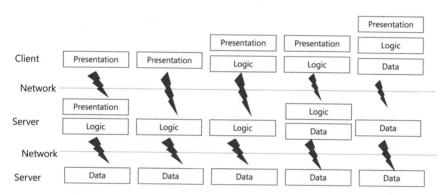

Fig. 4.55 Architectures with two network sections' component distribution

Regarding remote presentation, a web browser with JavaScript is a good example. For distributed logic, a browser running Java applets is an example of this architecture. In remote data architecture, the client makes calls directly to the database. The SQL flows through the network, as well as the answers. In a distributed database environment, part of the data is kept on the client side which is regularly synchronized with the server.

4.7.1.1 Two-Layer Versus Three-Layer Architectures

Three-layer (3L) architectures have, in general, the advantages over two-layer (2L) architectures presented in Table 4.3.

Table 4.3 Two-layer versus three-layer architectures summary

Quality	2 layer	3 layer
Security	−	+
Data encapsulation	−	+
Performance	−	+
Availability	−	+
Reuse	−	+
Ease to develop	+	−
Integration with legacy	−	+
Scalability and flexibility	−	+

Regarding **security**, three-layer architectures have the advantage since:

- 2L—security is done only in terms of data access.
- 3L—security is at methods access level.

Data encapsulation is better in three-layer architectures considering that:

- 2L— tables are traveling on the network (at least the structure of the data in SQL commands).
- 3L—only the methods and the results circulate on the network.

Although one more layer exists in three-layer architectures, **performance** is better since:

- 2L—much unnecessary network traffic is generated.
- 3L—there is no waste of network data; only the methods and results circulate on the network.

Availability is usually high in three-layer architectures since:

- 2L—SQL requests are made directly to a database server (it might reach a maximum number of "open connections").
- 3L—orders are directed to any application server.

Reuse is low in two-layer architectures since:

- 2L—client software must directly deal with the tables (in the DBMS).
- 3L—client software interacts with application servers methods (that hide the DBMS).

Development is easier and faster in 2L, since:

- 2L— low expertise is required.
- 3L—the separation of logic interface and application objects may be difficult in some cases.

Integration with legacy systems is very hard in two-layer architectures since:

- 2L—client software calls tables directly.

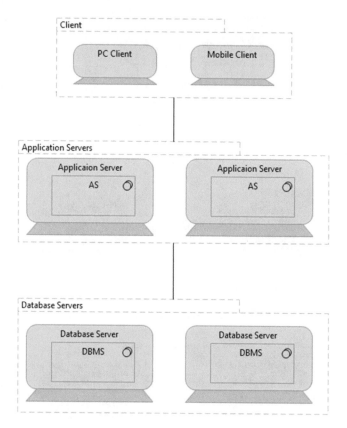

Fig. 4.56 Three-layer architecture

- 3L—Integration with legacy systems can be done by changing the application server.

Two-layer architectures have low **scalability and flexibility in hardware** considering that:

- 2L—Communication problems are raised (e.g., maximum DB connections reached).
- 3L—Scalability and flexibility are higher since clients call a service, not a process. The processes are launched on machines that may easily balance load. The logic is in the components that can be run on any server. There are components that ensure access to the database (ensuring the data integrity) (see Fig. 4.56).

Regarding security, the IT Architecture usually has three distinct security zones—Fig. 4.57.

Firewalls can limit accesses (who and what) between the parts of the network. In addition to security, firewalls are also important to reduce traffic on the network.

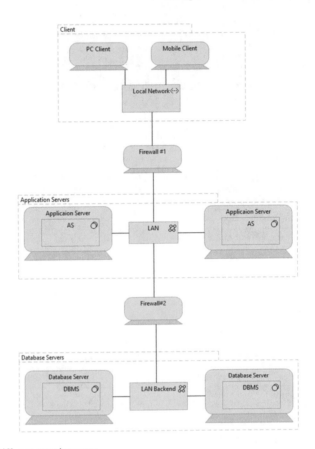

Fig. 4.57 Different security zones

Also notice that the same physical firewall can execute the role of two. For example, in a typical IT architecture for the Web, the same firewall can isolate different network segments—see the example in Fig. 4.58

4.7.2 Architectures for High Availability

Several patterns are available for increasing availability.

A possible approach to increase availability is accomplished using **backup servers** (see Fig. 4.59). This is the cheapest solution, but it has some problems, including:

1. Recovery is complex and slow.
2. A fault detection mechanism must be available: heartbeat which asks if the server is alive.

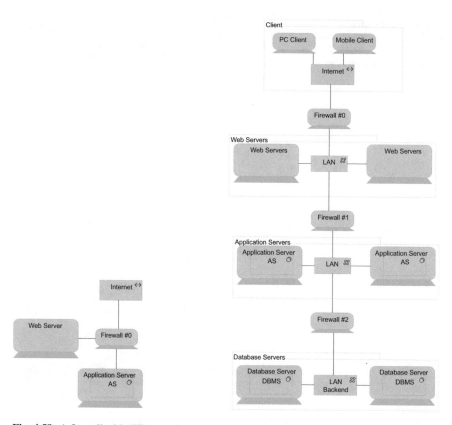

Fig. 4.58 A firewall with different roles

3. Re-processing of messages lost: there are no guarantees, since failure may have been on the message "sent," on the server, or on the server response or the processing of the response by the customer.

Passive Duplication is another approach for high availability (see Fig. 4.59) with the following characteristics:

1. It implies a standby server.
2. It is "transparent" to the user
3. Re-processing of lost messages—Reduces the Log and can reduce the time to replace the Network so that customers do not perceive. It is not used much.

Active-Active duplication is another approach where a "backup server" is used, but operating (see Fig. 4.60). It is "transparent" to the user and the best approach for stateless servers. It might have some loss in performance due to data update. It may be applied to a Database Cluster: both systems write to all disks. Problems might arise with Logs and Locks.

Fig. 4.59 Increasing
availability by using backup
servers (in the top) and
passive duplication (in the
bottom)

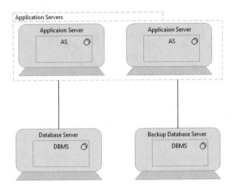

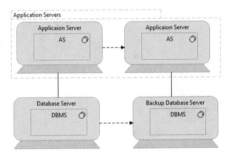

No architecture solves all problems, including those related to the connection to the outside. It's a business decision how to react when problems are detected.

4.8   IT Integration Patterns

4.8.1   Introduction

Integration was born as a technological possibility to connect multiple machines across networks but has become a way of overcoming the problems posed by the continuous development of business requirements. The scope moved from integration of technologies, for application integration and, more recently, for business integration.

Enterprise Architecture aims to solve similar problems, as Business processes, or significant parts of these processes, are not adequately supported by information systems; inconsistencies, incoherence, and replication exist in operational information; difficulties in the IS response to new business needs; and difficulties in the adoption of new technologies.

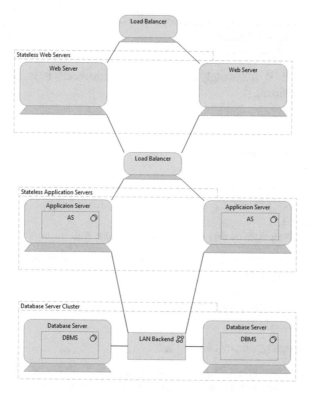

Fig. 4.60 Active-active duplication

We present next the major integration techniques from an architectural point of view.

4.8.2 File Transfer

One of the oldest integration technique is the file transfer. Its main goal is to exchange information between two systems using coding and decoding objects and a file. File Transfer Protocol (FTP) is a two-step technique:

- Encoding: Objects to file;
- Decoding: File to objects.

The main advantage of FTP is that it is a universal approach, since all operating systems and programming languages support the notion of file. However, it has several disadvantages, including:

- The complexity of encoding and decoding increases exponentially with the objects to be transferred.

- It can only be used to exchange objects whose type is relatively simple.
- The performance is limited.
- It implies the duplication of data.

This technique is still widely used despite its drawbacks (e.g., in some legacy financial transactions).

4.8.3 Screen Scraping

Screen scraping, screen harvesting, or form scraping has the main goal of extracting information directly from the user interface to a system in order to be used in another system (Fig. 4.61).

The main advantages of this integration technique are:

- Appropriate to integrate legacy applications where the code cannot be accessed or changed (e.g., COBOL applications on mainframes).
- There is no direct access to the data.
- It is not necessary to change the source application/system.
- Specialized applications exist for this purpose.

The disadvantages of screen scraping are:

- The user interface is not intended to integration.
- The user interface usually does not reflect the data type.
- It is not simple to simulate a (human) user using an application.
- The quality and performance of this approach are generally low, and the complexity is high.

Therefore, screen scraping is only used as a "last resource" technique for encapsulating (closed) legacy systems.

4.8.3.1 Web Scraping or Web Harvesting

Web scraping or web harvesting applies a similar approach of screen scraping to extract information from web pages. It is mostly used by web crawlers. Web pages are built with textual markup languages (HTML, XHTML), usually designed for human consumption. Its design often mixes content with presentation. Due to

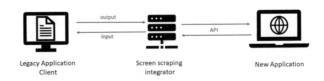

Fig. 4.61 Screen scraping

the widespread use of web scraping techniques, currently several "anti-scraping" techniques also exist.

4.8.4   Remote Procedure Call

Remote Procedure Call (RPC) protocol was created to support distributed programming based on the procedures called by clients that run remotely on the server. It is the simplest way of middleware. It provides the basic infrastructure to transform "procedure calls" into "Remote Procedure Calls" (RPC) in a transparent and uniform way (Fig. 4.62).

Currently, RPC is the "foundation" of almost all other forms of Middleware. "StoreProcedures" is a type of RPC to interact with Databases. Remote Method Invocation (RMI) is identical to RPC but applies to methods of objects (instead of procedures).

The synchronous architectures, as RPC, introduce high cohesion (tight coupling) between the caller and the called. The services and directory names try to minimize this effect, but do not eliminate it completely. This type of architecture presents specific problems in various areas:

- The management level of interaction between client and server is difficult (e.g., fault tolerance, availability, load balancing).
- The level of communication properties and services is hard to ensure (e.g., transactional behavior, compensation, exception handling).

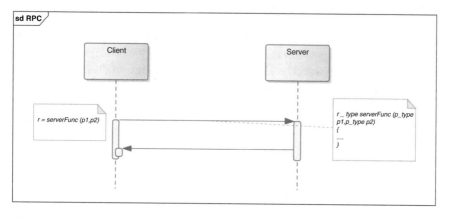

Fig. 4.62 RPC example

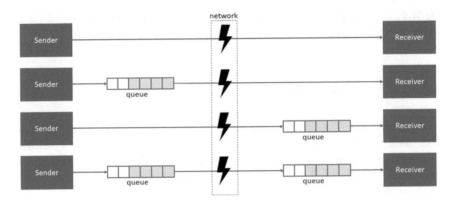

Fig. 4.63 Message queues

4.8.5 Message Queues

Message queues arise considering that the interaction does not always need to be synchronous. It provides access to transactional queues, persistent queues, and a set of primitives for reading and writing to local and remote queues.

Message queues provide a common ground for interoperability based on messages. In this paradigm, clients and servers interact using messages. A message is a set of structured data, characterized by a type, and parameters (set of pairs "name, value").

The interaction model is a publish/subscribe. Considering the possibility of defining routing logic for messages at the broker, there are several possibilities for message-based interactions. The publish/subscribe interaction is the most known and used one. In this pattern, the sender of the message does not send the message to any recipient—it just puts it in the queue. The recipients (interested) are responsible for subscribing a message type. The "queue" then ensures sending a copy of the message to all the subscribers (Fig. 4.63).

In model-driven messaging, client messages are placed in a queue, and when the recipient is ready to process, it invokes a function. Several benefits arise from queue model, including:

- Control when processing messages.
- Increased robustness to failures.
- Better distribution of applications across multiple hardware (for higher performance and availability).
- Message priorities setting.
- Interaction with the message queue system.

The main problems with message queues are:

- Asynchronous communication involves a programming model less intuitive than the RPC (programming events).

- The message queues servers are one more investment, management, and support costs.
- The message queue server is one more component of the architecture of the middleware that needs to be integrated with others.

4.8.6   Message-Oriented Middleware

In message-oriented middleware, the integration is performed using the routing information (messages) among systems. Applications receive and send messages to a message broker.

The messages, once received by the server, can be reformatted, combined, or modified in order to be understood by the target system. It is usually not necessary to modify the systems involved. The message brokers provide adapters for the most common applications.

The main goals of a Message-Oriented Middleware (MOM) integration are:

- Store and forward: message is persisted (saved) and delivered to the recipient (even in case of recipient application failure).
- Broker: all systems interact with a single point.
- Publish and subscribe model: there is a message subscribe queue.
- Assurance that the messages are delivered to the recipient, including two-phase commit protocols.
- Sorting capability.
- Ability to dynamically select the recipient based on the message content.
- Simulating synchronous operation: request/response.
- Confidential support through encryption.
- Sending events (e.g., unavailability of recipient).
- Ability to transform and filter messages as they move between the servers.

4.8.7   Data-Oriented Integration

One of the basic mechanisms for integration is data-oriented integration which includes:

1. Extracting the information from the source repository.
2. Processing or transforming information.
3. Updating the destination repository with the processed data.

The main advantages of data-oriented integration are:

- Simple mechanism to implement.
- There are access mechanisms independent of the technology.
- It does not require rework or application modifications.

The disadvantages of data-oriented integration are:

- It requires technical knowledge about the management systems databases because the operation of access and update may impact the consistency of the information.
- It may require to have knowledge about the inner workings of applications to ensure consistency of information.
- It may involve transformations between data types (possibly incompatible).
- The transformed data is not validated by the application that uses it.
- There is no guarantee of consistency between the replicated information (from repositories).

4.8.7.1 Integration via DBMS

The integration using database management systems (DBMS) defines an API for applications to access information. It converts the API commands in a language the database understands (e.g., SQL). The client sends the command to the DBMS. The DBMS processes the command and sends the result to the client. The client converts the response into a format understandable by the target application.

This interaction model can be seen as a dedicated RPC that interacts with a DBMS. Open Database Connectivity (ODBC) allows access to data in a DBMS, independently of the DBMS technology, the programming languages, and the operating system. It is a standard proposed by Microsoft in 1992. The API is independent of the DBMS. The same API is supported by multiple drivers seamlessly. The ODBC drivers depend on the specific database engines. There are multiple compatible implementations (directly or through bridges), such as Microsoft ODBC, JDBC, iODBC, and IBM i5/OS.

There are also interfaces based on the SQL standard defined in the Java platform to access relational databases. Java Database Connectivity (JDBC) is an API that defines a set of Java classes that allow an application to connect to a database.

ODBC is a mechanism mainly to access (remotely) to a Relational Database. It has been evolving to integrate various types of repositories in a transparent manner:

- relational databases
- non-relational databases
- text files (flat files)
- spreadsheets,
- email

It allows the creation of "Virtual Database," independent of the shapes of the sources of information.

4.8.8 Application Interface-Oriented Integration

The most commonly used packaged applications usually expose interfaces to access and process information. The trend is that the functionality of these applications is exposed through services rather than proprietary APIs.

Some (few) packages have well-documented interfaces allowing access to information and high-level processes. The main drawback of API integration is that each application defines a different interface. The interfaces are complex (and sometimes poorly documented). Additionally, version evolutions tend not to ensure backward compatibility. As an example, SAP Business Objects (BO) are objects that encapsulate data and processes associated with a business object (e.g., Material, Purchase Order, and Customer). External access to these data and processes is done through specific methods of these objects called Business Application Program Interfaces (BAPI). The BAPI in SAP Web Application Server are implemented as function modules that support the protocol RFC (Remote Function Call) and are described as methods of a SAP BO.

4.8.9 Transactions and Transaction Monitors

Atomicity, consistency, isolation, and durability (ACID) are the four primary attributes ensured by any transaction:

- **Atomicity**: Either all the tasks in a transaction occur or none of them occurs. The transaction must be completed, or else it must be undone (rolled back).
- **Consistency**: Every transaction must preserve the integrity constraints. It cannot leave the data in a contradictory state.
- **Isolation**: Two simultaneous transactions cannot interfere with one another. Intermediate results within a transaction must remain invisible to other transactions.
- **Durability**: Completed transactions cannot be aborted later or their results discarded. They must persist through (for instance) restarts of the DBMS or after crashes.

The properties of a DBMS apply only to transactions within its domain. In principle, the properties are no longer valid when an operation crosses more than one DBMS or when operations access data outside the control of the DBMS (e.g., on the server itself or in other layers of the architecture, including middleware). Therefore, the general rule is that whenever the data is distributed, the properties guaranteed by a DBMS do not apply.

To overcome the problem of the distribution of transactions, The Open Group defined the Distributed Transaction Processing Model (DTPM). This model aims to ensure that a distributed operation (i.e., that crosses multiple DBMS) meets the ACID properties. The model DTPM defines the XA interface. The XA needs

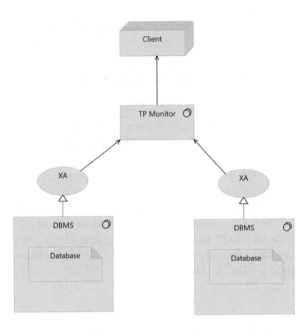

Fig. 4.64 Transactional RPC

to be supported by all nodes participating in a distributed transaction. The XA implementations ensure the atomicity of a distributed transaction supported in a 2 Phase Commit (2PC) transactional protocol.

The limitations of RPC can be resolved by making RPC calls transactional. In practice, this means that they are controlled by a 2PC protocol. As before, an intermediate entity is needed to run 2PC (the client and server could do this themselves, but it is neither practical nor generic enough). This intermediate entity is usually called a **Transaction Manager** (TM) and acts as an intermediary in all interactions between clients, servers, and resource managers. When all the services needed to support RPC, transactional RPC, and additional features are added to the intermediate layer, the result is a TP-Monitor (Fig. 4.64).

A TP-Monitor allows building a common interface to several applications while maintaining or adding transactional properties. A TP-Monitor extends the transactional capabilities of a database beyond the database domain. It provides the mechanisms and tools necessary to build applications in which transactional guarantees are provided. TP-Monitors are, perhaps, the best, oldest, and most complex example of middleware. Some even try to act as distributed operating systems providing file systems, communications, security controls, etc. TP-Monitors have traditionally been associated with the mainframe world. Their functionality, however, has migrated to other environments and has been incorporated into most middleware tools.

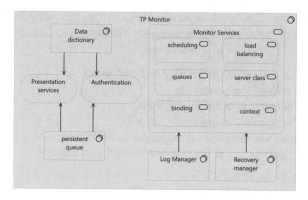

Fig. 4.65 TP-Monitor components

The typical features of a TP Monitor are:

- Features to support RPC (e.g., IDL, nameservers/directory, security, compilers Stubs, etc.).
- Transaction manager with features like logging, recovery, and locking.
- "System monitor"—responsible for the scheduling of threads, prioritization, load balancing, and replication.
- Execution environment for all the applications that use the TP Monitor.
- Specialized components for certain systems or scenarios (e.g., protocols for interaction with mainframes, queues).
- Variety of tools for installation, management, and monitoring of all components.

The main components of a TP Monitor are (Fig. 4.65).:

- Interface—API for programmatic interaction with client applications.
- Program flow—guards and executes programmatic flows possibly written in the proprietary language of the TP Monitor.
- Router—contains the mappings between the physical and logical resources.
- Communications manager—messaging system with delivery guarantees (and rollback) for communication with resources (e.g., databases).
- Wrappers—hides the heterogeneity of different resources.
- Transaction manager—supports the execution of distributed transactions (making use of 2PC protocol).
- Services—offers a comprehensive range of services to ensure high availability, performance, and replication, among others.

4.8.10 Business Process-Oriented Integration

4.8.10.1 Workflow-Oriented Integration

The term "workflow" is often used to designate a formal description of an executable business process. A workflow management system (WfMS) is a software platform that supports the design, development, implementation, and analysis of workflows. Workflows enable the automation of business processes across the organization. The features and basic functions of a WfMS are:

- Formalization authorization and approval of circuits.
- Digitization of business processes.
- Resource management of the organization.
- Obtaining the operational indicators and KPI.
- Security implementation and management of access control over the processes.
- Support automatic, semi-automatic, and manual activities.

The expected benefits of WfMS are:

- Cleared and structured processes.
- Easy explanation of problems or errors.
- Support for auditing and monitoring process.
- Transparent processes and perception of the path taken.
- Decentralization of work processes.
- Shared vision of the process flows.
- Support the collective work of the organization.
- Distribution of tasks according to the ability of the participants.

The integration using WfMS can be accomplished through two different architectures:

1. The workflow runs "on top" of the existing systems. The workflow provides a common interface, and operations may affect multiple systems. The workflow system keeps and manages the execution context of the process. Workflow systems should also allow to interconnect distributed processes in the organization (Fig. 4.66).

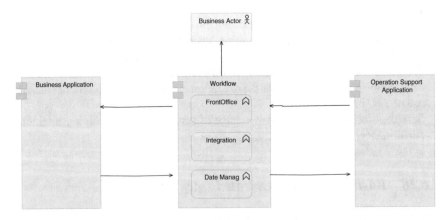

Fig. 4.66 Integration using a "WfMS on the top"

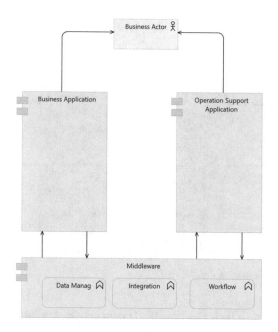

Fig. 4.67 Integration using "WfMS" as a Service Bus

2. When we face a scenario in which the integration of business processes is made only with participants who are systems/applications, the basic concepts of workflow are somewhat compromised. In this scenario (Fig. 4.67), the user interacts directly through existing application, and the WfMS is used to integrate applications (not to interact directly with the end user).

4.8.10.2   Business Process Execution Language

Business Process Execution Language (BPEL) aims to describe the interaction between business partners through sequences of synchronous and asynchronous messaging. It assumes that the interactions are long duration (long running) and have state. BPEL is based on the web services standards stack. It is supported by industry players such as IBM, Microsoft, SAP, and Oracle.

BPEL specifies the XML schema that contains the definitions of the flow of a business process. BPEL aims to generate executable code of the business process. It is an orchestration language (not choreography). Processes arise as service compositions. It defines processes that interact with the entities through web services (using WSDL to describe their contracts).

Business applications place requirements for integration and inter-operation. The current response to these challenges is based on SOA paradigm. Many enterprise applications expose their functionality through Web Services. But developing Web

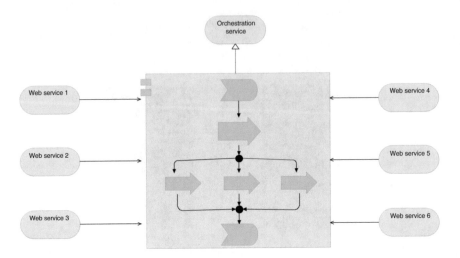

Fig. 4.68 BPEL orchestration

Services and exposing their functionality is not enough. A mechanism is needed to compose and orchestrate these functionalities (Fig. 4.68).

Within the organization, BPEL is used for setting standards for application integration, and for the specification of processes orchestration. Therefore, BPEL is used for the definition of the integration processes between systems that were isolated before. Outside of the organization (i.e., between organizations), BPEL is used for setting standards for inter-organizational communication (e.g., to support B2B), for simplifying integration with business partners, allowing explicit interorganizational processes that were previously implicit. BPEL orchestrates existing web services into a new (higher level) web service.

4.8.10.3   Orchestration vs Choreography

Orchestration is the specification of a flow from the perspective of a single entry point (single endpoint). As presented before, BPEL deals with Orchestration.

Choreography is defined as the exchange of messages, rules, and interactions between two or more entry points (endpoints) of business processes.

In Orchestration, only the central coordinator knows the process and the purpose of the process. A central process (which can also be a web service) takes control of the participants and coordinates the implementation of the different methods (web services) involved in the process. The orchestration is centralized through explicit definitions of operations and ordered calls to the web services involved. Web services involved do not "know" (and do not need to know) that they are involved in the composition of a process and that they are part of a business process at an upper level (Fig. 4.69).

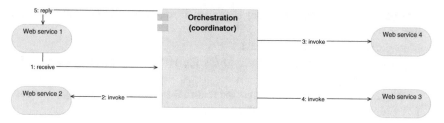

Fig. 4.69 Orchestration integration pattern

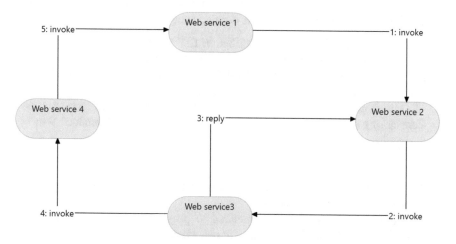

Fig. 4.70 Choreography integration pattern

In Choreography, there is no central coordinator. Choreography is a collaborative effort based on the exchange of messages in a process (usually public). All participants of the choreography have to worry about the process, the operations to be performed, the messages to be exchanged, and in which order messages should be exchanged. Each web service involved in the process knows when to run and meet other web services participants. At a minimum, each service knows the services with which it interacts directly—Fig. 4.70.

4.9   Exercises

Exercise 4.1

As presented in exercise 3.2, Lisbon Institute of Technology (LIT) established the following principles:

- Business units are autonomous.
- Customers have a single point of contact.

- Channel-specific components are separated from channel-independent components.
- Management layers are minimized.
- Common components are centralized (as the HR management process, or the course platforms).
- Messages with all the internal and the external systems are exchanged through LIT Enterprise Service Bus (ESB).

LIT CIO is considering different scenarios for supporting LIT Enterprise strategy and architecture. In one of the scenarios, the architecture described by Fig. 4.71 for supporting the course business process is being analyzed.

1. What architectural principles (described in LIT Strategy) are being violated in the architectural scenario described in Fig. 4.71? Justify your answer.
2. Review the architecture sketch of Fig. 4.71, and present a new one (in ArchiMate) that does not violate LIT architectural principles. Justify your answer.
3. LIT CIO is considering Orchestration and Choreography architectural scenarios. Considering the strategy described, which one would you recommend? Why?

Exercise 4.2

Several organizations in the public administration provide services to citizens that imply the use of the citizen's address.

Consider that N organizations intended to provide to citizens a single web interface (in the Internet) for the citizen to use whenever he or she wants to change his or her address; the goal is that the citizen can do "only once" the service and that change of address is propagated to the different organizations. However, each organization has its own systems (System S1,..., SN) that use different information technologies and different data models (Entity E1, ..., EN), and it is not feasible to change the data models of existing information systems.

Therefore, it was decided that each organization will build its own information service (IS1,...,IS10) to update the organization's data model and made it accessible to any other public entity, with specific data model for the address.

1. The architectural scenario of implementing a new Global Propagation System (GPS) to propagate an address to a list of information services (ISn) is being discussed. An architectural decision is whether if the GPS service will be implemented using an Orchestration or a Choreography approach. Assume that in any scenario, each organization Information System will only be integrated with a maximum of two other systems. Model in ArchiMate the two different scenarios.
2. What would be your recommendation for each of the architectural decision addressed in the previous questions (Orchestration vs. Choreography approach)? Justify your answer.

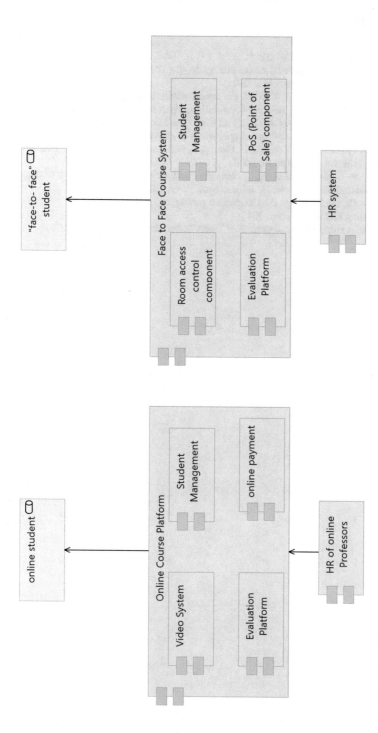

Fig. 4.71 LIT architecture scenario

References

1. The Open Group, *TOGAF Version 9.1,*, vol. 1 (Van Haren Publishing, 2011)
2. E. Proper, D. Greefhorst, Architecture principles—the cornerstones of enterprise architecture. *The Enterprise Engineering Series* (2011)
3. A. Vasconcelos, P. Sousa, J. Tribolet, Enterprise architecture analysis: an information system evaluation approach. Int. J. Enterp. Model. Inform. Syst. Archit. **3**(2), 31–53 (2008)
4. P. Sousa, Enterprise architecture alignment heuristics. Microsoft Enterp. Archit. J. **4** (2004)
5. ISO, *ISO/IEC, ISO 9126—Software Engineering—Product Quality* (2001)
6. R. Maes, D. Rijsenbrij, O. Truijens, H. Goedvolk, Redefining business—IT alignment through a unified framework, white paper, 2000
7. J. Sarkis, R. Sundarraj, Evaluating componentized enterprise information technologies: a multiattribute modeling approach. Inform. Syst. Front. (2003)
8. W. Inmon, Data architecture: the information paradigm (1993)
9. BEA, Scaling EJB applications, 2006
10. T. Mccabe, A complexity measure. IEEE Trans. Softw. Eng. **4**(2), 308–320 (1976)

Chapter 5
Enterprise Cartography

Pedro Sousa

Abstract This chapter describes Enterprise Cartography (EC) primitives. Thus, after an introduction to EC concepts, EC definitions are proposed (including enterprise model, enterprise meta-model, architectural sentence, alive artifact, transformation initiative, architectural maps, enterprise observation, knowledge base, as-was state, as-is state, to-be state, enterprise architect, and enterprise cartographer). Next, five EC primitives are described. The system representation and the EC formalization are presented next.

5.1 Introduction

Simply put, *EC* is the process of abstracting, collecting, structuring, and representing architectural artifacts and their relations from the observation of the enterprise reality. The expression "enterprise reality" refers to the present state of the enterprise. Traditionally, the observation of this reality is a subjective perception of an observer, and consequently, it is probable that there are different actors that perceive different realities of the same enterprise. So, the perception of the present state of the enterprise (the reality) must be sustained on relevant facts captured in logs and models and represented through artifacts based on previously defined and agreed upon models.

We refer to "architectural artifacts" as the enterprise's observable elements whose inter-dependencies and intra-dependencies express the architecture of the enterprise. Naturally, different institutions may consider various sets of artifacts as part of their architecture. To abstract, structure, and represent the architecture-related artifacts, one needs the whole set of knowledge and concepts implied in architecture visualization and representation. For example, the concepts of semiotic triangle [1, 2], the model of the architecture description presented in ISO IEEE 1471 [3], and a symbolic notation, such as the one used in ArchiMate [4], are concepts necessary to the production of EA views.

Ongoing transformation initiatives and their plans are an essential part of enterprise reality because they define the near future *TO-BE* of the enterprise if no further decisions are taken that might have an impact on them. This is a fundamental

© The Author(s), under exclusive license to Springer Nature Switzerland AG 2022
P. Sousa, A. Vasconcelos, *Enterprise Architecture and Cartography*,
The Enterprise Engineering Series, https://doi.org/10.1007/978-3-030-96264-7_5

concept that we call *emerging AS-IS*, which we define as the state of the enterprise after successful completion of ongoing transformation initiatives. This corresponds to the inertia of a body; if no contrary action is taken, inertia determines the body future position and speed. Similarly, if no opposite actions are taken, ongoing initiatives determine the TO-BE models of the Enterprise.

Given that in today's enterprises transformation initiatives are omnipresent, the concept of *Emerging AS-IS* is not only an essential capacity for the planning of the new transformation initiatives but also for monitoring ongoing ones. When driving a car, the faster the car is moving, the further ahead one should focus the eyes to match the longer time and distance one needs to steer it. Likewise, when steering an enterprise, the faster the enterprise is changing, the more important is to know the *emerging AS-IS*, as time flows.

Continuing with the car metaphor, if one knows the car situational reality (position, speed, and direction), then the car future's position, speed, and direction can be estimated unless some unforeseen action (e.g., break or turn) is taken. Much like the car's speed and direction, ongoing transformation initiatives are, in fact, the core elements of enterprise inertia, since they determine the future of the enterprise (the *TO-BE*). Since plans of ongoing transformation initiatives are observable artifacts, by observing the enterprise reality, one can predict the expected future enterprise state.

Enterprise cartography is a purely descriptive perspective, since it does not explicitly incorporate the purposeful design of the new enterprise artifacts, as one expects in EA. Such a difference is also evident in the definitions of the *architect* and *cartographer* roles. According to the IEEE Standard Glossary of Software Engineering Terminology [5], the term *architect* is defined as *"The person, team, or organization responsible for designing systems architecture"*, and in the Merriam-Webster dictionary,[1] the term *cartographer* is defined as the *person who makes maps*. So, an *architect* is essentially a person that designs and shapes intended changes to the architecture of the present enterprise reality, while a *cartographer* is essentially a person that aims at representing the reality as it happens, including such changes as they are occurring.

Capturing and representing organization changes as it happens is probably the most challenging aspect in EC since it implies doing representations of evolving artifacts. The real challenge comes when the practices of abstracting and representing the evolving enterprise occur at a rhythm that is slower than the actual rhythm of enterprise changes.

Furthermore, as presented in Sect. 1.3, a fundamental motivation for EC is to produce representations of the organization's TO-BE, given they are absolutely necessary to plan (today) the next transformation initiatives.

In the next section, we will present the key definitions and concepts that sustain EC.

---

[1] Merriam-Webster.

5.2 Definitions

In the context of EC, we consider the following definitions.

5.2.1 Enterprise Model

The Enterprise Model is a model of the enterprise based on a graph holding the enterprise artifacts as Nodes and their relationships as Arcs. Nodes and Arcs can hold additional information both the organization artefacts they represent. In formal terms, let an Enterprise E be modeled as a direct graph $G = (A, R)$ defined over the set of artifacts A and the set of their relationships R, where A represents the vertices and R the directed edges. Since A and R change over time, so does the graph G. Let $G_t(A_t, R_t)$ represent the value the of G at time t.

For simplicity, we assume that t is a discrete variable and that for each A_t, there is a valid R_t and vice versa. If we consider t to represent days, then this means that each day one has a new graph $G_t(A_t, R_t)$ as a model of the enterprise.

$$Enterprise\ Model: \ G_t(A_t, R_t) \tag{5.1}$$

The notion of an organization as a graph is just yet another very common way to represent an enterprise. Any model in TOGAF or ArchiMate can be easily represented as a graph, as long as we consider that nodes and arcs of the graph have types. Adding the types to nodes and arcs is what makes a meta-model, as presented next.

However, the notion of model evolution is not so common. Later, we also add a *life cycle* to nodes and arcs of the graph. The life cycle is about artefacts evolution, as in nature, from conception to gestation, from gestation to birth, from birth to dead. So, a node in the graph may represent some artefact of the organization that is not yet alive. For example, an application that is being developed is modeled as a node in state "under construction."

In this scenario, one needs to filter out the model of the organization as it is up and running. So, let us review Eq. 5.1 to consider only the productive nodes and relations and ignore the ones not yet productive or no longer productive, as in:

$$Productive\ Enterprise\ Model: \ PG_t(PA_t, PR_t) \tag{5.2}$$

where PA_t represents the set of productive artefacts at time t and PR_t represents the set of productive relations at time t.

In EA parlance, one does not use the terms nodes and arcs, but instead objects and relations or artefacts and references. So, we will use these terms later instead.

Both artefact types and artefacts *life cycle* will be detailed next.

5.2.2 Enterprise Meta-Model

Enterprise meta-model refers to the set of concepts one can use to build enterprise models. This means the set of types of artefacts used in the model and their possible relation types. Both artefacts and their relationship have a *life cycle*, whose states must also be defined in the meta-model.

The Enterprise Model establishes the subjects (artifacts, or nodes of the graph), the verbs (relations, or arcs of the graph), and their *life cycle* that can be used to express the architecture of the enterprise.

Examples of artifact types are *department, information system, service*, and *process*. Examples of relations are *realizes, uses*, etc. Examples of *life cycle* states are *productive* or *decommissioned*.

In formal terms, this means that both artifacts and relations have a type. Let each artifact $a \in A$ have a type $\tau \in \Gamma_t$, where Γ_t is the set of all types at time t. To find out the type of a given artifact or relation, one uses the function $type = TypeOf(instance)$ that states the type of a given instance, either an artifact or a relation.

Enterprise meta-model refers to the set

$$Artifact\ Types :\ \Gamma_t\ :\ \forall a\ \in\ A_t\ \exists\ \tau\ \in\ \Gamma_t :\ \tau = TypeOf(a) \qquad (5.3)$$

$$Relation\ Types :\ \Omega_t\ :\ \forall r\ \in\ R_t\ \exists\ \omega\ \in\ \Omega_t :\ \omega = TypeOf(r) \qquad (5.4)$$

Naturally, the set of types Γ_t and Ω_t may also change in time. For example, the evolution of ArchiMate, from version 1 to version 3, has introduced a significant number of new types and also changes the relations. The problem of meta-model evolution is a further discussed in [6–8]. In this book, for simplicity, we consider that the set of types Γ and Ω is constant over time.

5.2.3 Architectural Sentence

An architectural sentence is a well-formed proposition regarding the enterprise architecture. It must necessarily be expressed using the types, both artifact and relations types, as well as states both artifact and relations states, defined in the meta-model.

In our model, one considers two types of Architectural Sentences, one regarding relations and another regarding states, and both are necessary to define an Enterprise Architecture:

- *Relational Sentence* : $RS(t, a_1, a_2, r)$ that means that at time t the artifact a_1 refers artifact a_2 through relation r.

$$RS(t, a_1, a_2, r) : a_1 \in A_t \wedge a_2 \in A_t \wedge r \in R_t) \qquad (5.5)$$

- References can be unassigned using $RS(t, a_1, a_2, r, false)$ that means that at time t the artifact a_1 no longer refers to artifact a_2 through relation r.
- *State Sentence* : $SS(t, a_1, s)$ that means that at time t the artifact a_1 is in life cycle state s.

$$SS(t, a_1, s) : a_1 \in A_t \land s \in \Phi \qquad (5.6)$$

Using the examples given in the item *Enterprise Meta-Model*, the following are examples of architectural sentences:

- Sales *department uses* CRM *information system* at t_n
- Sales *department no longer uses* CRM *information system* at t_m
- CRM *information system* is *decommissioned* at t_p

In the above examples, the words in italic are elements of the *Enterprise Meta-Model*, and the non-italic words (Sales, CRM) are instances (subjects or artefacts) of the model.

Notice that in the examples given, an artefact has a name and a type. So, in the first example above, the Sales *department* and CRM *information system* match a_1 and a_2 of the Relational Sentence, and *uses* states the relation between them.

The sentences proposed above are enough to define a model of the enterprise as well as any changes of that model. A few remarks are appropriate to notice:

- A reference to a subject at a given time means the subject exists at that time in some state. There is no need for previous subject creation or elimination, since the subject creation is done implicitly in sentences and subject elimination is not required.

  For example, if the statement "Lisbon is the capital of Portugal on 01/01/2022" is pronounced on a date before 01/01/2022 and at that time Lisbon is not recorded in the model, then Lisbon is recorded in the model as being productive in 01/01/2022. If the statement is made in the distant future where Lisbon is not recorded, then Lisbon is recorded in the model as being decommissioned on 01/01/2022, with no productive date.
- All objects have at least one relation. In practice, one always declare objects related to some other object. Even so, if one really wants to have an object with no relation with other object, one can use a sentence that relates one object with itself.
- Any model $G_t(A_t, R_t)$ can be defined with a set of relational sentences RS and a set of state sentences SS. This means that:

$$G_{t_n}(A_{t_n}, R_{t_n}) = RS(t_m, a_i, a_j, r_k)$$
$$\cup\ SS(t_m, a_l, s_m)$$
$$\forall a_i, a_j, r_k, a_l, s_m$$
$$\forall t_m \leq t_n$$

(5.7)

The term $\forall a_i, a_j, r_k, a_l, s_m$ means for any artefact and relation, and the term $\forall t_m \leq t_n$ means for any time before t_n.

- Every change that occurs in the enterprise can be model by adding new Architectural Sentences to the previous model. There is no need for updates, or deletes. Any change can be modeled by adding new statement (facts) to the model.

Consider that $G_{t_n}(A_{t_n}, R_{t_n})$ is a model of an organization at time t_n. Any change the organization has undergone between any two moments t_n and t_{n+1} can be modeled by adding new Architectural Sentences to the model. One does not need to delete, remove, or update on any statement that was used to build up the model at t_n. Evolution is modeled just by adding new statements.

This means that:

$$
\begin{aligned}
G_{t_{n+1}}(A_{t_{n+1}}, R_{t_{n+1}}) = &\ G_{t_n}(A_{t_n}, R_{t_n}) \\
&\cup RS(t_{n+1}, a_i, a_j, r_k) \\
&\cup SS(t_{n+1}, a_l, s_m) \\
&\forall a_i, a_j, r_k, a_l, s_m
\end{aligned}
\tag{5.8}
$$

Given Eqs. 5.7 and 5.8, it also true that:

$$
\begin{aligned}
G_{t_{n+1}}(A_{t_{n+1}}, R_{t_{n+1}}) = &\ RS(t_m, a_i, a_j, r_k) \\
&\cup SS(t_m, a_l, s_m) \\
&\forall a_i, a_j, r_k, a_l, s_m \\
&\forall t_m \leq t_{n+1}
\end{aligned}
\tag{5.9}
$$

5.2.4   Productive Artefacts

A productive artifact is an artefact that contributes to the products and services that an organization realizes. This is different from the artefacts that contribute to the enterprise value, since in the former case we only consider artefacts that are operating and have a role in the current enterprise processes and services that creates value. In the second case, we must also consider the artefacts that are still under conception or under development but already have an impact on the enterprise value.

This means the artifact is reachable via the operational dependency graph of enterprise productive products and services. So, as a general rule, the productive state of an artifact is defined from a graph traversal and is not an intrinsic property of the artifact. The roots of this graph are usually the enterprise products and services that are active at a given moment in time. However, one cannot provide a strong rule for the definition of such roots or even the reachable criteria to define aliveness, since the relations are defined by the modeler, and its semantics is not known.

Consider the case where organization O has a product P that is realized by artefact A. If the modeler chooses to have a relation *realizes* between P and A, then one may infer that A is productive.

However, the modeler might chose to have instead a relation with the opposite meaning, for example, the relation *does not realize*. In this case, neither the existence of a relation between P and A does not mean that A is productive nor its nonexistence proves that A is productive. Therefore, one cannot use references to establish the artifact productiveness, without knowing its semantics.

5.2.5 Transformation Initiative

A transformation initiative is a set of planned and purposeful activities to change the enterprise artifacts as intended. A transformation initiative holds a set of architectural statements that change artefacts states after its successful completion. A common name for transformation initiatives is project. But many other initiatives normally outside the scope of projects, such as hiring staff, training staff, the creation of a new department, merges, and acquisitions, among others, are also transformation initiatives. Any change that has a purpose is a result of a transformation initiative. If it has a purpose, it must have a plan, which is nothing more than a set of architectural statements.

According to the previous definition of *Productive Artefacts*, ongoing transformation initiatives cannot always be considered to be productive artifacts of the enterprise, because they normally aim at transforming the organization and not to produce products or services directly. Nevertheless, for the purpose of being observable, it makes no difference whereas it is considered or not productive artefacts.

5.2.6 Enterprise States

One has defined the enterprise architecture at time t to be a graph as defined in Eq. 5.1.

However, quite often, one use the terms *AS-WAS*, *AS-IS*, and *TO-BE* to refer to past, current, and future states of the productive enterprise. So the actual meaning of each of this terms depends on the current date. So for a given current date t_c, one defines:

- The $AS\text{-}WAS(t)$ is the set of all productive artifacts, their relations, and states as observed at a particular point in time in the past t at time t (older than t_c).
  This means that $AS\text{-}WAS$ at time t in the past corresponds to $GP_t(AP_t, RP_t)$.

- *AS-IS* state of the enterprise is the current set of all productive artifacts and their relations at time t_c. The *AS-IS* corresponds to $GP_{t_c}(AP_{t_c}, RP_{t_c})$.
- *TO-BE(t)* state is the set of productive artifacts and their relations at some point in time in the future.

  This means that *TO-BE* at some time t in the future corresponds to $GP_t(AP_t, RP_t)$.
- *Emerging AS-IS(t_c, t)* state of the enterprise is the set of all productive artifacts, their relations, and states observed in the enterprise after the execution of ongoing and planned transformation initiatives as planned, from time t_c up to time t.

  So if a transformation initiative has in its plans to make an artefact productive at time t_1 ($t_c \leq t_1 \leq t$), this artefact will be part of the emerging AS-IS. Likewise, if some transformation initiative plans to make an artefact decommissioned at time t_2 ($t_c \leq t_2 \leq t$), this artefact will not be part of the emerging AS-IS.

5.2.7   Enterprise Observation

This concept relates to the ability to formulate architectural statements from the observation of the enterprise reality, including both productive and non productive artifacts.

The organization observable state at time t is $G_t(A_t, R_t)$.

5.2.8   Enterprise System

In Sect. 2.1.1, we present the basic notion of a system as being a set of components with a structure (the way components are connected), an environment (the list of external components or systems that interact with the system), and the system production (the artefacts delivered to the environment). We also add purposefulness as a condition so that a set or parts become a system.

Such as notion of a system can be formalized as follows[2]:

- Let $\sigma \in S$ be a System and S_t be the set of all systems at time t.
- Let a $P_t(\sigma)$ be the set of all artifacts a that *Is Part Of* system σ at time t. To find out which artefacts are part of the system, we consider that the components are *Is_Part_Of* of system. Such a relation stands for the *Aggregation Abstraction* [9].
- The Composition C of a system σ at time t is defined as:

$$C_t(\sigma) = \{ x : x \in S_t(\sigma) \} \tag{5.10}$$

- The Environment E of the system σ at time t is defined as:

$$E_t(\sigma) = \{x : x \notin C_t(\sigma) \wedge \exists y : y \in C_t(\sigma) \wedge (x \to y) \vee (y \to x)\} \quad (5.11)$$

- The Structure of system (σ) at time t is defined as:

$$S_t(\sigma) = \{<x, y> \in C_t(\sigma) \wedge ((x \to y) \vee (y \to x))\} \quad (5.12)$$

- The Integration of system (σ) at time t is defined as:

$$I_t(\sigma) = \{x, y : x \in C_t(\sigma) \wedge y \in E_t(\sigma) \wedge ((x \to y) \vee (y \to x))\} \quad (5.13)$$

5.2.9 Enterprise Roles

We define two enterprise roles with responsibility in the EA management:

- Enterprise Architect.
  A person that makes architectural statements regarding some point in time in the future (*TO-BE*).
- Enterprise Cartographer.
  A person that collects architectural statements from observations of the enterprise reality and produces architectural representations of the enterprise.

5.2.10 Enterprise System Representations

The representation of enterprise systems can be easily structured under the analysis of a system components graph and its environment.

A key aspect concerns with time. Since systems changes over time, so thus these representations. Thus, we consider that any representation always includes the visualization of all states between any two moments.

To exemplify the system representation corresponding to Eqs. 5.10 to 5.13, we use the organization "Global System" and its subsystems SA and SB as depicted in Fig. 5.1. SA is further decomposed in S01, S02 and S03, and SB in S04 and S05. In Fig. 5.2, we present the components of S01 and their relations with the components of other subsystems.

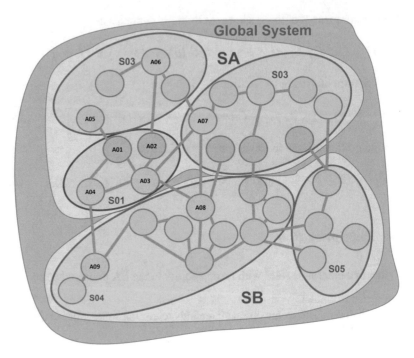

Fig. 5.1 Subsystems of enterprise "Global System"

Fig. 5.2 System S01 internal
and external dependencies

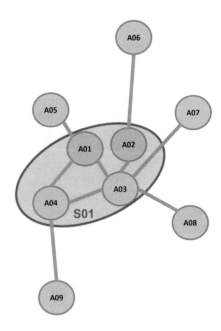

We consider the following representation patterns to describe an enterprise system:

- **Organic**. This represents how the system is placed along with other systems, normally in a hierarchical view whose root is the whole enterprise as single system and the leaves are the individual systems. This view often matches systems landscape views.

  Figure 5.3 presents an example of an organic view.
- **Context**. The context view of a system presents the external elements that relate directly with the system internal elements or with the system itself. External elements are often grouped by type, as presented in Fig. 5.4 for the case of system *S01* context view.
- **Structure**. The Structure view of a system presents the internal elements and how they are related with each other. Internal elements are often grouped by type, as presented in Fig. 5.5 for the case of system *S01* structure view.

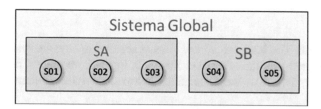

Fig. 5.3 Organic view of system S01 in the whole system

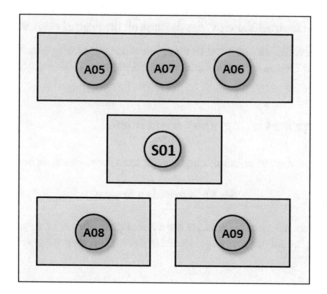

Fig. 5.4 System S01 context view

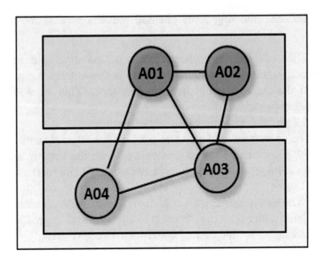

Fig. 5.5 System S01 structure view

- **Integration**. The integration view aims at presenting how the system elements are integrated with the external elements. In Fig. 5.6, we present the integration view for system S01, where relations between the internal elements are also displayed.

  Notice that even with the relations between internal elements presented, this view does not replace the structural view, because the internal elements displayed in the integration view are only those with relation to the external elements, whereas in the structural view, one displays all the internal elements.

The above views can be used to compose other views. For example, the well-known layered view is a composition of context views of different systems.

5.3 Enterprise Cartography Principles

We now present a set of principles that can be formulated based on one assumption:

An Enterprise is a System

If Enterprises are systems, and we are assuming the notion of a system in which a system must have a purpose as presented in Sect. 2.1.1, then we may formulate the following principles.

Fig. 5.6 System S01
integration view

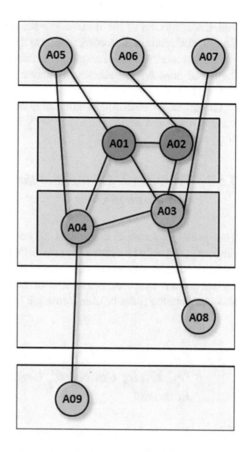

5.3.1   Principle 1: Transformation Initiatives Are Observable Artifacts of the Enterprise AS-IS

A transformation initiative is itself an enterprise artifact. This statement is in line with most architecture guidelines such as the *Work Package* concept in both TOGAF [10] and ArchiMate [4].

However, we go further and also state that the plans of transformation initiatives are also part of the observable enterprise. In practice, this means that the intention to build something is an observable artefact of the enterprise. How can such intentions be an observable artefact?

Since transformation initiatives must be purposeful ones, otherwise the resulting enterprise (i.e., system) would not have a purpose, they must have a purpose or a goal. The formulation of this purpose or goal is a definition of a desired or intended *TO-BE* state of the enterprise.

So, one can assume that transformation initiatives always have a plan or a road map to achieve it, no matter how simple, realistic, or achievable it is. If nothing else, then the definition of the desired *TO-BE* state of the enterprise is the plan. From Eq. 5.9, such formulation corresponds to a set of architectural statements.

In other words, a transformation initiative corresponds to two lists of artefacts—the list of artefacts to become productive and the list of artefacts to be decommissioned [11].

Of course, a transformation initiative can actually make unplanned changes and achieve undesired results.

5.3.2 Principle 2: Changes in the Set of Productive Artifacts Are Planned Ones

This principle states that artifacts do not become productive or non-productive randomly, but only as a result of transformation initiatives.

Since transformation initiatives are also observable enterprise artifacts (principle 1), an artifact becomes productive or non-productive as a result of observable statements in the plans of transformation initiatives.

5.3.3 Principle 3: All Enterprise Artifacts Have a Five-State Life Cycle: Conceived, Gestating, Alive, Retired, and Removed

Despite the fact that common EA notations (e.g., [4]) do not formalize artifacts states, it is convenient to have models that mix existing and not existing artifacts, to express model changes.

In this principle, we say that existing artifacts do not "fall from the sky," but go through an evolution process instead.

Let us first consider as *productive* the artifacts as the ones that are somehow involved in the enterprise business processes that produce value. In Fig. 5.7, we present the five states, their fundamental transitions, and their classification regarding productiveness: *Non-productive Yet*, *Productive*, and *No Longer Productive* states.

- *Conceived* state, as the first state of existence. It corresponds to a state where the artifact is planned but its materialization into a productive artifact did not start yet. A conceived artifact is an idea that exists *TO-BE* models (or plans) of some change initiative, even if itself is still in the conceived state.
- *Gestating* is the state when an artifact is being constructed or acquired to become productive. As conceived artifacts, gestating ones do not play a role in the enterprise transactions and processes. This state only differentiates from the conceived state by the fact that the change initiative that aims at putting the artifact into production has already started. An ongoing change initiative can be

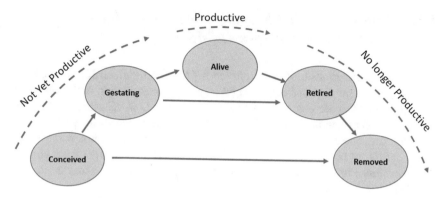

Fig. 5.7 Existence artifact life cycle

a productive artifact, since it can have an impact on other productive artifacts and is expected to produce value after its completion.

- *Alive* or *Productive*.[2] A Productive artifact plays purposeful roles in the enterprise to create value. Conceived and Gestation artifacts might have a relationship on productive objects, namely, in the ones that are conceiving or creating them. But their relation is a passive one, not a purposeful role as alive objects must have to create value. From Principle 2, it is clear that an artifact cannot be brought into existence as a productive; it always exists first as conceived before being productive.

- *Retired*,[3] is when an alive artifact no longer plays a role in the enterprise transactions and processes to create value. As in the conceived and gestation states, a Retired artifact may still have an impact on alive artifacts. In fact, even if it does not create behavior or value to the enterprise, it may be the target of several housekeeping activities that are necessary after being dead.

  The Retired state can be achieved directly after gestating state, without becoming productive. An artifact planned to become productive by a given transformation initiative might never be productive either because the initiative was canceled or because it simply changed plans and decided to no longer put that artifact into production.

- *Removed*. Represents the post-Retired state where the artifact has no impact in the remaining artifacts. A removed artifact is unable to interact with alive enterprise artifacts. An artifact can move from conception directly to removal when it never materialized in a gestation, meaning that it never went beyond an idea.

---

[2] In previous publications, the *Productive* stated was named as *Alive*.

[3] In previous publications, the *Retired* state was named as *Dead*.

5.3.4 Principle 4: The Emerging AS-IS Can Be Inferred by Observing the Enterprise AS-IS

The *emerging AS-IS* state differs from the *AS-IS* state by the artifacts planned to be brought into production/retirement by ongoing transformation initiatives. Since ongoing initiatives are enterprise artifacts, their plans (*TO-BE* models) are in the scope of the cartographer observations of the enterprise reality (principle 1).

Therefore, one can foresee the set of productive artifacts at some point in time in the future by consolidating the *AS-IS* with the *TO-BE* models of the ongoing transformations initiative whose completion date precedes the desired moment in time [11].

In other words, using Eq. 5.8, if $G_{t_{today}}(A_{t_{today}}, R_{t_{today}})$ is the enterprise *AS-IS* at time t_{today} and architectural statements RS and SS are the plans of the transformation initiatives ongoing (productive) between today and time t_m, then G_{t_m} will be our best guess of the enterprise *AS-IS* at time t_m.

Given that both RS and SS are part of the observable *AS-IS* of the enterprise, the principle is clear.

References

1. C.W. Morris, *Foundation of the Theory of Signs—International Encyclopedia of Unified Science*, vol. 1 (University of Chicago Press, Chicago, 1938)
2. J. Dietz, *Enterprise Ontology—Theory and Methodology*, 1st edn. (Springer, Berlin, 2006)
3. IEEE Computer Society, The IEEE standard 1471-2000 systems and software engineering—architecture description, 2000. superseded by ISO/IEC/IEEE 42010:2011
4. The Open Group, *ArchiMate®️ 2.1 Specification* (Van Haren Publishing, Zaltbommel, 2015)
5. IEEE, *Systems and software engineering—Vocabulary in ISO/IEC/IEEE 24765:2010(E)* (2010), pp. 1–418
6. N. Silva, M. Mira Da Silva, P. Sousa, An enterprise architecture model co-evolution operations catalog, in *Twenty-fourth Americas Conference on Information Systems (AMCIS 2018)* (New Orleans, 2018)
7. N. Silva, P. Sousa, M. Mira Da Silva, N. Silva, M. Mira Da Silva, P. Sousa. Lm2f: a life-cycle model maintenance framework for coevolving enterprise architecture meta-models and models, in *27th European Conference on Information Systems, Stockholm and Upsala* (Sweden, 2018)
8. N. Silva, P. Sousa, M. Mira Da Silva, Maintenance of enterprise architecture models, in *Business & Information Systems Engineering* (2020), pp. 1–24
9. C. Batini, S. Ceri, S. Navathe, Conceptual database design: an entity relationship approach (1992)
10. The Open Group, TOGAF version 9.1 (2011)
11. P. Sousa, J. Lima, A. Sampaio, C. Pereira, *An Approach for Creating and Managing Enterprise Blueprints: A Case for IT Blueprints*, vol. 34 of *Lecture Notes in Business Information Processing* (Springer-Verlag, The Netherlands, 2009), pp. 70–84

Part III
How We Do It: Supporting Methodologies and Technologies

Chapter 6
Enterprise Architecture Development Framework

André Vasconcelos and Pedro Sousa

Abstract This chapter presents TOGAF Architecture Development Method that supports organizations in defining, developing, and managing the enterprise architecture.

6.1 Introduction

Nowadays companies face important challenges in surrounding mutable environments. With relentless competition in almost all sectors, substitute products are available for customers.

The Open Group Architecture Framework, best known as TOGAF, is an enterprise architecture methodology and framework. TOGAF proposes a descriptive model to support the development of enterprise architectures called the Architecture Development Method (ADM) [1].

The ADM supports organizations in defining, developing, and managing their enterprise architecture.

6.2 TOGAF ADM

TOGAF is a framework for enterprise architecture. It provides an approach for designing, planning, implementing, and governing an enterprise architecture. TOGAF ADM describes a method for developing and managing the lifecycle of an enterprise architecture and forms the core of TOGAF. It integrates elements of TOGAF to meet the business and IT needs of an organization [1].

TOGAF Architecture Development Method (ADM) is an iterative method, considering the breadth of coverage of the enterprise, the level of detail, the extent of the time period (including the number and extent of any intermediate time periods), and the architectural assets to be leveraged.

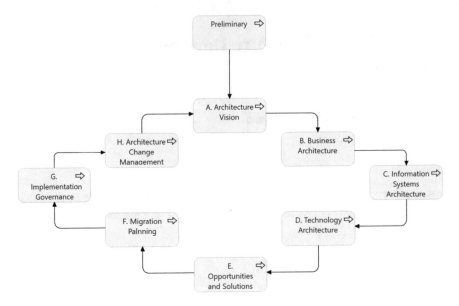

Fig. 6.1 TOGAF ADM phases (based on [1])

The ADM is a generic method since it is expected to be used by enterprises in a wide variety of different geographies and applied in different vertical sectors and industry types. TOGAF ADM phases are presented in Fig. 6.1.

6.2.1 Preliminary Phase

The first phase of the ADM has the main goal to determine the architecture capability desired in the organization, including the organizational context (including the organizations and business units involved), and the methods and frameworks relevant for the initiative.

In this phase, the architect is expected to establish the process and the tools to perform the EA project [1].

TOGAF recommends that the following steps are [1] followed:

1. Scope the organizations.
2. Confirm the governance and the support frameworks.
3. Define and establish the enterprise architecture team and organization.
4. Identify and establish the architecture principles.
5. Tailor TOGAF and, if any, other selected architecture framework(s).
6. Implement the architecture tools.

TOGAF ADM has to co-exist with other management frameworks that are present within organizations.

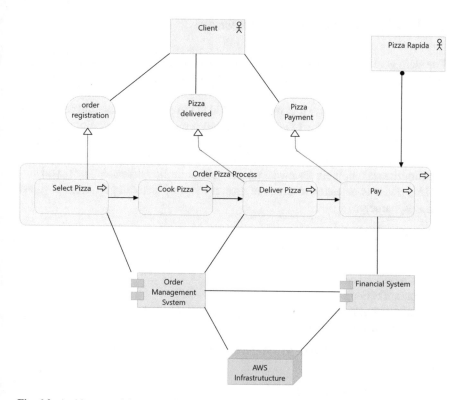

Fig. 6.2 Architecture vision example

6.2.2 Phase A: Architecture Vision

ADM phase A aims to develop a high-level vision of the capabilities and business value to be delivered, and to obtain approval to develop and deploy the architecture outlined in the architecture vision.

TOGAF [1] recommends to start by establishing the EA project roadmap, and identifying key stakeholders, concerns and requirements. Next the business goals and drivers should be modeled. The business capabilities are next described and the EA principles established.

In this phase the architecture vision is developed - see the example in Fig. 6.2.

Finally the target architecture with the KPIs and business risks are defined [1].

6.2.3   Phase B: Business Architecture

The main goal of phase B is to develop the target business architecture. The business architecture main focus is on the enterprise operation in order to contribute to the goals and drivers.

Thus, during this phase it is recommended [1] to develop a baseline description of the architecture, after the selection of reference models and viewpoints (Fig. 6.3).

TOFAF [1] recommends that a gap analysis is developed (between the baseline and the target architecture) addressing the impact in the architecture landscape.

After the stakeholders review an architecture definition document is created.

This phase is expected to produce several outputs, including different business catalogs, namely:

1. Organization/actor catalog
2. Driver/goal/objective catalog
3. Role catalog
4. Business service/function catalog
5. Location catalog
6. Process/event/control/product catalog
7. Contract/measure catalog

It is also recommended to produce matrices that relate business concepts, including:

1. Business interaction matrix
2. Actor/role matrix

Several business viewpoints (diagrams) are also expected to be delivered at this stage, including:

1. Business footprint diagram
2. Business service/information diagram
3. Functional decomposition diagram
4. Product lifecycle diagram
5. Goal/objective/service diagram
6. Use-case diagram (see Fig. 6.4)
7. Organization decomposition diagram
8. Process flow diagram
9. Event diagram

6.2.4   Phase C: Information Systems Architecture

The main goal of phase C is to develop the target information systems architecture. The Information Systems Architecture is expected to support the business architec-

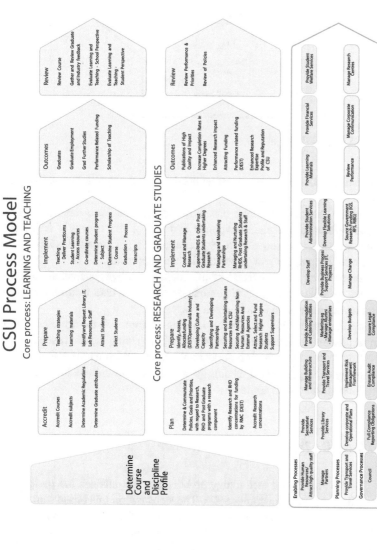

Fig. 6.3 Reference business model example (reprinted with permission from [2])

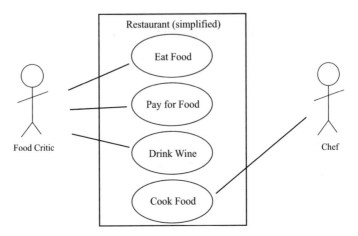

Fig. 6.4 Use-case diagram example

ture and vision. TOGAF considers together the data and the application architecture in this phase.

Regarding the data architecture a baseline data architecture is developed (after selecting the reference models, viewpoints and tools). Afterwards a target data architecture is also proposed and a gap analysis is performed leading to an architecture definition document (after stakeholders approval).

Several outputs may be produced in this step, including conceptual data diagrams, logical data diagrams, data dissemination diagrams, data security diagrams, data migration diagrams, and data lifecycle diagram.

Regarding the application architecture a similar approach is proposed [1] by developing a baseline application architecture (after selecting the reference models, viewpoints and tools). Afterwards a target application architecture is also proposed and a gap analysis is performed leading to an application architecture definition document (after stakeholders approval).

6.2.5 Phase D: Technology Architecture

Phase D develops the target technology architecture that enables the logical and physical application and data components. The steps within this phase start by the development of a baseline IT architecture (after selecting the reference models, viewpoints and tools). Afterwards a target IT architecture is also proposed and a gap analysis is performed leading to an IT architecture definition document (after stakeholders approval).

Examples of outputs from this phase are environment and location diagrams, platform decomposition diagrams, processing diagrams, networked computing/hardware diagrams, and communications engineering diagrams (Fig. 6.5).

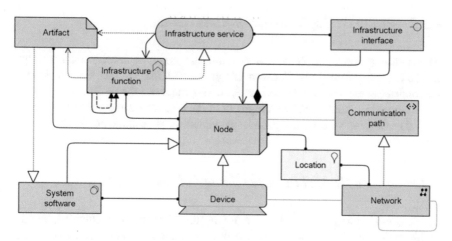

Fig. 6.5 Technology diagram example

6.2.6 Phase E: Opportunities and Solutions

The main goal of phase E is to generate the initial version of the architecture roadmap, considering the outputs from phases B, C, and D.

The recommended steps for Opportunities and Solutions phase [1] are the consolidation of the gap analysis, requirements and interoperability from previous phases. Afterwards the implementation strategy should be proposed (after a risk for business transformation assessment). An architecture roadmap, implementation and migration plan are expected to be delivered

6.2.7 Phase F: Migration Planning

In this phase the main goals are to (1) finalize the architecture roadmap and the supporting implementation and migration plan, (2) ensure that the implementation and migration plan is coordinated and (3) ensure that the transformation initiative and its benefits are understood by the key stakeholders.

TOGAF ADM[1] suggests that a business value is assigned to each work package. Then an estimation of the timings and resources should be developed, along with the prioritization of the initiatives, through a cost/benefit assessment. After these steps the architecture roadmap and implementation and migration plan are proposed.

6.2.8 Phase G: Implementation Governance

This phase ensures the conformance with the target architecture through the implementation of projects. Thus, in this phase, TOGAF [1] recommends to start by confirming the scope and priorities for deployment and the resources needed.

Afterwards a guide to the development of the solutions and compliance reviews should be developed, supporting the implementation of business and IT operations.

6.2.9 Phase H: Architecture Change Management

The last ADM phase ensures that the architecture lifecycle is maintained, that the architecture governance framework is executed, and that the enterprise architecture capability meets the requirements. Phase H should perform risk management activities, deploy monitoring tools and provide architecture change management analysis.

The requirement change along with governance and change processes are important activities of this final phase.

6.2.10 ADM Architecture Requirement Management

The ADM architecture requirement management ensures that exists and is performed through ADM phases and steps (when needed).

The major outputs of these activities are requirement impact assessment and architecture requirement specification.

6.2.11 Implementing the ADM

The ADM does not need to be implemented completely and sequentially from A to H phase. Figure 6.6 presents different iteration cycles that may be applied to the ADM.

Additionally, depending on the goal of the EA, ADM may be implemented at different depth and breadth of the enterprise (Fig. 6.7). For example, ADM may be used for supporting the implementation of a specific software system or for the development of the whole enterprise.

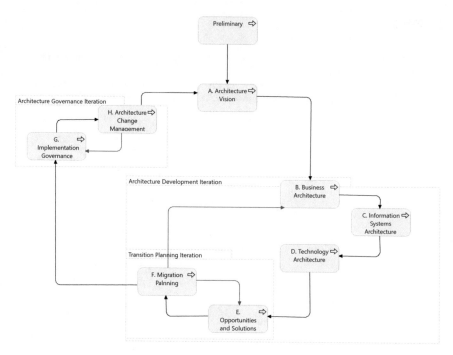

Fig. 6.6 Applying iteration to the ADM

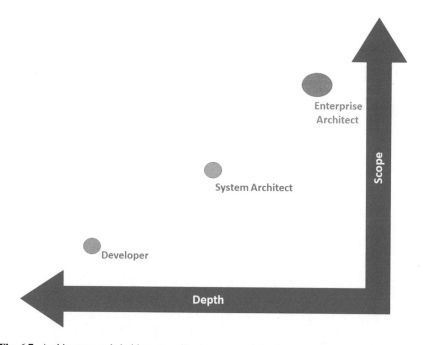

Fig. 6.7 Architecture stakeholders according to scope and depth

References

1. The Open Group, *The TOGAF Standard version 9.2*. https://pubs.opengroup.org/architecture/togaf9-doc/arch/chap02.html
2. D. Bedwell, C. Cox, H. Bryant, D. Ireland, *CSU Process Model* (Charles Sturt University, 2020). https://cdn.csu.edu.au/_data/assets/pdf_file/0003/51924/process-model-wpp.pdf

Chapter 7
Enterprise Strategy Design

André Vasconcelos

Abstract This chapter presents an enterprise strategy design approach supported in several techniques. Thus, the context of the strategy (and of the enterprise) is characterized considering the political, economic, social, technological, environmental, and legal factors. Then, the balanced scorecard is used to detail the vision into financial, customer, internal, and learning and growth objectives. The Business Model Canvas is next used for modeling the mission, strategies, tactics, business policies, business rules, requirements, and constraints of the EA. Finally, the EA is assessed through strength, weakness, opportunity, and threat analyses.

7.1 Introduction

The definition of the strategic elements that drive an organization is a management field of study and research. However, the strategy is not just central to the organization, but is also a key ingredient for justifying the key decisions when modeling the enterprise architecture. It is in this layer that the organization's vision and goals are defined, along with its mission, strategies, tactics, policies, requirements, and assessments. Therefore, the first step, when designing a new EA, should be the strategy design.

Thus, in order to design the organization strategy, we suggest that the process described in Fig. 7.1 is followed.

The enterprise strategy design process starts by looking "outside" of the enterprise, identifying external stakeholders (as customers, suppliers, competitors, regulators, etc.) and drivers (as economic changes).

Considering the enterprise context, the vision and the goals are established.

Afterward the enterprise should define its mission and set the strategies and tactics that are expected to achieve the goals previously defined. Finally, the enterprise directives and requirements are defined (that will be implemented in the EA).

Assessments should be defined in order to measure and control the outcomes achieved.

Next, we suggest the use of several methods to support the design of these steps.

© The Author(s), under exclusive license to Springer Nature Switzerland AG 2022
P. Sousa, A. Vasconcelos, *Enterprise Architecture and Cartography*,
The Enterprise Engineering Series, https://doi.org/10.1007/978-3-030-96264-7_7

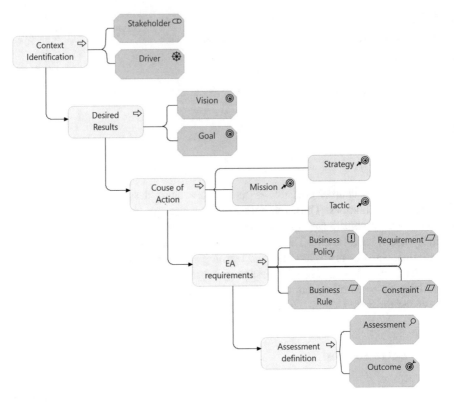

Fig. 7.1 Enterprise strategy design process

7.2   Context Identification

7.2.1   PESTEL

PESTEL analysis is used to assess the external environment of a business [1]. The external factors that may influence the enterprise are characterized into political, economic, social, technological, environmental, and legal (PESTEL) factors—see Fig. 7.2.

Political factors include the government policies that may influence business, including changes in tax policy, tariffs, and business licensing.

Economic factors consider how the economic outlook may influence business, including growth, interest rates, and inflation, among others.

Social factors include the cultural and demographic trends, including population growth rate and cultural factors, among others.

Technological factors assess the innovation, namely, R&D and technological innovation, among others.

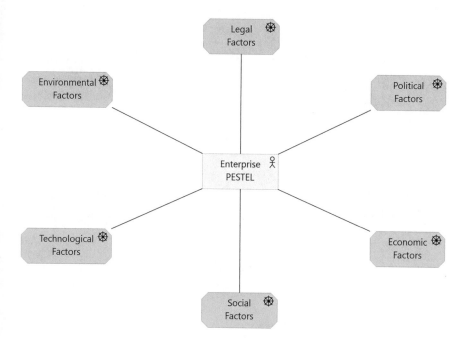

Fig. 7.2 PESTEL analysis

Environmental factors include the ecological impacts on business like weather conditions, climate change, and pollution, among others.

Finally, legal factors include the regulation and labor laws, among others.

7.2.2 External Stakeholders and Drivers

PESTEL analysis supports the identification of the external stakeholders' concerns (drivers).

Consider the example of a new pizzeria, Pizza Rapida, for the identification of the drivers and the stakeholders (Fig. 7.3).

Figure 7.4 presents the external drivers that may influence Pizza Rapida strategy definition, using the PESTEL analysis.

In addition to the PESTEL factors it is also important to identify the external stakeholders of the company. Figure 7.4 identifies four stakeholders (customer, pizza competitor, ingredient supplier, and transportation supplier) and their main concerns.

Finally, the internal stakeholders and their drivers should also be considered—see Fig. 7.5.

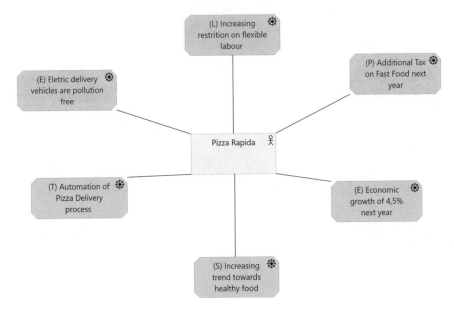

Fig. 7.3 PESTEL analysis of Pizza Rapida

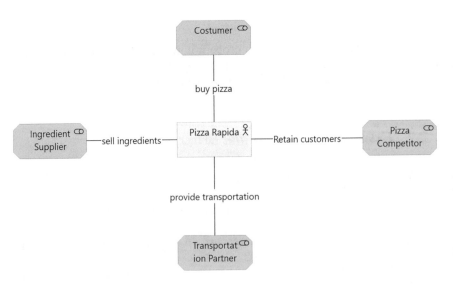

Fig. 7.4 Pizza Rapida context

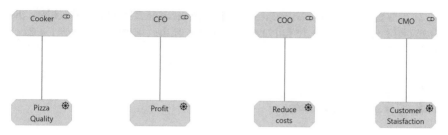

Fig. 7.5 Pizza Rapida internal drivers and stakeholders

7.3 Desired Result Definition

7.3.1 Balanced Scorecard

The balanced scorecard (BSC) was created in the 1990s by Robert Kaplan and David Norton [2] and is a strategic management method. The BSC adds to the traditional financial perspective three more perspectives.

The **financial perspective** identifies the short-, medium-, and long-term finance drivers and goals. This perspective addresses questions as the definition of acceptable results to the shareholders. Financial objectives support the other three perspectives of the BSC. Every measure selected must have a cause-and-effect relationship that culminates in improving the financial performance.

The **customer perspective** identifies the customer relationship and the market. This perspective translates the company's vision into specific goals for each market segment. Companies identify the customers and the market segments they have chosen to compete with. These segments are the sources of income of the company's financial goals.

The **internal process perspective** identifies the resources and capabilities needed to raise the internal level of quality. In this perspective the focus is on the quality of the internal processes, which are key to achieve excellence. The BSC's internal process perspectives should focus on the processes that will have the greatest impact on customer satisfaction and also on meeting the company's financial objectives. Managers must be able to identify which processes and competencies are expected to provide competitive advantages (e.g., differentiate itself from competition). These competitive advantages are delivered by the processes that the company performs, including planning, marketing, production, delivery, and after-sales processes.

The **learning and growth perspective** is the fourth BSC perspective. It is focused on the intangible goals of the organization, including the human capital (including skills and knowledge), information capital (including information systems and IT), and organizational capital (including culture and leadership, among others).

Notice that the BSC perspectives are interdependent. Therefore, to achieve the financial goals, you have to fully meet the needs of the clients (as well as the other perspectives).

7.3.2   Vision and Goals

After defining the organization's vision, the BSC method should be used to identify the goals, using the BSC four perspectives. In Fig. 7.6 the Pizza Rapida case study is presented.

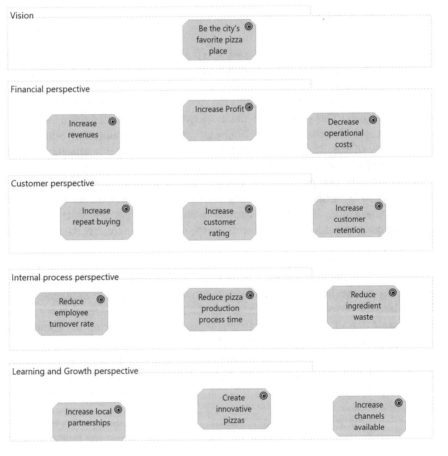

Fig. 7.6 Pizza Rapida vision and goals

Fig. 7.7 Pizza Rapida increased customer rating goal detailed into objectives

After identifying the (high-level) goals using BSC, each goal should be detailed in objectives that must have an explicit completion date and criteria for achievement (Fig. 7.7).

7.4 Courses of Action and Requirement Definition

7.4.1 Business Model Canvas

Business Model Canvas (BMC) is a technique to support enterprises describing their business models [3]. BMC help enterprises in structuring the market, by identifying the customer segments and the core value proposed to each segment, along with the expected revenues—see Fig. 7.8.

In order to use the BMC technique a team of 3–5 people, focused in the business, starts listing the top **customer segments** (considering the most profitable segments).

The **value proposition** is the second cell of the BMC to be addressed. In this step, the enterprise products and services are described, along with the needs addressed to customers. Products and service bundling should also be described.

The **revenues streams** are next described, including the value currently paid and the value customers may be willing to pay as well.

The **channels** used to promote, sell, deliver, and support the products and the services bought by each customer segment are also described in the BMC.

Customer relationship is another key item of the BMC, including the type of relationship for each customer segment and for each product and service (including self-service, dedicated personal assistance, co-creation).

The **key activities** that deliver the organization products and services (value proposition) should also be described.

The **key resources** (including people, knowledge, means, and financial resources) and **key partners** (central for the business) are also described.

Finally, the **cost structure** identifies the top costs to ensure the activities and the resources needed for business.

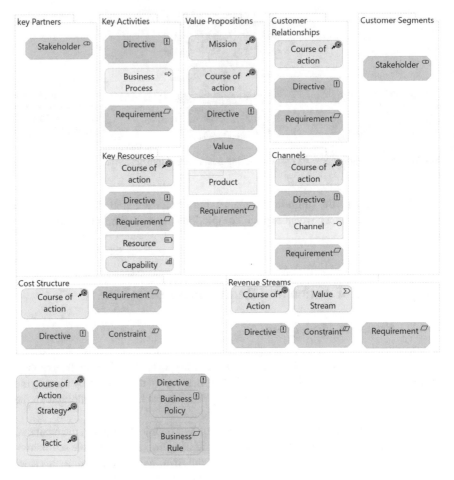

Fig. 7.8 Business Model Canvas

The BMC supports the elicitation of the strategies and tactics for each component of the business, presented in Fig. 7.8 as course of action. The business policies and rules (directives) and requirements are also identified using the BMC. Thus, using the BMC the mission, strategies, tactics, business policies, business rules, requirements, and constraints are identified.

7.4.2 Mission, Strategies, Tactics, Business Policies, Business Rules, Requirements, and Constraints

We present next the usage of the BMC technique to the Pizza Rapida case study (see Fig. 7.9).

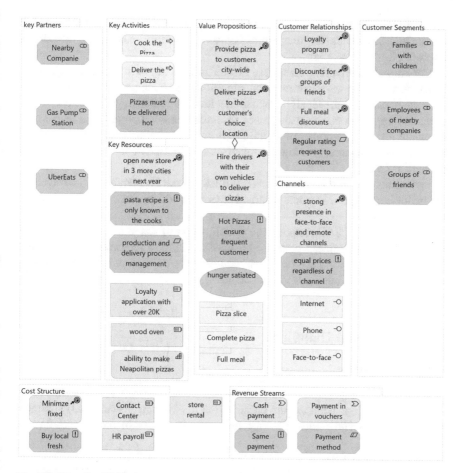

Fig. 7.9 Pizza Rapida Business Model Canvas

Pizza Rapida has three major customer segments: families with children, employees of nearby companies, and groups of friends.

As presented before, Pizza Rapida's mission is to deliver pizza to customers city-wide. Thus, as presented in the "value proposition" cell, the strategy is to deliver pizzas to the customer's choice of location, which is supported in the tactics "Hire drivers with their own vehicles to deliver pizzas." Pizza Rapida's three major products are the pizza slice, the complete pizza, and the full meal (including drinks, dessert, aperitifs, etc.).

The payment of the products is done in cash or other payment methods and using vouchers. The same payment methods are available in all channels.

The products are available using the Internet, phone, and face-to-face channels, and the prices are equal regardless of the channel. Promotion is strongly performed in the face-to-face and in the remote channels.

Customer relationship is developed through a loyalty program and discounts to groups and full meals. Regular rating is also requested to customers, in order to improve customer experience.

Cooking and delivering pizzas are Pizza Rapida's key activities that ensure hot pizza delivery. The key resources that support the BMC are a wood oven (used to cook the pizzas) and the loyalty application with over 20,000 downloads. The ability to make Neapolitan pizzas is also a key resource that is supported on a recipe only known to a reduced number of chefs. Pizza Rapida is looking to expand its stores in three new cities next year and has planned a major update in the production and delivery software.

Pizza Rapida minimizes fixed costs, and HR, contact center, and store rental are the major costs. Fresh ingredients are always bought from local suppliers and are also a relevant cost.

Notice that the BMC supports the identification of the mission, strategies and high-level tactic, business policies, business rules, and requirements. However, these elements (tactics, business rules, requirements, constraints) should be further characterized (in autonomous views/diagrams).

7.5 Assessment Definition

7.5.1 SWOT

The SWOT analysis supports the organization in assessing its (internal) strengths and weaknesses and (external) opportunities and threats in the market and in competitors.

This technique is based in a matrix with four cells (Fig. 7.10).

The **strengths** assess the unique resource and skills of the enterprise. On the other side, the **weaknesses** assess what could be improved in the enterprise (as human resources, business processes, information systems).

Opportunities assess outside trends that the enterprise may take advantage of, considering its strengths. **Threats** are the external factors that may have a negative impact on business.

7.5.2 Assessments and Outcomes

Figure 7.11 presents Pizza Rapida SWOT analysis.

In the top row the strengths (as the strong loyalty program, the revenue increase, and the unique ability to make Neapolitan pizzas) and weaknesses (as the profitability reduction and the high turnover rate) are described.

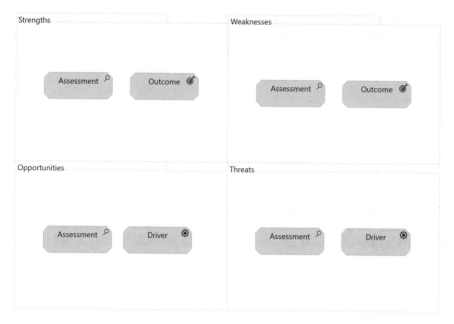

Fig. 7.10 SWOT template using ArchiMate

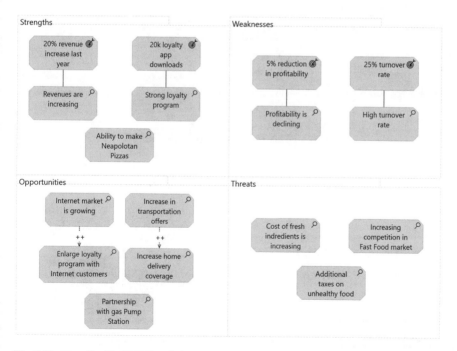

Fig. 7.11 Pizza Rapida SWOT analysis

The bottom row describes the opportunities (as the Internet market, the transportation offering, and the opportunity of partnership with the gas pump station) and the threats (as the increase in cost of fresh ingredients, the increase of fast food competition, and the possible additional taxes on unhealthy food).

7.6   Enterprise Strategy Design Overview

Figure 7.12 presents the overview of the strategy design process considering the four methods previously described.

Thus, the approach proposed to design the enterprise strategy starts by identifying the stakeholders and their drivers and concerns using the PESTEL analysis. Then, using the BSC, the vision and the goals are defined. The BMC is used for establishing the courses of actions (including the mission, strategies, and tactics)

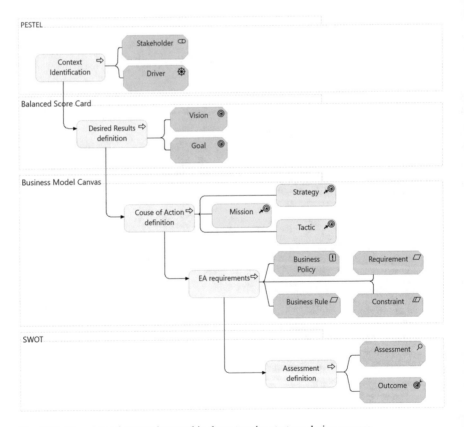

Fig. 7.12 Overview of approaches used in the enterprise strategy design process

and the EA principles and requirements. Finally, the SWOT analysis is used for assessing the strategy and its outcomes.

Notice, however, that in some EA projects, the organization strategy is already defined, or different tools are used for its definition. In that case the strategy elements (as mission, strategies, tactics, policies, requirements, and assessments) should be gathered from existing documentation.

7.7 Exercises

Exercise 7.1

South Hospital is a reference hospital in Europe.

The average age of the European population has been increasing. Population aging continues to be one of the most worrying factors in the old continent, leading to an increase in neurodegenerative diseases.

The Hospital has agreements with the main insurance companies. However, there has been a consolidation of health insurance market, with a concentration in two insurers that retain more than 80% of the market. Since the general population has health insurance, that has encouraged the screening and prevention of diseases.

However, poor eating habits have led to an increase in the percentage of obese population, with a higher frequency of heart attacks, diabetes, and other diseases.

The Hospital activity is supervised by the Health Regulatory Agency (HRA) that is imposing gender quotas on managerial positions.

Nowadays, technology has allowed the provision of health services through digital channels, from scheduling appointments to the remote execution of health-care services. Legislation such as the GDPR[1] has raised new challenges for South Hospital in accessing and sharing patient data, in the provision of integrated healthcare.

South Hospital is under high pressure to increase the profit margin from shareholders, considering the emergence of two new hospitals less than 50 km away and the reduction in the amounts paid by insurance companies for healthcare. One of the main concerns of the Human Resources Director is the hiring of doctors and nurses, as there is a shortage of these professionals.

1. Model South Hospital context.
2. Model in ArchiMate a PESTEL analysis of South Hospital.
3. Model South Hospital internal drivers and stakeholders.

---

[1] For further information on the EU General Data Protection Regulation (GDPR) please see https://eur-lex.europa.eu/legal-content/EN/TXT/PDF/?uri=CELEX:32016R0679&from=EN

Exercise 7.2

South Hospital seeks to be the hospital of choice for patients through healthcare excellence. Therefore, the Board of Directors approved the following goals:

1. By the end of next year, have a 10% market share increase.
2. Reduce operational costs by externalizing noncore activities (as cleaning) and by increasing efficiency (e.g., more efficient and environmentally friendly lighting).
3. Increase patient recommendation ratings by 15% each year.
4. Reduce 25% patient complaints each year.
5. Reduce average waiting times for medical appointments to less than 2 weeks.
6. Hire and retain at least two of the Top 10 medical doctors in each specialty in the country of operation.
7. Reduce nurses' turnover rate, 20% this year, 10% next year, and 5% in 2 years.
8. Have ISO 9001 certification.
9. In order to promote innovation, establish a long-term partnership with EU TOP 3 medical research centers, and execute 10% more clinical trials.

1. Model South Hospital vision and goals using a balanced score card approach.
2. Detail one of the goals into objectives.

Exercise 7.3

South Hospital provides specialized healthcare to people. In order to provide the best specialized healthcare, it hires top medical doctors in each specialty in the country. South Hospital provides exams, medical consultations, surgeries, and outpatient care and provides healthcare packs, which include two or more different healthcare services pre-paid, with a 25% discount.

Patients are segmented into private patients, patients with health insurance, and employees of companies with specific agreements.

South Hospital has a loyalty program, providing regular patients with various benefits (including free parking and discounted diagnostic consultations).

The opinion of patients is recorded on each healthcare and is an important factor in the computation of the employees' financial incentives.

The Hospital provides multiple channels (besides face-to-face) for the provision of its services, including a web portal, a mobile application, and a telephone not only for scheduling healthcare but also for the provision of some healthcare in an omni-channel approach (such as medical appointments and nursing follow-up, among others).

Complementary diagnostic exams, as well as outpatient medical activities, are the most important and profitable activities. The Hospital is governed by strict directives to always provide excellent healthcare, never reducing the quality of the services provided.

Insurers and general practitioners (who refer patients to the hospital) are central to the flow of patients. Besides having top medical doctors, South Hospital has a state-of-the-art facilities and equipment, which are key resources of the hospital. These resources ensure a unique ability to do medical diagnostics and treatments.

The major costs of the hospital are the specialized human resources and the capital costs (bank loans). The CFO has been following a path of reducing bank debt, retaining 50% of profits for this purpose.

Thus, payments are made by the insurance companies, up to 90 days after the healthcare, and immediately by the patient. The price of healthcare has a 20% discount on digital channels.

1. Model South Hospital Business Model Canvas

Exercise 7.4

South Hospital has top medical doctors in each specialty, being recognized as the leading hospital in making diagnostics.

It also provides healthcare services through multiple channels, having a strong presence in the digital channel, which opens the opportunity to provide medical services to patients in any place in the world.

The revenues and the profitability have been increasing in the last 2 years. Although revenue increase per year is about 25%, the profit increase is only 3%.

There is a shortage of health professionals in the market, namely, doctors and nurses, that is expected to be aggravated by the opening of two new hospitals nearby.

South Hospital has a high cost regarding HR and a high debt.

The consolidation of health insurance market (with a concentration in two insurers that retain more than 80% of the market) is a strong threat to the hospital.

The increase in neurodegenerative diseases and the aging of the population open the opportunity for continued health services for the elderly.

The increase in obese population is also expected to enlarge the healthcare services related to heart attacks and diabetes.

1. Model South Hospital SWOT.

References

1. A. Gillespie, *PESTEL Analysis of the Macro-Environment. Foundations of Economics* (Oxford University Press, USA, 2007)
2. R. Kaplan, D. Norton, The balanced scorecard—measures that drive performance. Harv. Bus. Rev. 71–79 (1992)
3. A. Osterwalder, Y. Pigneur, *Business Model Generation: A Handbook for Visionaries, Game Changers, and Challengers* (Wiley & Sons, Hoboken, 2010)

Chapter 8
Business Process Design

Sérgio Guerreiro, André Vasconcelos, and Pedro Sousa

Abstract This chapter introduces business process design approaches. After the introduction, process identification challenges are presented, along with activity identification, considering different concerns. Then, we present a method to design business processes. We explain how the core elements of a business process are elicited using a facilitator tool to be used by the business process stakeholders. From the elicited core elements two sequential stages are then triggered: (i) the business process discovery (in Sect. 8.2.3) using the SemantifyingBPMN framework and (ii) the business process enrichment (in Sect. 8.2.4). The SemantifyingBPMN framework is publicly available at https://github.com/SemantifyingBPMN/SemantifyingBPMN. Finally, Sect. 8.2.5 shows how a discovered (and enriched) business process could be experimented by stakeholders to enable better feedback and therefore minimize misunderstandings.

8.1 Business Process Design Overview

The same business process may be organized and composed in many different forms. Process identification and process discovery are well-known topics in business process management discipline [1]. The first attempts to identify the processes that should be considered in the organization and the second to find out the detailed model of the business process.

From a management perspective, process identification is based on a set of heuristics and methods. Thus, process identification may be performed by splitting different activities or having different nested processes, or having move business events that trigger other business processes. But, which one is the "right" business process design? In order to identify the "right" activities of a business process, we first need to set a common ground for process specification, classification, and analysis.

INESC-ID, Lisbon, Portugal

Instituto Superior Técnico, University of Lisbon, Lisboa, Portugal

© The Author(s), under exclusive license to Springer Nature Switzerland AG 2022
P. Sousa, A. Vasconcelos, *Enterprise Architecture and Cartography*,
The Enterprise Engineering Series, https://doi.org/10.1007/978-3-030-96264-7_8

8.1.1   Process Identification

A common issue that arises when modeling business processes is to know the difference between process, subprocess, activity, task, or operation. Firstly, it is important to notice that the number of levels (for hierarchical decomposition) is arbitrary. The basic concept of process is always the same: input—process—output. Depending on the modeling language the names for the business processes may be different (e.g., BPMN has activities, subprocess, task...).

A business process may be hierarchically decomposed, as the example in Fig. 8.1, or segmented through a common event, as presented in Fig. 8.2. Therefore, each process can be decomposed (hierarchically/vertically) in one or more additional "processes," and each process can be segmented (horizontally) in additional segments. Most authors use the term "process" as something that is made of a set of activities, and an activity as a "subprocess" (a process resulting from decomposition).

Process specification is an important tool for business process analysis, measurement, and automation. Several names are associated to hierarchical specification: processes, subprocesses, activities, tasks, and operation. It all refers to actions (verbs) that transform inputs into outputs. Thus, process specification is about identifying the processes that can be functionally detailed.

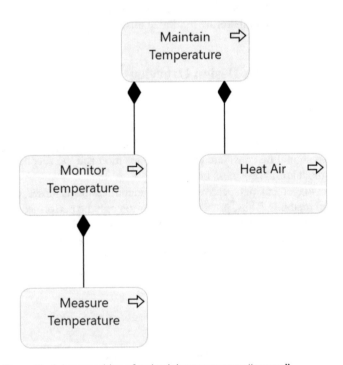

Fig. 8.1 Hierarchical decomposition of maintaining temperature "process"

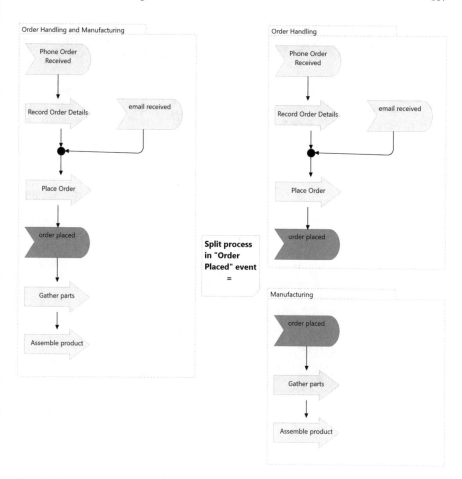

Fig. 8.2 Business process segmentation

8.1.2   Activity Identification

As in identifying business processes, we will see architectural issues related to the identification of the activities of a process. Consider the two scenarios presented in Fig. 8.3 as models of the same reality. What criteria should we use to decide between scenarios 1 and 2? How does such criteria relates with:

- the atomicity of activities.
- the artifacts being produced by activities.
- monitoring the process productivity.
- the systems supporting the activities.

So the problem to solve is to identify the criteria to be used when modeling the activities one observes in enterprises. The goal is to ensure consistency between

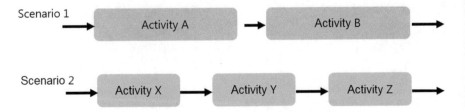

Fig. 8.3 Two modeling scenarios of the same reality

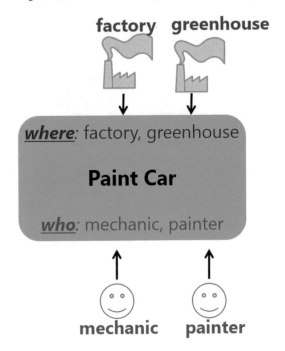

Fig. 8.4 High-level car painting process

models, making decomposing criteria independent of the models and matching models to the concerns of the stakeholders.

Let us consider the following example:

"At ABC Organization, the painting of a car is made by a painter and a mechanic. In the factory, the mechanic is responsible for straightening the metal before painting. Then the car is spackled by the painter and painted in a specializing painting greenhouse."

We could model the process as a single high-level process (Fig. 8.4).

If we look at the "where" concern we could split the process into two subprocesses, considering where the action occurs (see Fig. 8.5).

On the other hand, if the concern is on the actors involved, the split of task would be different (see Fig. 8.6).

Scenario 1
(Where)

Fig. 8.5 Car painting subprocesses according to the "where" concern

Scenario 2
(Who)

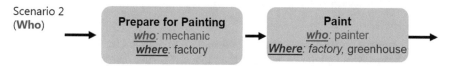

Fig. 8.6 Car painting subprocesses according to the "who" concern

Scenario 3
(Where, Who)

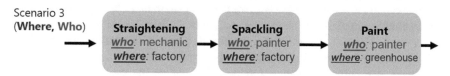

Fig. 8.7 Car painting subprocesses according to the "where" and the "who" concerns

Finally, if we combine both concerns the process would be split into three subprocesses (see Fig. 8.7).

Thus, the decomposition of the business process into activities changes with the concerns addressed. For managing spaces scenario 1 would be the right one, while to manage people, scenario 2 is the best one.

The idea that a process model is specific to a purpose is worrisome, given the effort that is usually involved in process modeling. Trying to detail activities as much as possible, as in scenario 3, is tempting, but often leads to processes that are too complex to be understood and lose their usefulness. This problem is solved by having a visualization tool that is able to produce the views of scenarios 1 and 2 based on a model of scenario 3 [2, 3].

A common concern is to monitor and control process productivity, by measuring the artifacts produced by each activity. We call *control points* to the exact places where measurements are performed within the process. Naturally, to ensure atomicity of activities, control points should not be placed inside an activity but rather between activities. In scenario 1 you can monitor the productivity of each site and in scenario 2 the productivity of each actor. In scenario 3, we can choose what we want to monitor.

Quite often, the handover of work between activities performed by actors belonging to different chains of command leads to lower productivity. We call **breakpoints** to these points. As a default practice, one can consider that there is a breakpoint whenever there is a handover of work between different actors. Naturally one should consider placing a control point in every breakpoint to monitor the points where lower productivity is likely to occur.

Fig. 8.8 Control viewpoint (why)

For example, in scenario 3, one can consider a breakpoint between "straightening" and "spackling", but not between the "spackling" and the "painting" once the actor remains the same.

An approach to identifying activities that allows a trade off between the complexity of the process model with the capability to monitor breakpoints is simply to assume that all activities between breakpoints can be modeled as one activity. In other words, you only change activities when the performing actors change the chain of command and control. But this approach is equivalent to scenario 2.

Finally, we define **_Critical points_** as points where the result of a process is perceived directly outside the enterprise. Any failure in these points is critical because it is potentially visible from the outside (i.e., it impacts the customer) which is not the case in an internal activity that the organization may try to mitigate the problem without involving the customer.

A similar approach can be used when the process model is focused on business strategy alignment, where the "why" (purpose) concern becomes dominant. Any sequence of activities contributing to the same purpose should be modeled as a single activity. In this way, each activity in the model addresses some concern managed by the enterprise (Fig. 8.8).

For the "what" concern, the main focus is on information. Therefore, the process is decomposed in order to ensure that there is a differentiation of the activities by the information they process. A sequence of activities that process the same information can be modeled as a single activity. Similarly, an activity that processes different information should ideally be decomposed into more specific activities such that each processes only one information (Fig. 8.9).

This also means that any behavior associated with an activity that processes some information must depend on that information. Consider the Activity "AB" presented in Fig. 8.10, which produces the "I" information, and then performs some tasks that are independent of both the "I" information and the "C" activity. In this case, the "AB" activity should be decomposed as represented at the bottom of Fig. 8.10.

The independence between activities B and C is an important fact, because in the first case (activity AB) it is stated that behavior B occurs before C, whereas in the second case, it can happen before, simultaneously or after behavior C.

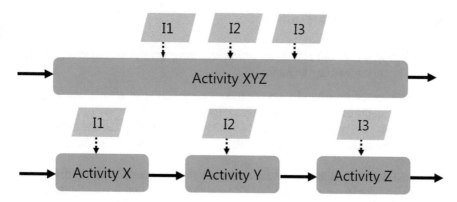

Fig. 8.9 Process decomposition according to the "what" concern

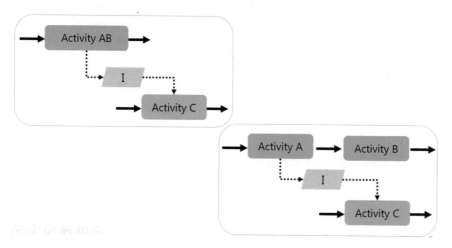

Fig. 8.10 AB activity decomposed into A and B according to the "what" concern

Several other identification criteria exist, according to the modeling purpose, including:

- Management, through control points
- Audit, namely, audit points
- Optimization, through identification and work-sharing between processes
- Automation, through manual vs. automatic activities
- Competence/skills
- And many others, such as quality, criticality, cost, safety, etc.

8.1.3 Activity Classification

Activities (or processes) can be classified into three categories according to their support in the information technology:

- Manual, when executed by one or more persons (human actors), for example, students doing an exam, people playing football, and people having lunch.
- Automatic, when they are performed by machines, applications, and autonomous IT (technological actors), for example, painting a car in "car production manufactory."
- Semi-automatic, as their implementation requires an interaction or collaboration between people and machines. At IT level this interaction is usually done by a GUI (graphical user interface).

The classification of activities in the categories above allows a more comprehensive process model, something that would otherwise not be possible. In fact, manual activities cannot be automated as such, and therefore are not included in the process models seen by IT. Automatic activities do not involve human resources and are therefore naturally excluded in human resources-centric business process models. In some notations, such as BPMN, automatic activities can still be further classified as services, decision tables and scripts.

8.2 A Methodology for Business Process Design

8.2.1 Foundations for Business Process Design Methodology

A holistic approach to deliver an automated governance is grounded in the well-known business process lifecycle consisting of discovering, designing, executing, monitoring, and optimizing. The execution phase could be supported in any available business process engine existing in your organization, knowing that the pre- and post-phases are guaranteed by this methodological explanation. Governed automation extends the ability of organizations to be aware about operational condition while also allowing you to reshape business processes whenever necessary.

The phases of discovering and designing are the capabilities of business processes elicitation, discovery, and enrichment.

The first capability aims at offering organizational awareness for business processes that are operating in place, and the second one is to be able to govern them, i.e., informing the organization stakeholders about current business processes and future predicted, operational conditions, in order to take informed actions to align with organizational goals whenever needed.

Moreover, the result of business process governance can be fed back to business processes elicitation, discovery, and enrichment to provide the capability of alignment between operation and architecture of your organization. Whenever an enhancement opportunity is identified at operation time, it could be incorporated back in your architectural design, closing the cycle enabling continuous improvement and optimization. The awareness for change is triggered by the monitoring and subsequent capability of intelligent simulation that predicts the future behavior of business processes. A manager is therefore able to take an informed decision about an improvement or a correction in the organization business processes.

The key benefit for decoupling these two capabilities is to be able to discuss, construct, and evolve the business process models independently from the operational data that is extracted from the software systems. In short, semantic understanding of business processes levers a fine-grained governance. Each capability is described in detail in the following.

A business process is a collection of events, activities, and decisions that brings value to the customers of an organization [1]. To achieve value a business process should deliver a new service or product that will be evaluated positively by all stakeholders. Therefore, a business process should account for the conversational and production aspects that occur within the execution course of a business process initiated by a customer. This concept of understanding the execution context of a business process is an uptake that will be used in the following descriptions.

The first step of the methodology starts by providing a facilitated way of eliciting the core elements of a business process, namely, the involved actors, the required activities, the business rules, the business objects involved, and the dependencies between activities. Decision points can also be included to specify how to proceed when some criteria need to be assessed.

The result of business process elicitation is a visual representation expressed in the business language domain, the language that is understood by the stakeholders of an organization, agnostic to any kind of technical language. No specialized knowledge, e.g., BPMN [4], BPEL, DMN, ArchiMate, or other specification language, should be required to understand the achieved representations of the elicitation step.

After that, the previous elicited elements are used to discover the details of the business process following the approach in [5]. The result is now a specialized representation using the BPMN notation. The automatically produced BPMN models entail all the knowledge captured before, and when multiple solutions are available, the user is asked about which model best fits the organization's purposes. The produced BPMN models are a representation of the happy flow of the business processes, including the expected behavior if all the business logic operates successfully without exceptions.

Finally, the previous BPMN models could be augmented, by user configuration, with exception handling capabilities. The advantages for enriching a BPMN model with exception handling capabilities are manifold. It allows an impact analysis of enclosing non-happy-flow situations in the business process, e.g., measuring the effort, and complexity, of dealing with such situations. Most time exception situations are handled manually, which entails an overhead to the organization. Moreover, enrichment also allows the identification of new and not previously discovered situations that might contain friction points requiring immediate attention.

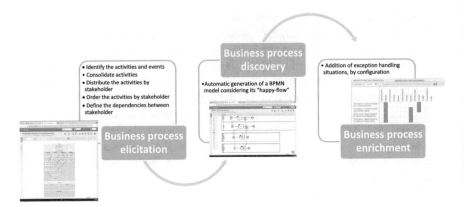

Fig. 8.11 Summary of the business processes' elicitation, discovery, and enrichment cycle

Figure 8.11 summarizes the business processes' elicitation, discovery, and enrichment cycle.

8.2.1.1 The SemantifyingBPMN Tool

The SemantifyingBPMN tool [5] articulates the BPMN concepts using a social interaction pattern inherited by DEMO theory [6], so that models can be discovered and enhanced with few extra complexities managed.

For a single business transaction of *producing a product*, at least two business actors need to be considered: the transaction initiator (TI) and the transaction executor (TE). As both actors are located in two different organizations, two BPMN pools are considered.

Figure 8.12 expands the business transaction steps included in a DEMO Ψ-theory basic transaction pattern, clarifying how the sequence of states originates a new P-fact in the world. Whenever an actor role is expecting a C-act from the other, a BPMN intermediate catching and an intermediate throwing message events are used. All the business transactions respect this pattern, even when some acts or facts are not observable. In that situation, the acts or facts are considered implicit in the execution of business transaction. This pattern allows a stable design for creating a network of business transactions considering a controlled increase in the complexity of the business process model.

8.2.2 Business Process Elicitation

Business process elicitation simplifies the business process modeling transforming it into a collaborative task. It works asynchronously, and remotely, to avoid long

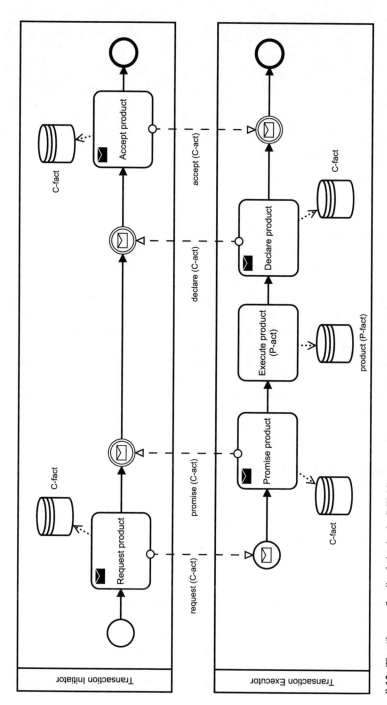

Fig. 8.12 The "happy flow" of the basic DEMO transaction pattern between two actors with separation between communication and production acts represented in BPMN

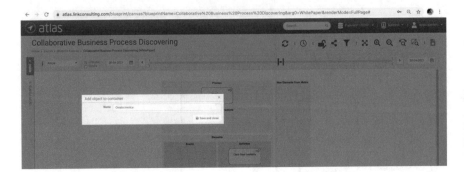

Fig. 8.13 Adding a new activity to the canvas. Activity "Check Stock Availability" is already created in elements

working hours spent in meetings. Each stakeholder adds information accordingly with their business knowledge, interests, and understanding of requirement changes.

On one hand, business process requirement changes are continuously imposed, and fast adaptations are expected to maintain their value. On the other hand, to be compliant with those evolving requirements, a huge number of possible design combinations for complete business processes are possible. The explosion of the number of those possible combinations hinders its development, management, and deployment (Figs. 8.13, 8.14, 8.15, and 8.16).

In detail, our business process elicitation encompasses the following five stages that can be executed without any prior order, presented in Table 8.1.

The following Fig. 8.17 depicts a collaborative canvas showing the result of the elicited business process.

8.2.3 Business Process Discovery

Business process discovery automatically generates business process model using the BPMN specification language. Business process discovery is grounded on the elicited elements designed by the previous business process elicitation phase: the involved actors, the activities and events that each actor is responsible for, and dependencies between activities.

To obtain such result, business process discovery starts by extracting the semantic that is available in the elicited elements and orchestrates them using a pattern-based approach that is able to offer a semantic definition for the business processes. The semantified patterns are pre-provisioned and account for all the conversational and production aspects of a single business process. Furthermore, business process discovery also identifies the network of business processes. This effect occurs whenever the execution of a business transaction depends on another one. A network

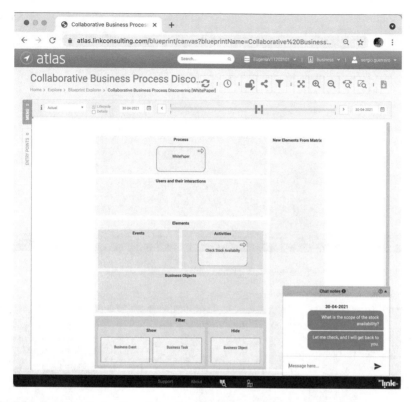

Fig. 8.14 Example of using the collaborative chat system for activity consolidation

is considered for instance a payment business transaction that succeeds a production business transaction.

Therefore, the goal of business process discovery is to facilitate the classical BPMN business process creation that requires BPMN specialized analysts to consume much effort in the design phase. In a classical and manual approach, whenever business changes anything inside a business process, then more design effort is needed. With this methodological approach, there is no need to include specialized analysts that understand BPMN. On the contrary, this approach offers a solution to involve the stakeholders that understand business language in a continuous collaborative cycle of elicitation and discovery.

Therefore, the collaborative business process elicitation is the knowledge source for the created BPMN business process that is produced on the fly. This solution promotes the trial-and-error approach until consensus is reached between business stakeholders. Figure 8.18 exemplifies an automatically discovered BPMN model which is produced from the elicited business process elements in the collaborative canvas. Any change in an element can be reflected in the BPMN model on the fly without requiring any BPMN modeling knowledge.

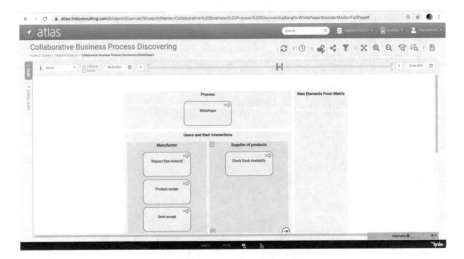

Fig. 8.15 Example of two stakeholders created with activities assigned

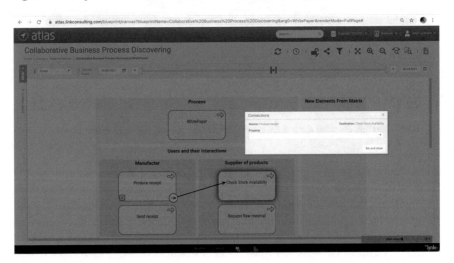

Fig. 8.16 Defining a handover dependency between activities

Figure 8.19 shows the ability of the solution to deal with BPMN gateways. Business processes are not only sequential flows of activities but can also contain decision points.

Table 8.1 Business process elicitation stages

Identify the activities and events	Each stakeholder can create any activity and event to articulate what they are doing even if they do not have full knowledge about the overall business process. This information is domain specific; therefore, different granularities can be found (usually in too complex processes). This issue will be consolidated in the next stage. More activities can be added as more detail is expected to a given model. This stage offers an agile and remote environment for any stakeholder to view, create, or update activities and events
Consolidate activities to check redundancies	Whenever activities and/or events are duplicated or with different granularity, consolidation is required. This step facilitates the presentation of the elicited activities and allows discussion between stakeholders using a collaborative chat system. Consolidation stage can be done iteratively until stakeholder consensus is reached
Distribute the activities by stakeholder	When some, or all, of the activities are identified, this step allows the assignment of each one to a specific stakeholder, using a simple drag and drop of elements in the collaborative canvas. The goal is to establish who (inside the organization) is responsible for each activity. The order of activities is not relevant at this stage. The activities could be distributed in an iterative manner in accordance with the elicitation phase
Order the activities by stakeholder	Within each stakeholder, their activities could be ordered accordingly with the business logic. The dependencies between activities are automatically established accordingly with the order. If needed, an activity can be dragged from one stakeholder to another
Define the dependencies between stakeholders	Handover represents a situation where a stakeholder depends on the other to finish his/her order of activities

8.2.4 Business Process Enrichment

Business process enrichment allows an agile addition of exception handling situations in the previously discovered BPMN business processes.

The usual solution encompasses a sequential, and manual, process of elicitation and design of the most relevant business processes using a business-dependent language. A high-level design is produced containing a partial view (also named as the happy flow) of the enterprise operation. Then, business processes are implemented in a software platform using a technology-dependent language. At this stage, revocations, declinations, rejections, and other non-happy-flow patterns are ad hoc included with a huge increase in complexity and unmanageability. Moreover, whenever a change in the implementation is needed, it becomes too difficult to trace it back to the initial business definition. Concomitantly, a change in business does not trace back to the implementation; a re-elicitation, redesign, and re-implementation are required. The effort consumed with these non-integrated solutions is high and not controlled in terms of costs.

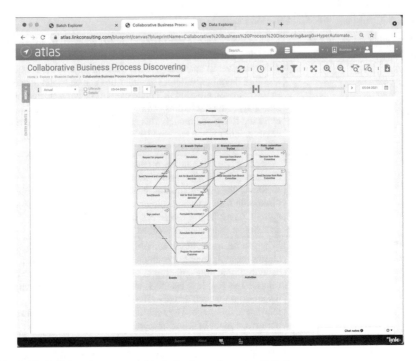

Fig. 8.17 Collaborative canvas with the business elements elicited

In practice, these exception situations are pre-provisioned and can be used by configuration in a BPMN model previously created by the business process discovery. As shown in Fig. 8.20, all the business process elements can be extended with exception handling situation and a new, and more complete, BPMN is generated.

Some examples of exception handling situations are exemplified in the following. For exemplification purposes, consider a business process where an actor role initiator requests the production of a new product or service to another actor role that is the executor.

Firstly, a decline of a request corresponds to an impossibility of promising the production of a new product, by an executor, e.g., due to lack of raw material stock. In these situations, it is a decision in the scope of the initiator actor to finish the business process by discontinuing the communication with or insisting on the new, or the same, request. This conversation could end up in a deadlock situation. The deadlock is avoided with common sense between the actors. This situation could consume huge organization efforts—a customer insisting on the request of a product that will not have the stock replenished. This extreme example shows well the impact of identifying, by configuration, a set of catalog exceptions, instead of arriving to that knowledge by process mining many months later.

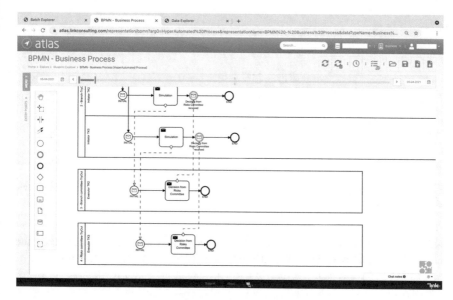

Fig. 8.18 Automatic business process discovered from the elements of Fig. 8.17

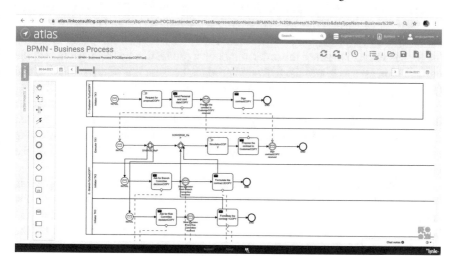

Fig. 8.19 Automatic business process discovered including gateways

Symmetrically, a rejection could be issued by an initiator after the new product had been delivered to him/her, for instance, if the delivered product is defective. In that situation, the executor decides if the rejection is acceptable, and if so, a stop and refund is emitted. Otherwise, a delivery is re-emitted to the initiator actor. Its difference to the previous declination situation is that, now, the new product already has been produced, and its production involved costs. Therefore, the cost must be

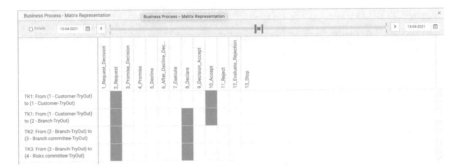

Fig. 8.20 Business process enrichment, selecting the desired extensions to generate a new enriched model

assigned to one of the two actors involved. Usually, if the cost is incurred by the executor actor, then a stop is issued and the business transaction execution ends.

Furthermore, any actor, either initiator or executor, could revoke any previous activity. For instance, a request could be revoked, e.g., when the customer does not want the previous order product anymore. In this situation, it is on the role of the executor to decide if it is acceptable to revoke and then roll back all the previous executed activities, or if the revocation request is unacceptable and the actor initiator needs to keep its order. Other revocation examples are when the organization no longer has stock to produce the order, although a production has been promised; the organization asks to return the delivered product, because it is badly produced; and the actor initiator rejects the previously accepted product due to malfunctioning.

The impact of rolling back the activities of a business transaction is most of the times delayed in the software implementation stage due to the complexity associated to its enforcement in a BPMN model. Revocations are pre-provisioned, allowing them to be added by configurations to any BPMN model previously created by the business process discovery.

In short, this methodology offers business process models automatic completion, in a systematic manner, so that models can describe far more situations with few extra complexities managed. Those exemplified exception handling situations can be added to the model by request and on the fly increasing the awareness for the organization business processes.

8.2.5   Extending to Business Process Prototyping

Allowing stakeholders to experiment a new system at early stages of its development enables better communication and therefore minimizes misunderstandings in the development team that are usually very costly to correct at the end of a project. When a nondesirable behavior is identified in the last mile of the project, it could drive to project failure and stakeholders' dissatisfaction. The reasons for failure are

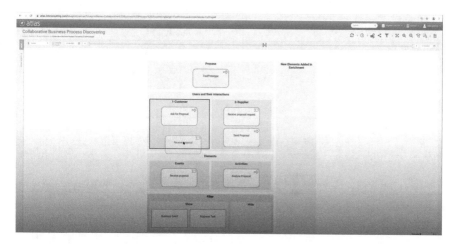

Fig. 8.21 Collaborative canvas

manifold; some examples are misunderstanding about the desired system behavior, bad communication or documentation, failure in the requirement elicitation, and regulatory changes during project development, among others.

Combining our collaborative business processes discovery and enrichment solution with the ability of producing on-the-fly prototyped business processes that are executable and could be really experimented by stakeholders leverages a whole new way of achieving a common understanding among all the project participants. Furthermore, it allows the dynamic adjustment of business process design, for instance, adding a rejection situation, and then an immediate prototype update is delivered and ready to be experimented again.

Let us have a look at a step-by-step example.

1. **Design the business elements in a collaborative canvas.**
   Discover the business process capturing the specific details from the business perspective using a simplified business language composed only of the involved actors, the activities each actor is responsible for, and the events triggering the collaboration between actors. A collaborative canvas facilitates the drag and drop of elements directly to any actor (see Fig. 8.21) without the need to learn a new specification language. Moreover, you can specify the business objects that are already identified as being of core importance for your business. Misalignments and misunderstandings are easier to identify and solve due to the simple representation used. Discovery also enables the communication between business analysts working remotely, avoiding the exchange of multiple business process models, but providing a single point of trust.

2. **Generate the happy-flow business process model in BPMN.**
   The provided detail in this collaborative canvas is used to discover the existing business transactions between actors on the fly automatically (see Fig. 8.22) using the language most widely used by industry—the BPMN specification lan-

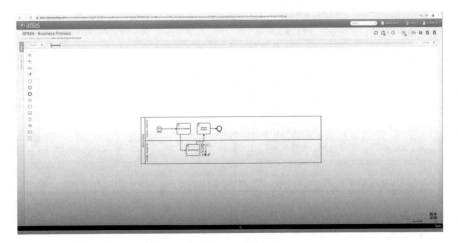

Fig. 8.22 Viewing the generated happy flow in BPMN

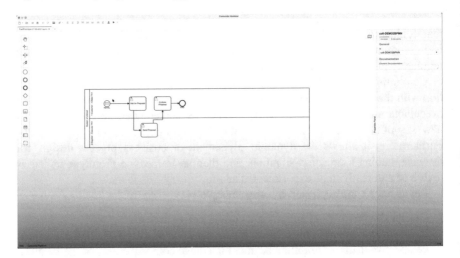

Fig. 8.23 Loading the BPMN model and deploying in an execution engine

guage. Therefore, discovery facilitates creating a shared semantic understanding between the different business analysts of an organization. A change in business is only a matter of changing the canvas and re-generating the BPMN model.

3. **Export the BPMN model and deploy it in Camunda engine.**
   Next, load the BPMN model (see Fig. 8.23) in Camunda modeler (provided by the Camunda Platform Community Edition) and then deploy it. The deployed model can be consulted in the Camunda cockpit (see Fig. 8.24). Integrations of Atlas with other platforms are foreseen.

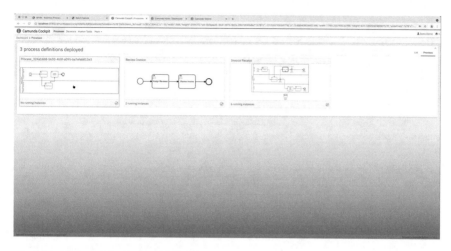

Fig. 8.24 Listing all the deployed BPMN models

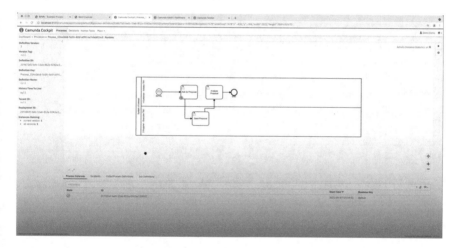

Fig. 8.25 Viewing the execution state of each business process instance

4. Instantiate the deployed BPMN model and try it. This is the step where you are able to experiment directly your generated business processes without any interference. To that end, instantiate the BPMN model (see Fig. 8.25) and use Camunda task list and Camunda cockpit to follow its execution (see Fig. 8.26).
5. Enrich the happy-flow business process model. After that, the business process enrichment generates a business process model enriched with an inherited business process pattern. In step 2, the model discovered is only based on the elements previously captured in Atlas collaborative canvas, but it could now be extended by the choice of the business analyst (see in Fig. 8.27). Enrichment leverages a controlled and known management effort to increase the complexity

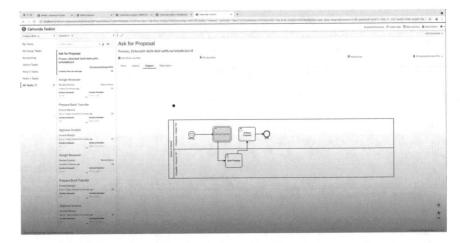

Fig. 8.26 Consulting the user-assigned task list

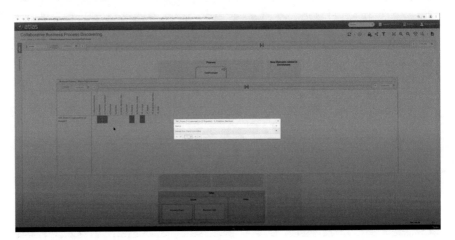

Fig. 8.27 Business process enrichment, selecting the desired extensions to generate a new enriched model

of the designed business processes. With enrichment the exception situations can be added to the model by request and on the fly. It is also recognized that BPMN defines clearly how to articulate its concepts but usually involves the investment of learning a new language that entails extra costs. With this approach learning BPMN is needless.

6. Repeat steps 2–5 as you need, with this on-the-fly prototyping creation solution.

8.3 Exercises

Exercise 8.1

Consider the following process, held between a client and "Pizza Rápida" restaurant.

After feeling like eating a pizza the customer selects the pizza and proceeds with the order. The bartender receives the client request transmitting it to the chef.

The chef after cooking the pizza places it at the disposal of "the delivery boy" that delivers it to the customer. The customer pays the pizza (the payment is received by the "delivery boy").

The customer eats the pizza and hunger is satisfied.

1. Draw an ArchiMate or BPMN collaboration diagram for the process above.
2. Identify the control points, the break points, and the critical points in the model.

Exercise 8.2

Consider the following process (modeled in ArchiMate) of the Navy—see Fig. 8.28.

1. Identify the control points, the break points, and the critical points in the model.
2. Describe two distinct criteria for identifying activities, which may be applicable to "P4" business process (including the objectives of the criterion, the results of its application, the preconditions to be checked, and its method of application).

Exercise 8.3

Consider the following processes P3 and P8 (modeled in ArchiMate)—see Fig. 8.29

1. Identify the control points, the break points, and the critical points in the model.

Exercise 8.4

Consider the process shown in Fig. 8.30, which represents the client sending a complaint letter. Assume that the communication between task 1 and task 2 is made by telephone. Also assume that the communication between task 3 and task 4 is performed using the system S3.

1. Identify in the diagram with a "C" critical points of this process. Justify your answer.
2. Identify the break points of this process in the diagram with a "B." Justify your answer.
3. Assume that there was a problem in the organization's performance when providing support to the customer complaints in a timely manner. Explain what you would do to realize the source of this problem.

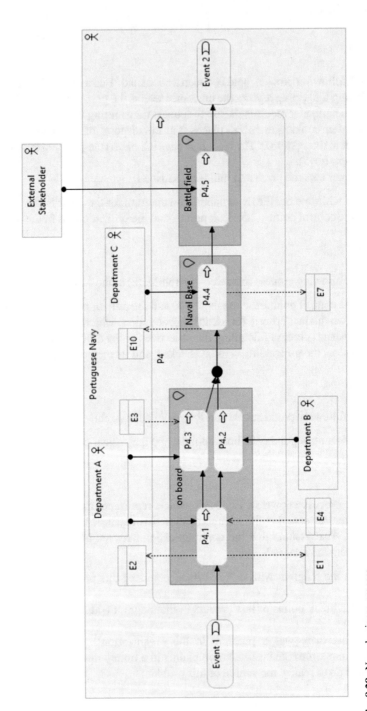

Fig. 8.28 Navy business process

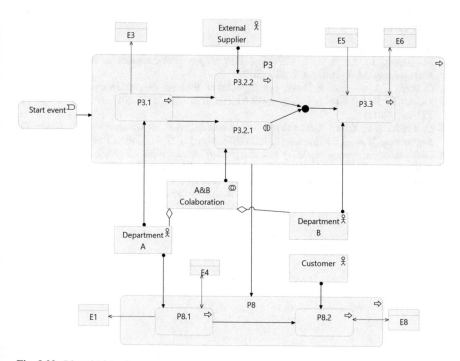

Fig. 8.29 P3 and P8 business processes

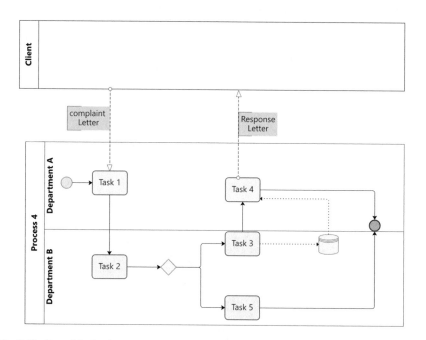

Fig. 8.30 Complaint business process

References

1. M. Dumas, M. La Rosa, J. Mendling, H.A Reijers, *Fundamentals of Business Process Management*, vol. 1 (Springer, Berlin, 2017)
2. C. Pereira, A. Caetano, P. Sousa, *Ontology-Driven Business Process Design, 1 International Federation for Information Processing* T. Skersys et al. (Eds.): I3E 2011, IFIP AICT 353, pp. 153–162 (2011)
3. D. Cardoso, P. Sousa, *Generation of stakeholder-specific BPMN models, 9th Enterprise Engineering Working Conference (EEWC 2019)*, May 21, 2019 – Lisboa, Portugal
4. OMG, *Business Process Modeling Notation (BPMN) Specification 2.0* (2010)
5. S. Guerreiro, P. Sousa, A framework to semantify BPMN models using DEMO business transaction pattern (2020). arXiv preprint arXiv:2012.09557
6. J.L.G. Dietz, H. Mulder, *Enterprise ontology: A Human-Centric Approach to Understanding the Essence of Organisation* (Springer Nature Switzerland AG, 2020)

Chapter 9
Information Architecture Design

Pedro Sousa and André Vasconcelos

Abstract This chapter presents two approaches for designing the information architecture. Thus, after introducing the topic and its similarities and differences, the top-down and the bottom-up information architecture design primitives are described. In the following section, using the design primitives, the top-down and the bottom-up approaches are presented, along with an example. Afterward, we discuss the benefits and challenges of each approach and suggest how to mix them. Finally, some information architecture design exercises are proposed.

9.1 Approaches for Information Architecture Design

The definition of an organization's information architecture is a complex task that normally one cannot do in one step. It takes many interactions and involves many different persons. Quite often it is done in small steps, each step being related to different projects or transformation initiatives. Being an ongoing process, it is critical to have a design method so that one can continue the process where the previous ones have achieved. Over the years, an organization's information architecture is constantly evolving with contributions by different individuals, and the existence of a method simplifies both the construction process and the maintenance and evolution of the information architecture.

The design of the information architecture is similar to the conceptual design of an information repository. By conceptual design, we refer to models that are independent of any technology used in the management of information repository, whether object-oriented, relational, or non-relational. The similarity lies in the fact that in its essence, the information architecture of an enterprise is a conceptual model. As we have seen in Sect. 3.3.3, information architecture is defined around the concept of informational entity, which is no more than a state associated with an identifier. The identifier is necessarily defined by business information. For example, stating that Maria is customer number 33 contributes nothing to the identification of the customer if code 33 is not known in the business context; on the contrary attributes such as the name, citizen number, and fiscal number are usually known in the business context, and if they are unique to each customer, they could

P. Sousa, A. Vasconcelos, *Enterprise Architecture and Cartography*,
The Enterprise Engineering Series, https://doi.org/10.1007/978-3-030-96264-7_9

be identifiers of the information entity. Besides this "detail," there are no major differences from defining the key attributes of an entity in entity-relationship model.

In essence we have two generic approaches to the design of information architectures. The *top-down* and the *bottom-up*. Both are precise and rigorous approaches, but also flexible because they can be applied to a variety of situations. Additionally, their co-existence in the design of a model is also possible.

As presented by Batine, Ceri, and Navathe in [1], both approaches define a set of primitive functions sharing the following properties:

- Each function transforms a given architecture model (the input model)—and information from the enterprise and its environment—and produces another architecture model (the output model).

    So designing an information architecture is a sequence of transformations each applied to the resulting model of the previous transformation.
- Each transformation maps business concepts of the input model to business concepts of the output model.

    During designing, one is either detailing or abstracting concepts, but the resulting concepts (either more detailed or more abstracted) also exist as business concepts. So, in both cases, each step establishes the relationship between business concepts at different levels of detail or abstraction. For example, in detailing the concept of an employee, one transforms *employee* into *employee* and *employee contact data, employee bank data, employee career data*, and so on. On the reverse direction, one may abstract *employee contact data, employee bank data*, and *employee career data* into the concept of *employee*.
- Concepts in the output model comply with all constraints of the concepts in the input model.

    This means that all relations or dependencies applied to the concepts abstracted or detailed persist in the resulting concepts.

Next we describe the primitive functions to be used in top-down, bottom-up, or even mixed approaches to design information architectures.

9.2 Design Primitives

9.2.1 Top-Down Design Primitives

Top-down design primitives take an artifact as an argument and decompose it into a set of artifacts of the same nature. So one has the following key top-down primitives Fig. 9.1:

- *Entity generation* primitive. This primitive takes no argument and produces an information entity.

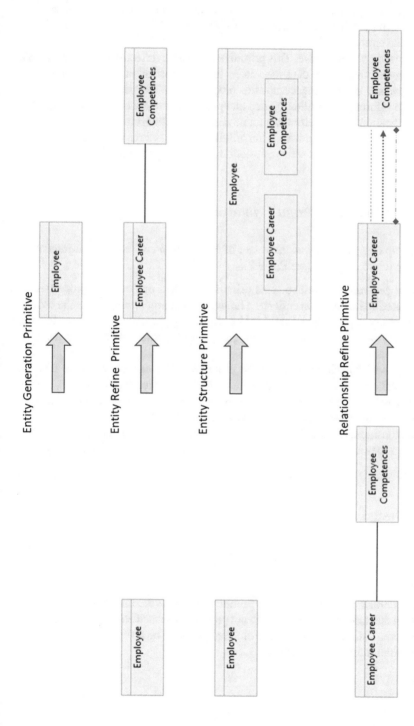

Fig. 9.1 Top-down primitives for information architecture modeling

- *Entity refine* primitive. This primitive takes an information entity as an argument and produces two related information entities, which may or may not include the original entity.
- *Entity structure* primitive. This primitive receives an information entity and adds a property that holds data associated to the information entity. At this point we are not considering composite properties, as they can be achieved with nested information entities. Notice that properties are not entities since they lack identification and therefore cannot be part of a relationship.
- *Relationship refine* primitive. This primitive receives a relationship between two entities and produces a series of relationships among the same entities.

9.2.2   Bottom-Up Design Primitives

Bottom-up design primitives take a set of information entities as an argument and compose it into an entity (see Fig. 9.2):

- *Entity generation* primitive. This primitive receives one or more properties and produces an information entity as a holder of such properties. Notice the creation of an entity implies the definition of its identifying properties. Therefore, to create an entity one must use as argument the set of properties that make up the entity identification.
- *Entity enrichment* primitive. This primitive receives one property and one information entity and produces the entity with one more property.
- Relationship generation. This primitive receives two information entities and produces the same entities related by a new relationship.
- Relationship abstraction. This primitive receives a set of relationships between two entities and produces the same entities related with a new relationship.

9.3   Design Approaches

9.3.1   Top-Down Design Approach

Top-down design starts from the high-level entity, where one can then apply the *entity generation* or *entity structure* primitives to refine the initial entity.

Given that top-down primitives do not produce unrelated entities or relationships, all concepts in the final information architecture must be reached by the refinement of the initial information entity.

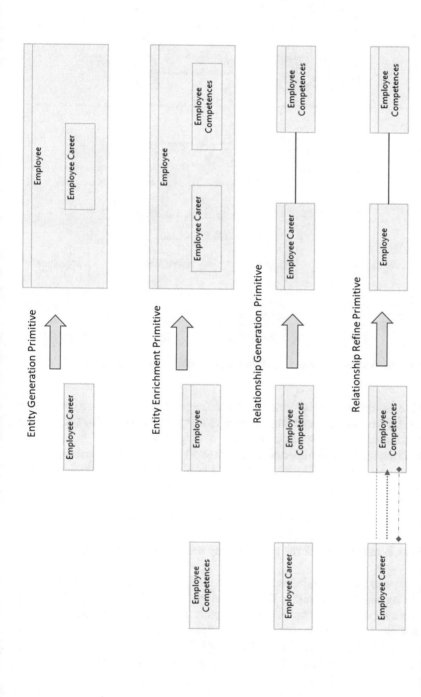

Fig. 9.2 Bottom-up primitives for information architecture modeling

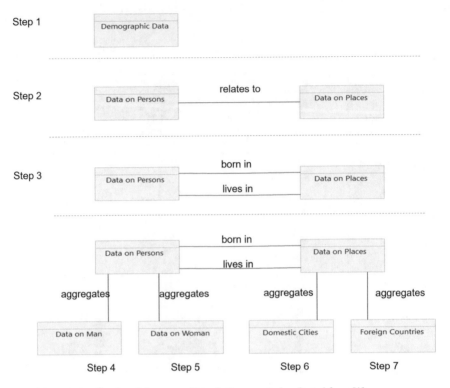

Fig. 9.3 An example of applying a top-down design approach, adapted from [1]

In the top-down approach, one does the refinement step by step and one concept at a time, ignoring the remaining concepts at that step. This simplifies the process because it reduces the scope of each step.

However, the top-down approach requires to start with a highly broad and generic entity, and continue to refine it with the right level of genericity concepts, which is truly difficult to those not fully familiar with the scope of the information being architected.

Thus, if one does not fully understand the context being modeled, the first steps of the top-down approach would lead to models that will not address the necessary concepts, because some of the concepts may not have been included in the initial steps.

We present an example in Fig. 9.3, where the *entity generation* primitive uses the generic concept "Demographic Data" in the model in the first step. In the second step one uses the *entity refine* primitive to refine the concepts underneath the initial one, namely, *Data on Persons* and *Data on Places*, using the *relates to* relationship.

In the third step one refines the *relates to* relation into *born in* and *lives in*, using the *relationship refine* primitive. In step 4 one uses the *entity refine* primitive to refine the *Data on Persons* entity into *Data on Persons aggregates Data on Man*. The same applies for steps 5, 6, and 7.

9.3.2 Bottom-Up Design Approach

In the bottom-up approach, one starts from elementary and simple concepts grouping them into more complex concepts that in turn can be grouped into even more complex concepts. At each step, one is creating new concepts, not refining existing ones as in the top-down approach.

Thus, in the bottom-up design approach, one starts by collecting properties and then identifies properties with high inter-dependency, meaning those that belong to the same concept (or information entity in this case). To group properties into entities one uses primitive entity generation and entity enrichment primitives. Using the bottom-up approach one can propose to add a concept as long as one has some properties to match an identifier for such new concepts.

In Fig. 9.4 we present a similar example to the one used for the top-down design approach, but now using the bottom-up design approach. One first identifies the simplest concepts, and properties, and aggregates them into groups with a strong affinity. Despite this gathering of information requires business knowledge, since bottom-up starts with simplest concepts, they are normally easy enough to start with. In this case one must relate the properties to Man, Woman, Country, and City into entities *Data on Man*, *Data on Woman*, *Country*, and *City*.

Step 5 of our bottom-up example is illustrated in Fig. 9.5. It looks into *Data on Man* and *Data on Woman* and recognizes that a more complex concept (*Data on Persons*) could be used to abstract the previous ones in a single one. Steps 5 to 7 are used to build such abstraction. First, one must find some form of common identification between man and woman. Considering the ID person property, using the *entity enrichment* primitive, the *Data on Person* entity is created.

Next, in step 6, one states that *Data on Persons aggregates Data on Man*. Finally, in step 7, one does the same operation with *Data on Woman*, as illustrated in Fig. 9.6. Notice that the previous relations of the entity *Data on Persons* are not lost during the use of *relationship generation* primitive in step 7, and so after step 7, *Data on Persons aggregates* both *Data on Man* and *Data on Woman*.

Finally, in Fig. 9.7 we present the remaining steps. Steps 8 and 9 follow the same logic as steps 6 and 7, but now regarding the abstraction of concepts *Country* and *City* into a more complex one *Place*.

In step 10 one recognizes the existence of the *born in* relation between concepts *Data on Person* and *Data on Places* and uses the *relationship generation* primitive to establish it. The same happens in step 11 with the relation *lives in*.

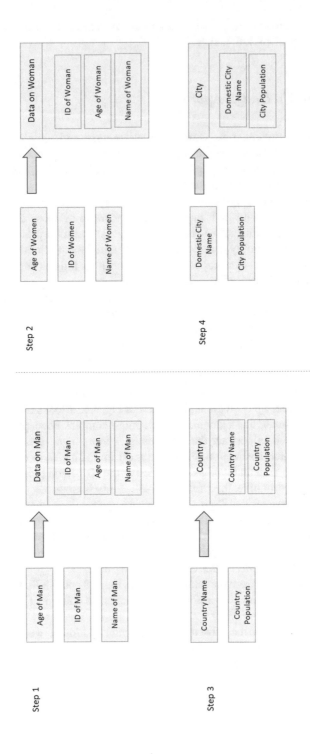

Fig. 9.4 An example of applying a bottom-up design approach, steps 1 to 4, adapted from [1]

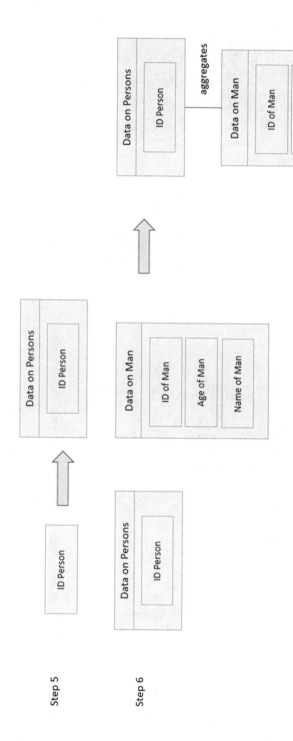

Fig. 9.5 An example of applying a bottom-up design approach, steps 5 and 6, adapted from [1]

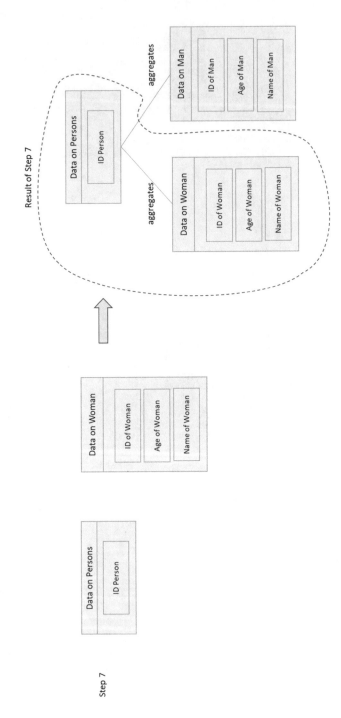

Fig. 9.6 An example of applying a bottom-up design approach, step 7, adapted from [1]

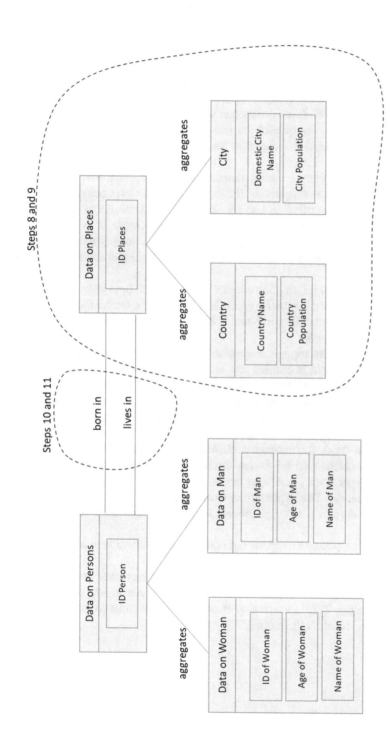

Fig. 9.7 An example of applying a bottom-up design approach, steps 8 to 11, adapted from [1]

9.3.3   Discussion

Quite often, the decision between bottom-up or top-down approaches depends on many factors that must be taken into consideration. Consider the case where the information architecture is being designed starting from a business process model, for example, in BPMN. In this case, one would start by detailing the information required by each activity of each business process. Such information should be modeled as data objects associated to each task in the BPMN diagram of each process.

The level of detail of such information determines the approach one should adopt. If data objects hold a description of the data required for each activity at the level of the properties (lists of), then one should use the bottom-up approach to gather such lists of properties into more abstract concepts. Otherwise, if the level of detail of the existing data objects contains generic, high-level concepts, then one needs to use the top-down approach to refine such concepts into simpler and more property-based entities.

If the design of the information architecture starts with both low- and high-level concepts, then we must use both approaches. Fortunately, the basic *bottom-up* and *top-down* approaches can be combined in many forms to overcome each weakness and exploit their strengths.

The strength of the top-down approach is to allow parallel and independent refinement of information entities into more detailed and rich ones. The biggest weakness of the top-down approach is that the quality of the final design depends on the quality of the initial concepts. If one starts with an incomplete or bad initial set of entities, one cannot recover from such handicap. For example, if someone has airplanes and boats as initial concepts, and has forgotten the concepts of "common parts" between them, then common elements such as light lamps and electrical appliances cannot be derived during the top-down design process. Instead, one gets airplane light lamps, boat light lamps, airplane electrical appliances and boat electrical appliances. The impossibility to recover from the lack of key concepts at the very beginning of the design process is the major limitation of the top-down approach.

Notice that proposing a common light lamp from observation of boat light lamps and airplane light lamps is a bottom-up primitive.

On the other hand, bottom-up approaches have a very easy and simple start, because they start with simpler concepts that one needs to use to derive more complex concepts. This is fairly easy if one knows the business and knows what concepts are relevant for the business.

In practice one uses both bottom-up and top-down approaches. Two scenarios are common:

- One starts from the most relevant concepts and expands from those concepts using both top-down and bottom-up primitives.
- One starts with a top-down approach to refine the most relevant concepts and then use the bottom-up approach to integrate resulting schema into a single one.

In both cases one could overcome the limitation of both bottom-up and top-down approaches. Nevertheless, at all times, one knows if we are refining or abstracting concepts.

9.4 Exercises

Exercise 9.1

Sell.Everything is a startup company that sells products to customers, just using a mobile app, supported in artificial intelligence and machine learning to better target products to customer. Products are directly shipped by Sell.Everything suppliers to customers.

1. Just considering the information above, which design approach would you recommend for designing the information architecture?
2. Just considering the information above, present the high-level information entities for Sell.Everything.
3. Using the approach that you recommended, present a possible information architecture that could be derived from the high-level information entities. Present your assumptions and the design primitives used.

Exercise 9.2

The "neighborhood store" is a retail chain present in neighborhoods with high purchasing power. According to the neighborhood store IT department, the following information is needed to manage the business:

- Customer unique id
- Customer name
- Customer tax number
- City of the customer
- Street of the customer
- Zip code of the customer
- Customer mobile
- Customer email
- Store type
- City of the store
- Street of the store
- Zip code of the store
- Store unique id
- Stock item
- Stock description
- Stock category
- Stock item quantity
- Bill number
- Bill type
- Bill description

1. Just considering the information above, which design approach would you recommend for designing the information architecture?
2. Just considering the information above, present the information entities for the neighborhood store.
3. Using the approach that you recommended, abstract the entities into two to five information entities (present your assumptions).

Exercise 9.3

Consider the following business process diagram that describes the loan application, for businesses, at bank Onolut (Fig. 9.8).

The loan application at the Onolut bank takes into account the bank records of the company, as well as the records of its administrators. Additionally, the company's business plan is carefully analyzed. In addition to the supporting documentation required by the banking regulator for granting loans to companies, Onolut bank requires an independent assessment of the business plan by external experts, for loans above 100,000 euros.

1. Just considering the business process diagram of Fig. 9.8, model the current information architecture.
2. Just considering the text description above (without considering the process diagram), model the current information architecture.
3. Considering the partial information architectures, present a consolidated model of the current Onolut information architecture.

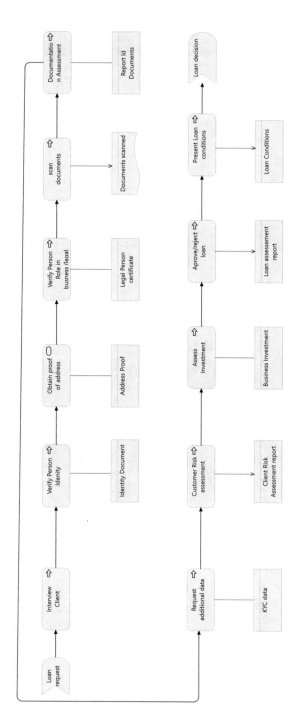

Fig. 9.8 Loan application, for businesses, at bank Onolut

Reference

1. S. Batini, C. Ceri, S. Navathe, *Conceptual Database Design, An Entity-Relationship Approach* (Addison-Wesley, Boston, 1991)

Chapter 10
Information Systems Architecture Design

André Vasconcelos and Pedro Sousa

Abstract This chapter presents information systems architecture (ISA) design techniques. Thus, information planning techniques are described including information systems architecture (ISA) analysis, ISA design, and ISA project development approaches. In Sect. 10.2 information systems portfolio management is discussed. Section 10.3 introduces service design techniques. At the end of the chapter are proposed several exercises using some of the techniques introduced through the chapter.

10.1 Information Systems Architecture Planning

The process of defining the information systems architecture (ISA) aims at delivering a "good" architecture of the information systems (IS). So, one should first clarify the characteristics of a good ISA and how they depend on the ISA design practices.

One characteristic of a good ISA is that the information systems should be as much independent of the organizational structure as possible. This means that management should be able to change the organizational structure of an enterprise without requiring changes in the information systems. In the early days of IT, due to a common "bad practice" to design and tailor IS to each organizational unit, the resulting ISA had a strong dependence (cohesion) with the organizational structure. This was minimized with the increase of the IT function in organizations and the need to have an integrated view of the organization's information.

Another characteristic of a good ISA is the absence of multiple replicas of the same information that can be updated individually but it requires extra effort or developments to keep the replicas consistent whenever one of the replicas changes.

Information redundancy has been a very common situation and is indeed responsible for a significant portion of the total developments and manpower that are required to keep the business running. It results from considering IS primarily as a means of "processing," supporting the activities of the business processes, but discarding the requirements for proper information management. As a result, data becomes private to organization's information systems; poor management of data

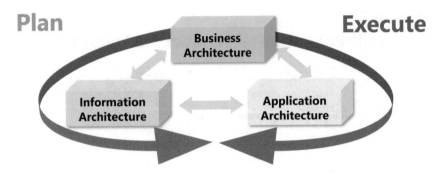

Fig. 10.1 Plan and execute application lifecycle

leads to redundancy, inconsistency, and complex integration between information systems.

Both situations could be easily avoided if one had a view of the information architecture before designing the ISA. Quite often organizations follow a three-phase adoption of information systems. In phase one, they start by implementing information systems, and then, in phase two, they integrate the information systems. A third phase occurs when organizations build data-centered systems as data warehouses and data management systems as a way to provide global and consistent view of data across several systems. This sequence is presented in red arrow in Fig. 10.1.

The effort and complexity of the second and third phases would have been greatly reduced, if not eliminated at all, if the information systems had been designed based on a view of the information architecture. In turn, to design a proper information architecture, one needs to have a view of the process architecture. Thus, to properly plan the IS landscape, one needs to follow the green arrow in Fig. 10.1.

A very common error many enterprises have made has been starting the implementation of applications to support the business needs without planning ahead the information and the business processes, in order to define the *right* applications, i.e., the right ISA.

Therefore, the ISA (plan) should be derived from the business process and from the global information needs, in order to ensure stability and full support to business needs. On the other side of the equation, the implementation of applications (after the ISA is planned) should be developed considering business needs (among other factors). Information cannot be managed and understood in the context of a single process or a single system! One can only align IT with business if the information is considered a *first class citizen*, side by side with business processes and systems. Information architecture is key to define the ISA, since processes have higher rates of change than information.

Change is constant in organizations, in technology, in business process, and in organic structures. However, the information required for business is independent and more stable than the business processes, the technology, and the organic

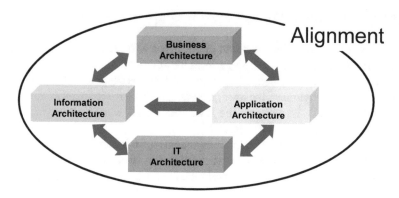

Fig. 10.2 Alignments in information systems architecture planning. Adapted from [1, 2]

structures! This means that the information systems architectures that were designed based on information architecture are (potentially) more stable.

10.1.1 Information Systems Architecture Alignment

An aligned architecture aims at reducing the costs of its overall implementation, operation, and maintenance. Architectural heuristics and principles serve as a guide for assessing the state of alignment between architectures. However, they are not mandatory rules and there are indeed many situations where one should not follow them because of very specific and contextual reasons. But even in these cases, architectural heuristics and principles are very useful because they force designers to explain and evaluate the decisions with greater detail when they take decisions that go against the heuristics and simplify the explanation of the decisions when they are aligned with the heuristics (Fig.10.2).

A heuristic is defined as a technique based on experience or observation that aims to assist the resolution or the discovery of defects. In what concerns ISA design, heuristics can be grouped into three major groups, as presented in light gray bidirectional arrows in Fig. 10.1. We present next three categories of alignment heuristics between:

- Business and information architectures
- Business and application architectures
- Information and application architectures

As we will show, these alignments are orthogonal, meaning that they are independent of each other. Each can be fully achieved or not at all achieved, regardless of the others.

10.1.1.1 Alignment Between Business and Applications

The alignment between business and applications aims at reducing the resources organizations require to allocate to perform the activities of the business processes, including the resources associated with the applications supporting those activities.

The higher the alignment, the lower the effort actors have to spend in mechanized or repetitive operations, and also the lower the resources needed to maintain the applications supporting the business.

Automation is often seen as higher alignment, since it reduces the effort humans have to perform the business process's activities. However, automation is not always recommended in the perspective of cost/benefit, since its cost may not compensate for the effort it reduces to humans.

But the effort required to perform the activities of a business process is not restricted to the actual execution of each activity. The handover of activities between the different actors participating in a given business process is a huge source of wasted time and related inefficiencies.

Workflow systems are examples of systems which essentially promote this type of alignment. These systems can be standalone applications or integrated into a suite (e.g., ERP, CRM).

Thus, besides the automation they may bring to actual activities, business process automation by workflow engines completely automates handover activities. They also enable the management of the actual process and the actor becomes fully observable and traceable and therefore easily optimized.

However, business and application alignment is not synonymous to extensive and mandatory business process automation. One should always consider the costs/benefits of such automation.

Even with no automation, in a fully aligned business architecture and application architecture, information is inserted only once, thus reducing effort and also preventing errors.

The following alignment heuristics between business and application architectures should be considered [1]:

- Each activity of a business process should be supported by a single application.

   The rationale for this heuristic is that it reduces the context switch between applications with different interfaces and probably the need to insert information already inserted in other application.

   The other aspect of this heuristic is that no activity should be left unsupported by a given application. Even for activities that are mostly non-automated, like a brainstorm meeting to reach a consensus decision, it is useful for management purposes to record when they started, when they were completed, and what the result was, and thus, they could benefit from being supported by some application, namely, workflow systems.

   One could extend further this heuristic and state that all activities of a business process should be supported by a single application. However, such a heuristic would hardly be followed because there are many processes that cross many areas within the organization and thus a business process will likely be supported by different applications. For example, an order to pay process will likely cross product catalog and financial applications.

Finally, there is another advantage this heuristic enables. Most activities include several steps or procedures to be made. If they require any transaction properties, either all or none of the steps are done, then these transaction properties are harder to achieve if that activity is supported by multiple applications than if it is supported by a single application. This results from the fact that, in the first case, one requires a distributed transaction mechanism, while, in the second case, one needs a single-node transaction mechanism (which is significantly simpler).

- Each functionality provided by a given application should be used by at least one activity.

  This heuristic states that all application functions are purposeful and are used in some activity.

  Having application functionalities that are not used means that some code was specified, coded, tested, maintained, and hosted in some node with no actual benefit for the organization. Unused code makes applications more complex and difficult to maintain, test, and evolve. Thus, unused functionalities have no benefits to organizations.

- Different applications should not provide the same functionality.

  This heuristic avoids functional redundancy among applications. Having to implement the same functionality in different applications is clearly a waste of organizational resources.

  However, the more one follows the first heuristic, the more likely one will comply with this heuristic. In fact, if two activities supported by two applications need to use the same functionality, it is either duplicated in each application, or it exists only in one activity and both activities must use the same application for that particular functionality.

- The characteristics of the activities are in accordance with the features of the systems that support them (e.g., scalability, availability).

  This heuristic is implied in both previous heuristics. On one hand, it states that the functionality should be available whenever needed. This includes fulfilling the performance required by the business.

  On the other hand, it states that application functionalities should not be available when they are not needed. For example, if some application function is only required once a year, for example, at Christmas time, then one should not have it available during the all year because it represents a waste of resources. This is easier to achieve in recent technologies as *Kubernetes*[1] that supports on-demand deployment of applications, thus saving resources when they are not needed.

---

[1] https://kubernetes.io/.

In a fully aligned business and application scenario, the time and effort businesspeople spend to run the business should mostly be spent in reasoning and decision-making functions. On the contrary, misalignments force businesspeople to perform extra and mechanic work such as:

- Inserting the same data multiple times in different applications.

  This misaligned is often mitigated by the use of a specific application to do repeated insertions of the same information whenever required. These applications are often called "robotic process automation" engines.
- Authenticating multiple times, one for each application users need to access. This misalignment is often mitigated by the use of a specific application that automatically authenticates the user in multiple applications. These applications are often called "single sign on."
- Recovering from a failed operation across multiple systems, requiring careful human analyses to roll back to a coherent state.

  As far as we know, there are no applications in the market to mitigate this misalignment.
- Overcoming inappropriate or the absence of application functionality, for example, printing hundreds of invoices one by one because applications do not have an interface for multiple printing in one click.

Notice that the alignment between business and applications in the above context does not imply a flexible and agile application architecture. A measure of a flexible and agile application architecture must assess the resources and time that organizations must spend to keep the business and applications aligned when business changes.

This means that we can have a perfectly aligned business and application architectures at a given point in time, but when the business changes, the time or the resources needed to re-adapt the applications to maintain the perfect business and application architecture alignment are so high that the organization simply can no longer maintain such alignment, leading to a scenario that more resources are needed considering the maintenance efforts of the applications supporting the business.

10.1.1.2 Alignment Between Business and Information

The alignment between business and information aims at ensuring that business has the information it needs to operate. Therefore, the information entities defined in the information architecture should be aligned with the business processes *inputs* and *outputs*.

The focus is on structuring the information necessary to conduct business, both in operations and in management information. One example is the decision of approving an order placed in a procurement process. What is the information that the decision maker will use to approve or reject the purchase order?

The alignment between the business and the information does not imply that there must be some system that provides the necessary information, but instead that the required information is mapped in the information architecture.

Next, we present a few examples:

- A first example is the concept of "customer" in a company. This word ("customer") may exist in the description of different activities with different meanings. If the management decided to give a 10% discount in future sales for customers that have bought over some amount, they do not necessarily mean to give such discount on customers that have not paid any of their products, or that are in legal dispute with the company, or even that have returned and asked for immediate refund of all products they have bought in credit.
- Another example is the concept of "product" in a company. For the sales department, a product is something they can sell. When they cannot sell, it is no longer a product. However, for the legal department, a product is something the company is selling or has sold in the past. In fact, a product that is no longer sold by a company, and thus is out of any store or site, may still be a full product for the after-sales department or to the legal department.
- Yet another example is the word "locomotive" in a train company. For the marketing department, the locomotive standing in front of the company headquarters counts as a locomotive that they must paint and maintain with the company image, but it does not count as one locomotive for the operations department since it is not used to pull any wagons.

We will see in the next sections that having a clear understanding of the information entities, both in terms of its identification and its properties, is very relevant to plan information systems and thus to decide which information systems better fit into a given organization.

The following alignment heuristics between business and information architectures should be considered:

- Information entities must contain all the information necessary for the activities of the processes, regardless of them being manual or automatic activities. This heuristic states that all information must be mapped in the architecture, to make sure it complies with organizational rules and management procedures, such as the ones implied by the heuristics presented next.
- All processes refer to information entities as they are presented in the information architecture; thus, synonyms and antonyms are not allowed when referring to information entities.

  This heuristic states that when different business areas use a given term to refer to information, they all agree in what it stands for.
- All processes read, create, or update at least one information entity.

  Since processes input and output information, it is mapped into information entities. This heuristic states that a process must have input information and must produce some output data. In fact a process without input date is either a clock, a random number generator, or something similar. Likewise, a process with no output has no purpose, since one could not even distinguish between the case where it has been executed from the case where it was not executed at all.

- Each information entity is created, read/updated, and deleted by at least one process.

This heuristic states that every information entity must have some purpose for the business, both as input and as output.

Generally, all information entities are created, updated, and then read by at least one process different from the one that created/updated them. An entity that is not read means that there is no purpose of it being written. In fact, there is no point in writing something that will never be read.

Likewise, an entity that is not created is something that never changes and one can ignore the processes that have created them because such processes will be executed once; for example, the information entity holding the plan and seat number in a cinema theater. Such information entity is defined during the theater planning and construction and only changes after reconstruction. Thus, it remains immutable during the cinema's day-to-day operations. In this case, most likely one will not find any process created or updated in the organization's process landscape.

Nevertheless, even in the above case, the COVID crises showed that such entities do need to be updated in day-to-day operations, limiting the seats that could be sold to ensure the social distance determined by the law on a weekly or monthly basis.

Information and business architectures are aligned when businesspeople have the information they need to run the business. This means it is accurate, with the right level of detail and on-time information. Unlike the previous misalignment, here the impact is neither time nor effort, but the impossibility of getting the adequate piece of information relevant for the business.

10.1.1.3   Alignment Between Information and Applications

The alignment between information and applications aims at the effectiveness of information management by the information systems. The overall outcome is the reduction of resources organizations must spend in managing, maintaining, and operating information systems.

A first concern of this alignment relates with completeness, making sure that all information handled by applications is mapped in the information architecture and vice versa. A second concern is about redundancy. The existence of multiple replicas of the same information in different systems is a common problem because each replica has structure, syntax, and semantics usually different in different systems, making it difficult to integrate and to keep consistency whenever one replica changes.

An ERP (enterprise resource planning) system is a good example of an aligned application and information architectures. By having a single database, ERPs do achieve a highly aligned application and information architecture, because there are no information replicas within the ERP to keep it coherent and updated. However, this does not mean that ERP workflows are aligned with the business processes, or stated differently, this does not mean a high business and application alignment.

The following alignment heuristics between information architecture and application architectures should be considered[1]:

- Each information entity is managed by a single system. By management we mean firstly managing the entity identifiers, both assigned identifiers, as well as managing the set of attributes that are immutable and ultimately identify the information entity. For example, when a client is created in the *CRM* (customer relationship management) system, the CRM must assure:

  - That no other client has the same set of identifying attributes, including when considering the clients already deleted
  - That any assigned identifiers differ from all identifiers ever assigned, including those assigned to deleted clients
  - That the set of identifying attributes remain unchanged throughout the entity lifestyle

    This actually might not be so simple for some entities because some attributes that one consider as unchangeable might be changed in some broader context. A person may change sex and name during his or her life, the parents may also change sex and name, and even countries may change name, split apart, or merge.

- Each attribute of an entity should not be updated by more than one system. However, different attributes of the same entity may be updated by different systems.

  Consider again the client in the *CRM* system. Despite the fact that client identification must be performed by the *CRM*, client properties as financial status could be updated or even deleted by the billing system, as long as it stays associated to the client identification.

  Such updates could be done autonomously by the billing system independently of the *CRM* system. However, in what concerns validation, it might imply interactions between the *CRM* and the billing system. The heuristic also states that the same data, financial status in the previous example, should not be updated in any other systems.

- Entities must be changed in a transaction, meaning they all change or none changes, should be managed by a single system.

  This heuristic simply states that whenever possible one should favor local transactions rather than distributed ones. However, quite often this heuristic cannot be fulfilled because it would lead to a single system doing everything.

  An *ERP* is an example of a complex system holding a wide range of organization information entities that are managed by a single system, assuring the fulfillment of this heuristic.

In fully aligned information and application architectures, IT staff only spent effort and time coding business functions and logic. On the contrary, any misalignment between information and application might require IT staff to do extra coding for:

- Keeping multiple replicas of the same data coherent, because they are updated by multiple applications
- Assuring coherency from multiple transactions, because a single business process crosses multiple applications
- Gathering information from multiple systems and coding rules to produce a coherent view of the organization's business information
- Transforming data structures when data migrates between applications

Besides the extra work from the IT staff, misalignment might also lead to extra work to business staff, for example:

- Inserting the same information multiple times in different systems
- Recovering from failing transactions across different systems, requiring detailed human analysis to roll back to a coherent state in each system

10.1.2   Information Systems Architecture Design

In this section we present a method to design information systems architectures based on the heuristics presented in the previous sections, thus having the desired characteristics.

The CRUD matrix is a very common way to represent in a matrix the relationship and dependencies between behavior and state. For the purpose of designing information systems architectures, the behavior represents business processes, the state represents information entities, and the cells represent the dependencies between business process and information entities. These relationships may be "create," "read," "update," or "delete" (CRUD) relations.

There is no granularity defined for business processes or information entities. So, behavior could represent macro processes, processes, or activities and the information may be "macro" entities, entities, or attributes. Each cell specifies the action access (CRUD) to the information—"create", "read", "update," or "delete" (CRUD) action, as presented in Fig. 10.3.

The "create" of an information entity implies at least the creation of the entity identifier, or identifying attributes. The remaining attributes can be updated afterwards. On the other hand, the "delete" of an information entity implies at least the invalidation of the identifier of the entity. After a "delete" the entity can no longer be used. An "update" of an information entity means to change the state of an attribute of that information entity (Fig. 10.4).

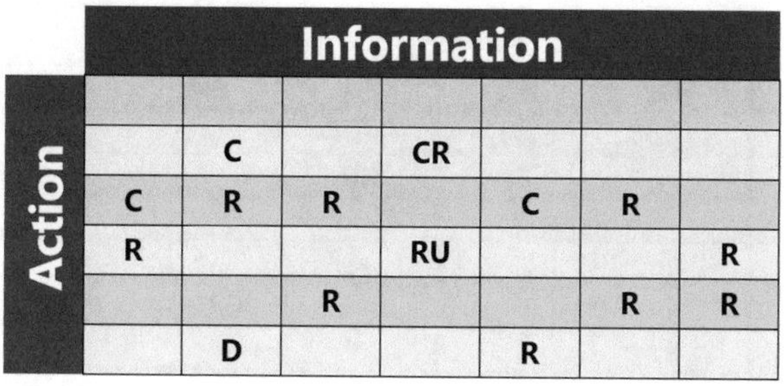

Information							
	C			CR			
C	R	R			C	R	
R			RU				R
		R				R	R
	D				R		

(Action)

Fig. 10.3 An example of the **CRUD** matrix

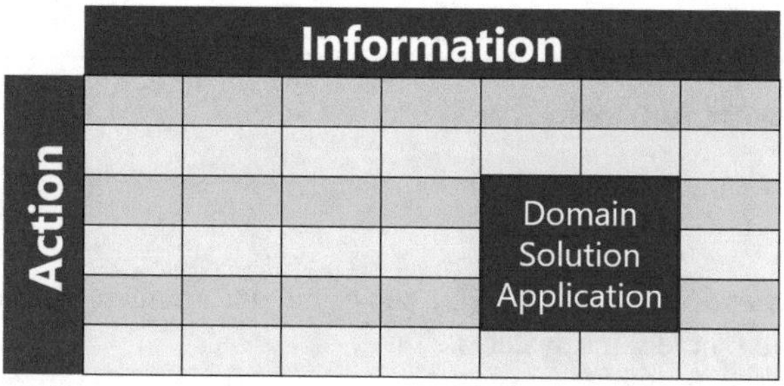

Information							
				Domain			
				Solution			
				Application			

(Action)

Fig. 10.4 Representation of a solution in the **CRUD** matrix

It is important to notice that the "delete" of all the information of an entity is an "update," not a "delete." What is at stake with the create/delete of an information entity is its existence and *not* the value of its attributes or properties.

All entities are created (C), read (R), and deleted (R). The vast majority are also updated (U). On the other hand, all processes read (R) and usually update (C/U) information entities. There may be "special" processes that deal with private information (not relevant company-wide) that may not create or update information entities.

10.1.2.1   Rules for Designing the ISA

In order to define systems that are enduring and resistant to business changes, a set of basic rules must be followed:

- Rule 1

  - Processes that create or delete (C/D) the same information entities should be supported by the same systems.
  - Therefore, one should aggregate the processes according to the entities created by them.

	E1	E2	E3	E4	E5	E6
P1	CRUD	CRUD	CRUD			
P2		R	RU			
P3		R	CRUD			
P4			R			
P5				CRUD	RU	
P6	R	R			RU	
P7					CRUD	
P8	R	R			R	R
P9					R	CRUD
P10					R	CRUD

Information Entity spans E1–E6; **Process** labels P1–P10.

Fig. 10.5 The initial **CRUD** matrix example

- Rule 2
  - The processes that update (U) the same information entities should be supported by the same systems.
  - Therefore, one should aggregate the processes that update information entities with those that create them.
- Rule 3
  - Systems should be as simple as possible (minimization of each area).
  - Afterward, at the technological level, we can choose to implement several system clusters in a single information system. Thus, we expect to find the maximum number of information systems that could exist for the enterprise processes and information entities.

Therefore, the business system planning (BSP) method defines the following major steps for creating the system/application clusters:

- **STEP 1**: Delete irrelevant (similar) columns or rows.
- **STEP 2**: Next put together processes that create the same entities.
- **STEP 3**: Next put together processes that update (U) entities with the processes that create the entities (C).
- **STEP 4**: Identify the "application clusters" considering that the applications (systems) should be as simple as possible.

Let's apply these steps to the matrix in Fig. 10.5.

The initial matrix is built considering each business process and the information entities it creates (C), reads (R), updates (U), or deletes (D). A possible business process view of P1 and P2, for the matrix in Fig. 10.5, is presented in Fig. 10.6.

- **STEP 1**: First, we should delete irrelevant columns or rows. Equal rows and columns should be joined together (P9 and P10), as presented in Fig. 10.7.

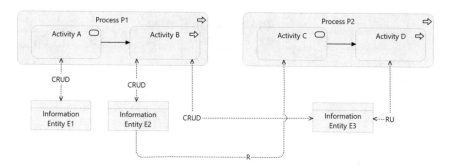

Fig. 10.6 Possible business process view of P1 and P2 relationships with information entities E1, E2, and E3

		Information Entity				
		E1	**E2**	**E3**	**E4**	**E5**	**E6**
Process	**P1**	CRUD	CRUD	CRUD			
	P2		R	RU			
	P3		R	CRUD			
	P4			R			
	P5				CRUD	RU	
	P6	R	R			RU	
	P7					CRUD	
	P8	R	R			R	R
	P9+P10					R	CRUD

Fig. 10.7 CRUD matrix without irrelevant rows and columns

- **STEP 2**: Next we should put processes together (by moving lines) considering the entities created by them (P1 and P3 moved), as presented in Fig. 10.8.
- **STEP 3**: Then we should move to adjacent rows processes that update (U) entities with the processes that create them (Fig. 10.9).
- **STEP 4**: Finally, we should be able to identify the application clusters in the matrix. For that purpose we need to know if the processes are atomic (or transactional) or end-to-end.

   In atomic processes all the steps (behavior) of the process must be performed in the same system (since it is hard and expensive to ensure atomicity properties if the process is performed in different systems). On the other hand, in end-to-end business processes, different organization stakeholders (usually from different departments) are involved, and atomicity is usually not required. Thus, end-to-end processes are not required to have a single system supporting all the steps (behavior) of the process.

Process	Information Entity					
	E1	E2	E3	E4	E5	E6
P1	CRUD	CRUD	CRUD			
P3		R	CRUD			
P2		R	RU			
P4			R			
P5				CRUD	RU	
P6	R	R			RU	
P7					CRUD	
P8	R	R			R	R
P9+P10					R	CRUD

Fig. 10.8 CRUD matrix with process P3 moved up

Process	Information Entity					
	E1	E2	E3	E4	E5	E6
P1	CRUD	CRUD	CRUD			
P3		R	CRUD			
P2		R	RU			
P4			R			
P5				CRUD	RU	
P6	R	R			RU	
P7					CRUD	
P8	R	R			R	R
P9+P10					R	CRUD

Fig. 10.9 CRUD matrix with updates close to creates

Thus:

- Assuming the processes are atomic, we want that each activity is supported by just one system (see Fig. 10.9). In this case, we identify three applications. The first one supports processes P1, P3, and P2 and manages entities E1, E2, and E3. The second system supports P5, P6, and P7 processes and entities E4 and E5. And the last system supports P9+P10 and manages entity 6.
- On a different scenario, if processes P1 to P10 are end-to-end processes (non-transactional), we could have different systems supporting each process (see Fig. 10.10).

In Fig. 10.11 we present the integration flow among systems, considering the end-to-end scenario.

The integration flows are identified considering the "R" (reads) outside the system clusters. The system that supports the process (P1 ... P10) must integrate with the system that manages the information entity (E1 ... E6). For instance, the

Information Entity						
Process	**E1**	**E2**	**E3**	**E4**	**E5**	**E6**
P1	CRUD	CRUD	CRUD			
P3		R	CRUD			
P2		R	RU			
P5				CRUD	RU	
P6	R	R			RU	
P7					CRUD	
P9+P10					R	CRUD
P8	R	R			R	R
P4			R			

Fig. 10.10 Application clusters for atomic activities (P1 to P10)

Information Entity						
Process	**E1**	**E2**	**E3**	**E4**	**E5**	**E6**
P1	CRUD	CRUD	CRUD			
P3		R	CRUD			
P2		R	RU			
P5				CRUD	RU	
P6	R	R			RU	
P7					CRUD	
P9+P10					R	CRUD
P8	R	R			R	R
P4			R			

Fig. 10.11 Application clusters for end-to-end processes (P1 to P10) with integration

green system that manages process P3 must be integrated with the light blue system
(that manages E2) to read (R) E2 (needed in process P3).

Each cluster of cells in the matrix can represent a domain, solution, application,
or application component—depending on the granularity of the "ingredients"
(columns and lines). If the matrix is made of macro processes and macro entities, the
solution will be a domain application architecture. If it uses entities and processes,
the cluster represents a solution architecture; if the CRUD matrix is made of
activities and information entities (or attributes), the results are application clusters,
as presented in Fig. 10.12

10.1.3 Information Systems Architecture Project Approach

The main goal of information systems planning is defining the desired future for
the organization's information systems. It explains how IS should be supported by
IT. The main result of information systems planning is the information systems

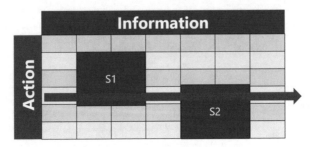

Fig. 10.12 Processes and systems in the **CRUD** matrix

architecture. There are several methods and approaches for planning the information systems.

Spewak's [3] approach to enterprise architecture planning (EAP) has a strong relationship with the Zachman framework. It has been adopted and adapted by various institutions according to their needs. The EAP, according to Spewak, defines the upper levels of the Zachman framework [4], and the data columns, functions and location (network). Spewak's approach delivers three architectures (data, applications, and technology), using the business model as a starting point for the enterprise architecture specification. Thus, the approach aims to define the ISA and a plan to implement it.

Spewak proposes a four-layer approach for EAP. The first layer is focused on the planning and the second layer on the "AS-IS" (at an IT and business level). The third layer settles the "TO-BE" architecture. The fourth layer defines the implementation plan (Fig. 10.13).

The activities described next can be done in a high-level manner or in a more detailed manner. This is particularly relevant in the discovery of the models of level 2, *where we are today*. If too abstract, one may overlook many important aspects that later can have huge impacts on time and effort. If too detailed, one may spend a lot of time in the gathering of information necessary to produce them, when the models produced will be already obsolete.

One cannot ignore the fact that organizations do not stop evolving while phases 2 and 3 are being developed. Therefore, the longer they take, the higher the changes will occur, and the more obsolete the resulting models will be.

So, the whole EAP should be realized in a few months (e.g., 2 to 4), depending on how fast the organization is changing. That was already a problem 30 years ago, when organizations changed at relatively slow paces. Today it is indeed a major issue, since organizations change at a much higher pace. This risk is the fact that when one concludes the EAP project, its initial models of the organization AS-IS are already obsolete, leading to the invalidation of the whole project.

This is where enterprise cartography comes in, by providing the organization with models of the AS-IS updated on a weekly or monthly basis. Such a capacity not only reduces the effort and time required to get the AS-IS models, but also

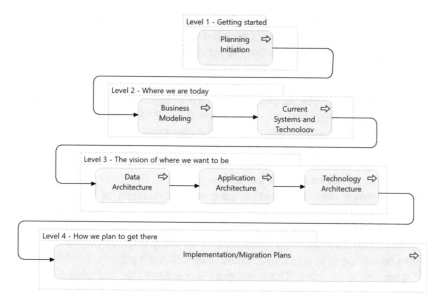

Fig. 10.13 Spewak's approach to enterprise architecture planning

allows the assessment of the changes that have occurred when proposing a plan to achieve the organization desired TO-BE states.

10.1.3.1   Level 1: Getting Started

There are two major goals at this stage. The first is the work plan that specifies the steps needed in order to achieve the objectives of the EAP, including the development of the architectures and the implementation plan. The second goal is to ensure the support and the cooperation of executives and managers in the organization, including through the allocation of resources in order to achieve a successful EAP.

There are seven steps in this phase:

1. Determine the scope and objectives of the EAP. At this stage the scope and objectives of the project are officially defined for the project team and for the management. Issues like the scope of the project (e.g., all company versus a business unit or subsidiary) must be defined during this step.
2. Create a vision. After defining the scope of the project (including the meaning of the word "organization") and after identifying the business areas that will be included, this step serves to conduct a study on the background of the enterprise, systems, and opportunities. This information is used to create a vision for the future of the business information systems. Understanding the business and the enterprise is very important to get a good support to define architectures that enable the implementation of the vision.

3. Adopt a methodology. The result of this step is a methodology adapted to the business needs. The methodology provides the general ideas for the project work plan and the training sessions for the team. Every step of every phase must be specified including source documents, guidelines, roles, responsibilities, and the estimated effort.
4. Get the resources. The purpose of this step is to ensure the IT infrastructure (including computers and software) supports the EAP. This step involves producing reports and any programs that are necessary to prepare the product to be used. There is no single product that is perfect for the EAP. A range of products will be used as a tool to support the methodology of the EAP. The objective is to have an integrated set of tools that enable the EAP data exchange.
5. Join a planning team. It's probably the most important step of this phase. There are four principles that should be followed when choosing a team: (i) A good and effective leadership helps overcome many problems. (ii) Team members must be credible. (iii) They must be committed to the success of the project. (iv) They must be willing to cooperate and collaborate with each other.
6. Prepare the work plan. The work plan is the timetable and plan for all the activities of the team. It is critical for the EAP to be completed on time.
7. Obtain the agreement, the commitment, and the funds. Calculate the total EAP project cost. Include the estimated times of each team member, consultants' fees, the cost of computation, and the cost of materials and tools.

10.1.3.2   Level 2: Where We Are Today

Layer 2 of the EAP approach has two main phases: (i) business modeling and (ii) a survey of the current technologies and systems.

The first phase of the "AS-IS" architecture is business modeling. It is the process of defining the business. The aim is to provide a broad base of knowledge about the business models. Business modeling is divided into two parts: a first, preliminary, followed by a complete model. The preliminary model identifies the business processes and the business units involved in these processes.

Three steps are required for modeling the business:

1. Document the organizational structure. The purpose of this step is to document the structure of the organization and identify who and where they carry out the "business function." This information is important in two ways for the EAP: (i) it identifies people to be interviewed and (ii) it determines the extent to which data and application systems are shared.
2. Identify business processes. This step defines the structure of the business model. It is one of the most important steps in the EAP, because defining the business is essential for defining further architectures.
3. Document the model and distribute it to the parties involved in the business in order to get feedback. The models are distributed to check whether the definitions and relationships are accurate, so that the next phase runs smoothly.

In this phase the organization is necessary in order to complete the business model including:

- What information is used to perform each business process (function)?
- When are the business processes (functions) executed?
- Where are the business processes (functions) executed?
- How often are the business processes (functions) performed?
- How may the execution of the business processes (function) be improved?

There are five steps to perform the study of an organization:

1. Schedule interviews. At this stage all the necessary interviews are scheduled and time recorded in accordance with the work plan.
2. Prepare the interviews. To prepare for the interviews, "forms and templates" are created that serve as guides during the interview process.
3. Conduct the interviews. It is important to conduct the interviews at the time planned to maintain a good image and reputation of the team. It is also important to fill the forms during interviews, so at the end, the interviewer can check the data with the respondent. Errors at this stage could jeopardize the credibility of the business model.
4. Enter the information in the toolset. All the information acquired in the course of the interviews is introduced into the toolset and verified. Although this step sounds simple, it is not. The reason is that many of the products used as toolset do not have the capacity to handle large amounts of data. This situation is usually referred to as "data entry bottleneck."
5. Distribute the business model. At this stage the business model is completely distributed to the organization's managers.

The second phase of the "AS-IS" architecture is the current systems and technology, also called information and resource catalog (IRC). The IRC does not go into exhaustive detail for all systems. The steps to build the IRC are:

1. Determine the scope, objectives, and work plan.
2. Prepare for data collection. At this stage you must determine the type of data that will be compiled and develop forms to assist in data collection.
3. Execute the data collection. At this stage the developed forms will be distributed. The applications will be linked to the business processes supported, as defined in the business model. Applications will also be related to technology platforms defined in the previous step.
4. Enter the data. The purpose of this step is to enter the information into the forms.
5. Validate and review the IRC (sketch). The integrity of the information on the current applications, as well as on the technology platforms, should be checked before being distributed.
6. Draw the diagrams (views), including the application level diagrams that graphically show the flow of input and output for each system. They provide an insight into the IRC showing how applications are interlinked.

7. Distribute the IRC. After the data have been verified in the IRC and schemes designed and revised, they must be distributed and made available to the organization.
8. Administer and maintain the IRC. In order to be used as reference information, the IRC must be kept updated.

10.1.3.3 Level 3: The Vision of Where We Want to Be

This stage presents the vision of three architectures: (i) information architecture, (ii) application architecture, and (iii) technology architecture.

The information (or data) architecture (IA) identifies and defines the main types of data that support the business processes defined in the business model. The steps that should be performed to develop the IA are:

1. List the candidate entities. The purpose of this phase is to identify power data entities required to support the business (things, concepts, places, people, or events).
2. Define the entities, attributes, and relationships. The purpose of this step is to create a standard definition and a description for each information entity in the architecture of data and provide a graphic illustration of their interrelations.
3. Link the entities with the business processes. The purpose of this step is to determine which entities are created, deleted, updated, or read by business processes.
4. Distribute the data architecture.

The application architecture is not a system design, but a definition of what the application will do to manage data and provide information to people running the business processes of the company. The recommended steps to develop this architecture are:

1. List candidate applications. Identify all possible applications, necessary for data management as well as to support the business. Use the business system planning ("CRUD matrix" method—see Sect. 10.1.2) to identify possible applications.
2. Define applications. The purpose of this step is to provide a standard definition for each application in the application architecture. In this step each application definition is based solely on the business model and the architecture of data and is independent of who uses the application, how the application works, and where it is located or operated.
3. Relate the applications with the business processes.
4. Analyze the impact on existing applications. The purpose of this step is to determine the impact of applying existing applications defined in IRC. This step is sometimes performed as part of the implementation phase/migration because it compares existing applications with future applications.
5. Distribute the application architecture. In this step the organization is informed about the applications that have been set up and asks opinions or suggestions. This step is sometimes combined with the technology architecture.

The technology architecture defines the types of technology, i.e., platforms, that will support the business. The technology architecture according to Spewak [3] should not be a requirement analysis or a detailed network or software design. It must first define the types of technology, i.e., platforms that will support the business. According to Spewak, the technology architecture is a conceptual model that defines platforms, not draws the software. Spewak suggests that at this stage (technology) specialists are integrated in the EA project team.

The steps suggested to develop the technology architecture are:

1. Identify the principles and the technology platforms. The purpose of this step is to identify the principles underlying the architecture and the technology platforms required to support an environment of shared data. The principles will determine the types of platforms and set the direction for the acquisition of technology.
2. Set platforms and distribute them. After the principles for the technology architecture are defined, the aim of the second step is to determine the strategy to distribute applications and data, and define the technological platform that will be the setting for the applications and data that support the business.
3. Relate platforms with applications and business processes. This step provides a "justification" for the technology platform linking it to the business processes that will directly benefit from it.
4. Distribute the technological architecture. At this stage we intend to confirm the technology architecture is reasonable and acceptable. The application architecture can be distributed along with the technology architecture on a single document.

10.1.3.4 Level 4: How We Plan to Get There

The final stage is the definition of the implementation plan. The goal is to formulate and prepare an implementation plan for the architectures. The steps for this stage are:

1. Sequence the applications. The purpose of this step is to establish priorities and to reach a result that defines the order in which the applications should be implemented. There is a fundamental principle to follow: "Applications that create data must be implemented prior to applications that use the data."
2. Estimate the effort, and produce a calendar. The aim now is to estimate the amount of effort required to implement and the resources needed and produce a project plan to implement the architectures.
3. Estimate the costs and plan the benefits. The economic benefits, profit, or return rates are factors that lead organizations to make the decision on accepting the plan. Some organizations based their decision on monetary factors.
4. Determine success factors and make recommendations. Implement a data sharing environment with quality, where people have access to data requests involving changes. In order to make changes, decisions have to be made. This step will determine the success factors needed to implement the architectures and plans, and provide indicators to support management decision.

10.2 Application Portfolio Management

In the previous section we have seen the alignment criteria of an ISA and an approach to plan and develop such architecture.

However, many organizations fail to proceed with such an approach, because they are unable to build and maintain the required process and information architectures.

So, they rather adopt a more incremental approach to decide the TO-BE of their information systems. *Application portfolio management*, or simply **APM**, is an incremental method to evolve the portfolio of applications, based on business, technical and financial aspects.

So, whereas ISA is an engineering approach to design an architecture, APM is a management approach to identify the applications with highest negative impact, as perceived by its stakeholders.

However, the APM approach has some advantages.

- It may include a broader range of factors than the ISA, such as cost or technology.
- It is easier to apply incrementally and periodically than the ISA. This is an important aspect because, due to the constant evolution of organizations, architectures designed by an ISA approach tend to get out of alignment with time, thus requiring a periodic redesign of the application architecture.

We first present the analysis usually performed in an APM initiative, then we present the corresponding decisions and finally a method for an APM project approach.

10.2.1 APM Analysis

Quite frequently, existing applications violate the most basic rules of information systems architecture planning. Therefore, some of the analyses aim at checking the existence of symptoms of misalignment caused by bad design decisions [5–8], including:

- **Redundancy Analysis**. In this analysis one looks for signs of duplication, or multi-existence of the same artifact. Such a duplication can be observed at the following levels (see Table 10.1):

    - **Functional Redundancy**. Existence of alternative ways of doing the same functions
    - **Technological Redundancy**. Multiplicity of equivalent technologies
    - **Informational Redundancy**. Existence of multiple of alternative sources to obtain the same information

Table 10.1 Redundancy (duplication, waste) analysis

Analysis type	Symptoms	Analyze	Supports recommendations of	With potential impact on
Functional redundancy	Existence of alternative ways of doing the same functions	Groups of applications with equivalent functionality	Discontinuation of applications and/or features	– Maintenance cost reduction
				– Greater resource management capacity, by reducing the learning curve
Technological redundancy	Multiplicity of equivalent technologies	Potentially redundant technology groups	Reduction in the number of equivalent technologies	– Greater negotiation skills with suppliers
				– Greater resource management capacity, by reducing the necessary skills
Informational redundancy	Existence of multiple alternative sources to obtain the same information	Groups of applications with redundant information	Reduction in the number of information sources	– Reduction of maintenance and operating costs implied by maintaining information
				– Coherence across different sources

- **Obsolescence Analysis**. Here, one looks for aged, non-supported, or no longer efficient artifacts (see Table 10.2):

    - **Functional Obsolescence**. Existence of application features that are no longer used, because the business no longer requires them.
    - **Application's Obsolescence**. Applications that have decreasing usage or even have no usage at all.
    - **Technological Obsolescence**. Technologies that are rarely used or are in the process of not being usable. Another aspect of technology obsolescence is the lack of support from vendors.
    - **Informational Obsolescence**. Existence of applications with information not usable either because it is no longer required or because it is no longer kept up to date.

- **Capacity**. In this quality the applications are assessed considering (see Table 10.3):

    - **Application Capacity**. Absence of evidence of lack of licensing

Table 10.2 Obsolescence (age, inoperability)

Analysis type	Symptoms	Analyze	Supports recommendations of	With potential impact on
Application obsolescence	Rarely used or unusable applications	Degree of use of each application	Discontinuation, replacement, or improvement of applications	– Reduced maintenance costs
				– Reduced infrastructure costs
Technological obsolescence	Technologies rarely used or about to be unusable	Technology quality of each application	Discontinuation, replacement, or technological migration	– Reduction of maintenance costs, by reducing the necessary skills
				– Reduced infrastructure costs
				– Risk reduction skills
Informational obsolescence	Existence of applications with obsolete information	Obsolete information applications	Discontinuation, replacement, or improvement of applications	– Reduced maintenance costs
				– Reduction of operating costs, by reducing the necessary infrastructure
				– Risk reduction

- **Support Capacity**. Absence of delays in supplier response
- **Computation Capacity**. Absence of evidence of lack of performance

- **Alignment**. The alignment of an application may be assessed considering:

  - **Automation**. Reduced application support to the business areas
  - **Usability**. High learning curve and delay in the execution of operations
  - **Information Alignment**. Difficulty in obtaining the necessary information
  - **Technological Alignment**. Misalignment with possible enterprise technology guidelines

- **Cost**. The cost of an application is usually assessed considering:

  - **Maintenance**. The cost to maintain and support the application
  - **License**. The cost of license and the licensing model (when applicable)
  - **Acquisition**. The cost to implement, customize, and install the application, considering the enterprise requirements

Table 10.3 Capacity (volumetry)

Analysis type	Symptoms	Analyze	Supports recom- mendations of	With potential impact on
Application capacity	Absence of evidence of lack of licensing	Applications with potentially excessive licensing	Reducing the volume of licensing	– Maintenance cost reduction
Support capacity	Absence of delays in supplier response	Applications with inadequate support from supplier	Defining and monitoring adequate SLA with suppliers	– Support cost reduction
Computation capacity	Absence of evidence of poor performance	Applications with potentially excessive computational resources	Education of computational capacity made available to applications	– Reduction of operating costs

10.2.2 APM Indicators

The indicators that are typically used to assess the suitability of an application are cost, business relevance, and technical quality. The cost is based on the acquisition, license, and maintenance as previously presented. With regard to business relevance and technical quality, they are calculated on the basis of other indicators (see Fig. 10.14), which should be weighted according to their availability, quality and specificities of the enterprise.

10.2.2.1 Business Relevance

Business relevance defines how important an application is for the enterprise, and is computed based on the weighted average of several indicators, as for example:

- **Functional Coverage**

  - User Satisfaction. Degree of satisfaction of application's users.
  - Business Satisfaction. Value for the business, perceived by management.
  - Internationally. Ability to support multiple instances, languages, currencies, etc.
  - Functional Redundancy. Degree of Functional and Informational redundancy with other applications.

- **Usability**

  - Ergonomics. Ergonomics of interfaces and concepts perceived by the User

Fig. 10.14   Example of an application score card with a set of APM indicators

- – Performance. The degree of impact that performance has in business outcome
  or production. The key issue is assess how much more productive the users
  would be with the increase of application's performance.

- **Usage**

  – Number of Users. Number of effective users that use the application to do
    their tasks.
  – Criticality. Criticality perceived by the management of organic units. The key
    issue is how much additional effort would be required to keep the business
    running if this application ceases to perform.

10.2.2.2   Technical Quality

This indicator expresses the technical quality of an application. As with business
relevance, technical quality is computed based on the weighted average of several
other indicators, both absolute (intrinsic to the application), as well as relative to the
enterprise needs. For example, if in average, an application is not available one hour
per week, their availability should be better rated in the case it is only used once a
week, and with no hard timing requirements, than in the case it is used on a 24*7
paradigm.

- **General**

  – Availability. The degree of impact that application unavailability has in
    business outcome and production. Similarly to performance, the key issue is

to assess how much more productive the users would be with the increase of application's availability.
- Maintainability. Average resolution time for corrective and evolutionary maintenance requests. It assesses the capacity to evolve the application, either with internal or external expertise.
- Age. Number of years since the application is in production.

- **Adaptability**

  - Configuration. Degree of configuration the application has received since the it is in production.
  - Customization. Degree of customization performed since the it is in production, weighted by the customization approach (low code, script, programming language, etc)

- **Technology**

  - Development Technology. The technology required for the application development and execution.
  - Integration Technology. The technology available for integration with other applications, such as REST Services, SOAP, file transfer, file sharing, etc.

Additionally, enterprise-specific indicators may be added, as for example the quality and coverage of the documentation.

The indicators presented above are standardized into a five-level qualitative category as: very low, low, normal, high, and very high or similar.

These indicators are aggregated into three top indicators, as indicated in Fig. 10.14:

- **Business Relevance**. Resumes how relevant or important the application is for the organization
- **Technical Quality**. Resumes the technical quality of the application
- **Cost**. Resumes the cost elements of the application

The weight of each indicator may change from organization to organization and should be carefully adjusted so that the aggregated indicators are meaningful.

Once computed, the top indicators are plotted in the business/technical/cost charts as presented in Fig. 10.14. Traditionally, the technical quality and business relevance are plotted as X,Y coordinates and the cost is translated into a circle diameter. The color is left for some categorization, as functional domain.

In this chart, applications are divided into four major quadrants, and the goal of the proposed actions is to move applications to the right-top quadrant and reduce costs as much as possible (see the example in Fig. 10.15).

- **Lower-Left Quadrant**. Applications in this quadrant have low business relevance and bad technical quality. They should not consume significant organizational resources, neither financial nor human resources.
- **Lower-Right Quadrant**. Applications in this quadrant have good technical but low business relevance. So, it might be a good investment to increase

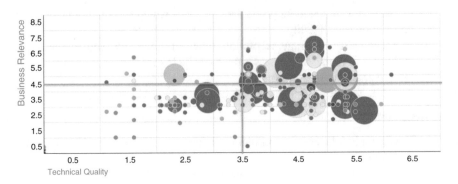

Fig. 10.15 Example of an APM analysis chart

their business relevance, by incorporating more functionalities required by the business. Otherwise, given their low business relevance, one should not spend resources on them, unless they can support additional functionalities required by the business, thus increasing their business relevance.

- **Higher-Left Quadrant**. Applications in this quadrant have high business relevance, but a low technical quality. One should either improve their technical quality or simply replace them by a better quality one.
- **Higher-Right Quadrant**. Applications in this quadrant have high business relevance and a high technical quality. So, keep them as they are.

Regardless of the previous analysis, cost is always a factor to take into consideration. Traditionally, given the list of decisions from a business relevance/technical quality perspective, one starts to consider those dealing with applications with higher costs, and simply leave the actions on low-cost applications for later.

Apart from any transformation initiative to improve the business relevance/technical quality chart, one can always optimize the costs spent on the applications by improving the application's sourcing. Application sourcing includes the cost of maintenance, licensing, and hosting. To optimize sourcing one needs to ensure that we are not acquiring more capacity than is needed, including:

- **Maintenance Capacity**. The costs on maintenance, either corrective, evolutionary regardless of whether it is done by the organizational resources, or outsourced to external resources, depend on several factors that might be reduced without affecting the business. For example, the readiness of the maintenance team is observed when the requested changes are performed.

  A conservative approach is to consider that if the internal users do not complain about the maintenance readiness, then it is a sign that it may be higher than needed and one might consider to reduce it. For example, one may attempt to do a small reduction and after 1 year assess if there were any complaints or reported business impacts.

- **Licensing Capacity**. When software license is involved one must confirm that all licenses are actually needed, or if installed capacity may be reduced. An analysis of application logs for login operations may reveal the actual license usage.
- **Hosting Capacity**. This is mostly about the cost of infrastructure used to run the application. CPU and communications are among the higher costs.

  Very much like the maintenance capacity, if there are no complaints that the application is slow, then it probably can run a little slower, thus saving hosting costs. However, this might be a dangerous assumption for heavily used applications, because a bit slower may imply a lower productivity of hundreds of users, yielding much higher costs on personal than the actual savings in hosting.

10.2.3 APM Actions

After calculating the indicators presented in the previous section and selecting the applications to be transformed, it is necessary to make a concrete proposal for the changes to be made to each selected application. A characterization of the most common changes is presented next.

- **Retire**. The application should be discarded.
- **Replace**. The application should be discarded and its functionality should be supported by another application or applications. The replaced application(s) might be new or existing ones whose functionality would be increased with the functionality of the replaced application.
- **Re-platform**. The technology of the application should be upgraded or improved, but the application remains unchanged. Typical scenarios include upgrading operating systems, databases, and application servers and libraries. One may even consider that the change of application language is a re-platform action, for example, from COBOL to Java, since it can be mostly automated and therefore is a technological transformation. Another common re-platform action is the adaptation or migration to the cloud infrastructure.
- **Restructure**. Restructure means changing the application structure or architecture. Restructure includes changing from a two-layer to a three-layer paradigm, or also to the cloud. Quite often restructure comes along with re-platform, but they can be seen as distinct actions.
- **Optimize Sourcing**. This action aims at adjusting the readiness and quality of the teams maintaining the applications to the proper level. It can be the reduction or the increase, depending on business needs and observed impact of the current level of sourcing.
- **Optimize Capacity**. As with sourcing optimization, capacity optimization aims at better adjusting the computing infrastructure (CPU, memory, disk communications) to the actual application needs. It can be increased or decreased.

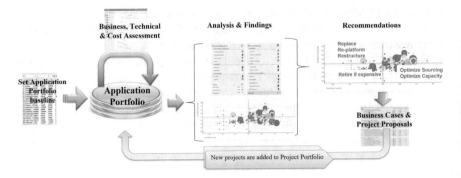

Fig. 10.16 APM project key steps

10.2.4   APM Project Approach

An APM project typically has the following steps (Fig. 10.16):

- **Set Application Portfolio Baseline**. In this step, the list of applications is prepared with the appropriate level of detail, and the existing information associated with each application is compiled in order to minimize the information to be collected through the stakeholders.
- **Business, Technical & Cost Assessment**. In this step, one prepares the questions to be answered by each application's stakeholders, providing the information necessary to calculate the intended indicators. One also needs to identify the stakeholders to be questioned regarding each application. Questions should be mostly indirect and focused on the impact. For example, one does not ask the person responsible for an application if it is critical, but what would have to be done if the application stopped working. Similarly, one does not ask users if an application is slow, but rather how much more productive they would be if the application were faster.
- **Analysis & Findings**. Here, the aforementioned analyzes are carried out and the candidate applications to be the target of a transformation project are identified.
- **Recommendations**. Each identified application will be analyzed and the possibility of its transformation is evaluated. Often, recommendations are related to a group of applications, particularly when it comes to consolidating several applications into one.
- **Business Cases & Project Proposals**. Finally, each recommendation is evaluated in detail and if it is consistent, a transformation project is defined, which will add to the company's portfolio of projects.

10.3   Service Architecture Design

We discuss next how services that fulfill the goals of a service-oriented architecture (SOA) are identified, namely:

1. A service encapsulates a reusable business function.
2. Services have explicitly defined interfaces (contracts) independent of the implementation.
3. Services are loosely coupled and communicate with each other (choreography, orchestration) through protocols independent of the location and of the technology.
4. After a business function has been defined as a service, each service is instantiated in one place and invoked (remotely) in this site by all the applications that use it (thus there are no replicas with potential independent evolutions).

As presented in Sect. 3.3.6, services in the service layer can be structured according to their potential for reuse, as:

- Solution layer services
- Core business layer services
- Utility layer services

As one could expect, service architecture design can follow different approaches. In the bottom-up approach, one starts by creating elementary services around existing applications. In the second stage, these services are aggregated into more complex services. However, this practice leads to the proliferation of services, since it ignores the dependency between applications that support each service. No rules or guidelines for the implementation of new applications are defined in this approach and it ignores the alignment between business information and applications. The bottom-up approach only allows the definition of a set of services that make sense to the set of existing applications in the organization.

In a "top-down" approach to service identification, one starts by the application processes existing in each application and then proposes the Core Business Services (see Fig. 10.17) that better matches application processes needs and that allows an higher potential for reuse.

Finally, the core business services are decomposed in utility services (increasing the reuse).

The top-down approach ensures a high reuse of services for enterprise architectures done from scratch. However, if existing services are available, the middle-out approach is recommended because it considers existing services (see Fig. 10.18).

In the middle-out approach the services realized by core applications are identified first (usually by the IT department). Afterwards, a top-down approach is followed, identifying the business processes and the supporting applications. Next, the core business services are defined by identifying the sequences of automatic activities and the sequences of activities that are common to more than one business process. Finally, the results from the first step (existing IT services) and from the

1. Specify the processes supported by each application.

2. Identify Core Business Services:
   - identify sequences automatic activities.
   - Choose sequences or sequence of fractions with higher potential for reuse.

3. Decompose the Core Business Services in Utility Services, increasing the reuse of these

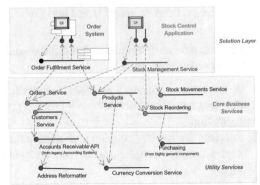

Fig. 10.17 Top-down approach to service identification (Reprinted with permission from Link Consulting, SA)

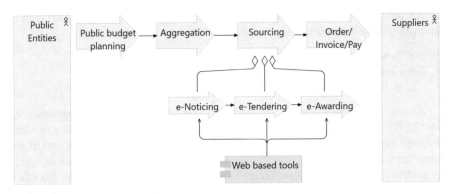

Fig. 10.18 Middle-out approach to service identification

last top-down step are merged into utility services. In this final step the existing IT services and the "required" services (that result from the breakdown of core business services) are compared, and, when possible, the current IT services are reused and aggregated, and only when not available or possible, new services are implemented.

10.4 Exercises

Exercise 10.1

Consider the following example of the relations between information entities and business processes—see Fig. 10.19.

Perform the following steps to identify the "application clusters":

1. Delete irrelevant columns or rows.

Information Entity

	E1	E2	E3	E4	E5	E6	E7
P1	CRUD	CRUD	CRUD				
P2		R	RU				
P3		R	CRUD	R			R
P4			R				
P5				CRUD	RU		CRUD
P6	R	R			RU		
P7		RU			CRUD		
P8	R	R			R	R	
P9					R	CRUD	
P10					R	CRUD	

(left margin label: **Process**)

Fig. 10.19 CRUD relations between information entities (E1 ... E7) and business processes (P1 ... P10)

Information Entity

	E1	E2	E5	E4	E3	E6	E7	E9	E10	E8
P1		CRUD	RU	S1				R		R
P2			RU	CRUD	R				R	
P3	R			R	R	R	R	R	R	
P4	R	CRU		R		R	CRUD		UD	S2
P5					CRUD	CR	R	R		
P6				S4			UD	CRUD S3		S5
P7	R		RU		CRUD	R				CRUD
P8	R	R	RU	CRUD	R			S6 R		S7
P9	R		R				R	CRUD	CRUD	R
P10	R							RU	R	

(left margin label: **Process**)

Fig. 10.20 Information entities, business processes, and current application clusters for the Navy

2. Next, put together processes that create the same entities.
3. Next, put together processes that update (U) entities with the processes that create the entities (C).
4. Identify the "application clusters" considering that the applications (systems) should be as simple as possible, considering three different scenarios:

   a. P1 to P10 are "end-to-end" processes.
   b. P1 to P10 are atomic activities.
   c. P1 to P10 are "end-to-end" processes, but P1 to P3 are processes with high affinity (developed by the same teams).

Exercise 10.2

The Portuguese Navy Enterprise Architecture is summarized in the CRUD matrix in Fig. 10.20.

The information architecture is described by the information entities E1 to E9; and the business process architecture is described by business processes P1 to P10. The CRUD matrix in Fig. 10.20 represents the dependencies (create, read, update, delete) among business processes and information entities. Assume that processes P1–P10 are transactional activities, except for P4 and P7 that are end-to-end business processes. The existing systems of the Navy are identified in the matrix as S1 to S7.

1. Based on the contents of the CRUD matrix, give a concrete example of a misalignment for each alignment dimension between architectures, namely, "processes and information architectures," "information and application architectures," and "process and application architectures."
2. Redesign the CRUD matrix above and identify the maximum number of information systems by applying the alignment heuristics among the processes, information entities, and information systems (business system planning method).
3. List all the integration relationships between each of the systems identified.

Exercise 10.3

Considering the CRUD matrix of Tota Tola company, including the current systems (S1–S5), processes (P1–P10), and information entities (E1–E10). All processes (P1–P10) are atomic—see Fig. 10.21.

1. Consider the alignment dimensions among the architectures presented in Fig. 10.22.

   Which architecture dimensions are misaligned, considering the CRUD matrix? Justify your answer by providing specific examples from the CRUD matrix and the information provided.
2. Propose a new CRUD matrix for the future architecture of Tota Tola, identifying the information system clusters, using the BSP method. Remember that you

	E1	E2	E3	E4	E5	E6	E7	E8	E9	E10	E11
P1				R						UD	
P2	CRUD		R			R		R			
P3		R		R				R		R	R
P4		CRUD	RU								
P5				CRUD							
P6				R			R	CRUD			
P7				UD							
P8		UD							CRUD		
P9	CUD				CUD					RU	
P10									CRUD		

Fig. 10.21 CRUD relations between information entities, business processes, and systems (S1 …S5)

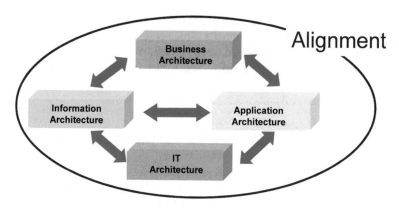

Fig. 10.22 Architecture alignment dimensions

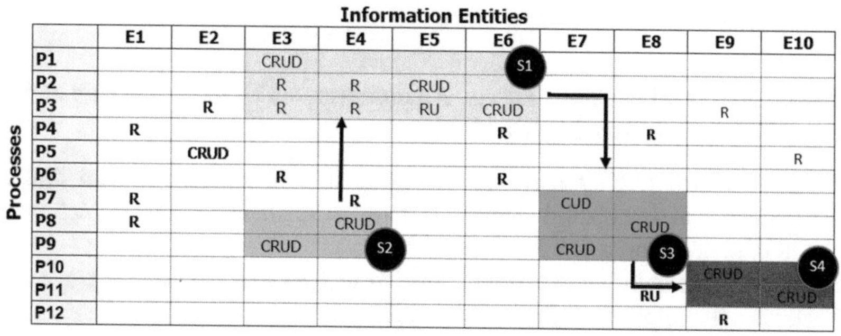

	Information Entities									
	E1	**E2**	**E3**	**E4**	**E5**	**E6**	**E7**	**E8**	**E9**	**E10**
P1			CRUD			S1				
P2			R	R	CRUD					
P3		R	R	R	RU	CRUD			R	
P4	R					R		R		
P5		CRUD								R
P6			R			R				
P7	R			R			CUD			
P8	R			CRUD				CRUD		
P9			CRUD	S2			CRUD	S3		
P10									CRUD	S4
P11								RU		CRUD
P12									R	

Processes (row axis label)

Fig. 10.23 CRUD matrix

should propose systems as small as possible (which means the maximum number of information systems). Also identify the integration among the system clusters.
3. Considering only the information above, in which order would you propose the systems to be implemented? Justify your answer.

Exercise 10.4

Consider the following CRUD matrix with atomic activities P1 to P12 and information entities E1 to E12—see Fig. 10.23.

Consider also the four applications identified in the matrix and the respective integrations.

1. Based on the contents of the CRUD matrix, give a concrete example of a misalignment for each alignment dimension between "processes and information architectures," "information and application architectures," and "process and application architectures." Justify your answer.
2. Identify which of the following architectural implications are a consequence of the principle "Data are maintained in the source application."

a. The source application for all types of data is known.
b. Applications acquire data from the source application.
c. Replication of data is accepted when properly motivated.
d. Replicas are never updated, unless a controlled synchronization mechanism is in place.
e. Data are not copied before it is finalized (completed).

    Justify your answer.

3. Identify in the CRUD matrix above where the principle stated in the preceding paragraph is not fulfilled. Justify your answer.
4. Now identify the correct systems by redesigning the original matrix to ensure the architectural principle above and the alignment heuristics (when possible). Use the BSP (business system planning) method and identify the integration between the systems, as well.

Exercise 10.5

Consider the following CRUD matrix. All processes are atomic, except P4 and P10 (that are end-to-end)—see Fig. 10.24.

1. Propose a new CRUD matrix, identifying the information system clusters. Remember that you should propose systems as small as possible (which means the maximum number of information systems).
2. Considering only the information above, in which order would you propose the systems to be implemented? Justify your answer.

Exercise 10.6

Consider the following CRUD matrix—see Fig. 10.25:

1. Faced with misalignments in the CRUD presented, propose a new set of systems that ensures a complete alignment between architectures. Identify the maximum number of possible information systems. Also identify the proposed integration.

Information Entities

	E1	E2	E3	E4	E5	E6	E7	E8
P1			RU		R	CRUD	RU	
P2	CRUD				R			
P3		R						
P4		CRUD		RU				
P5			CRUD					
P6	R	R		R		R		
P7	RU				CRU			
P8	R			RU				
P9				R		CRUD		
P10							U	U
P 11	R					R		RD

(Left vertical label: **Processes**)

Fig. 10.24 CRUD matrix

Information Entities

	E1	E2	E3	E4	E5	E6
P1	CRUD	RU				
P2		RU	R	R		
P3		CRUD	RU			
P4			CRUD	CRUD	CRUD	
P5	R		R		CRUD	
P6			R		RU	
P7		R			RU	CRUD
P8					R	
P9		R	R	R		R

S1	C17	S3	E19;G22	S5	D24;H25
S2	D17;D19	S4	G23;H23		

Fig. 10.25 CRUD matrix

References

1. P. Sousa, Enterprise architecture alignment heuristics. Microsoft Enterp. Architecture J. 4 (2004)
2. P. Sousa, C. Pereira, *Enterprise Architecture: Business and IT Alignment* (Santa Fe, New Mexico, 2005)
3. S. Spewak, H. Steven, Enterprise architecture planning: developing a blueprint for data, applications and technology, Wiley-QED, 2nd edition, September 1, 1993, ISBN-13: 978-0471599852
4. J. Zachman, A framework for information systems architecture. IBM Syst. J. **26**(3), G321–5298 (1987)
5. G. Carvalho, P. Sousa, Business and information system misalignment: diagnosis, therapy and prophylaxis techniques based on syndromes. Int. J. Comput. Sci. Inf. Syst. **4**(2), 140–157 (2009)
6. G. Carvalho, P. Sousa, Using a medical sciences perspective to harness business and information system misalignment, in *16th European Conference on Information Systems (ECIS)* (2008)
7. G. Carvalho, P. Sousa, Business and information systems misalignment model (bismam): an holistic model leveraged on misalignment and medical sciences approaches, in *RD International Workshop on Business/IT Alignment and Interoperability (BISTAL'08)*, France (2008)
8. G Carvalho, P Sousa, Business and information system misalignment: diagnosis, therapy and prophylaxis techniques based on syndromes. Int. J. Comput. Sci. Inf. Syst. **4**(2), 16 (2008)

Chapter 11
A Method for Enterprise Cartography

Pedro Sousa and André Vasconcelos

Abstract This chapter describes a methodology for developing enterprise cartography in enterprises. The purpose is to support enterprises when producing *AS-IS* and *TO-BE* architectural views with minimal human effort.

As seen in Sect.1.3.1, enterprise cartography has been a reality in various domains, but often with a very limited scope and a predefined set of concepts, focusing mostly on past views of the enterprises.

We aim to implement a mechanism as automatic as possible to produce architectural views of current (AS-IS) and future (*TO-BE*) enterprise states, according to the progress of ongoing and planned transformation initiatives, as depicted in Fig. 11.1.

The upper part of Fig. 11.1 illustrates a scheduling of projects (or transformation initiatives), where one can see that project X execution is scheduled to begin and end at Tm and Tn, respectively, and project Y is expected to end between those dates. In the lower part of the figure, on the left, different types of information sources are presented. Their differences will be discussed in Sect. 11.1.3. At the bottom of the Fig. 11.1, on the right, one shows examples of architectural views generated on-the-fly based on the information collected and existing in the knowledge base (*KB*), which holds the information collected from the different information sources. Each architectural view has a time slider that changes the contents of the view according to the selected point in time. For example, if one moves the time slider to Tn, the generated view will show the expected outcome of project X, as well as the expected outcome of any other project that is planned to end between the current date and Tn. Likewise, whenever a project changes it's conclusion date, the generated views will change accordingly.

In terms of the model described in Chap. 5, both projects and information sources are generators of architectural sentences (Eqs. 5.5 and 5.6) that are loaded into the KB holding the enterprise's architectural model (Eq. 5.9). The architectural views correspond to combinations of the base views (see Sect. 5.2.10) and the time slider allows the generation of views at selected moments in time.

© The Author(s), under exclusive license to Springer Nature Switzerland AG 2022   265
P. Sousa, A. Vasconcelos, *Enterprise Architecture and Cartography*,
The Enterprise Engineering Series, https://doi.org/10.1007/978-3-030-96264-7_11

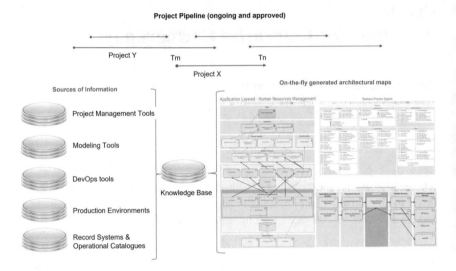

Fig. 11.1 An overview of the intended *EC* project

To assemble the mechanism depicted in Fig. 11.1, we need a tool[1] that is capable of generating architectural views relative to a given point in time. But this is not enough. Such a tool needs to be fed with a continuous flow of information (architectural sentences) that is coherent with the set of concepts and states defined in the meta-model.

In the following sections we present a method to feed the *KB* with the necessary information and produce corresponding architectural views. Similar to many other methods of extract, process and load, typically known as ETL processes, this process addresses specific issues due to the fact that the end result must be an enterprise architecture.

11.1   Phases of the EC Approach

In Fig. 11.2 we present an approach for developing enterprise cartography in an enterprise. It follows quite a straightforward sequence of stages, in a circular manner, so that at each iteration one may increase the scope of the previous iteration. The idea is that in each iteration one deals with a set of concerns, from the requirements to results and then iterate again to address new concerns.

---

[1] Such as Atlas from www.linkconsulting.com.

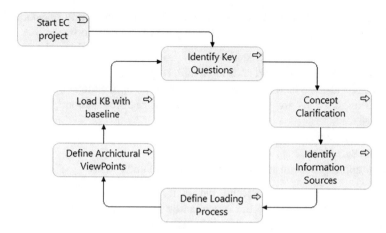

Fig. 11.2 The approach for enterprise cartography

11.1.1   Phase 1: Identify Key Questions

In this phase one tries to establish the list of artifact types (concepts in meta-model) one needs to track down in this iteration. The more the artifact types, the more complex and slower and the more effort required in the iteration. Each artifact type must be fully clarified as well as the multiple manifestations it can exist in the organization.

To identify artifact types, we do a list of questions to be answered at each interaction. Using questions to determine the meta-model helps focus and simplify the explanation of the value to enterprise stakeholders.

For example, let us assume the following list of questions:

- What business processes support each organization capability?
- What applications support each business process?
- What technologies support each application?
- What applications process people's private data?

This list of questions leads to the clarification of the following concepts: *business processes, capability, application, technology,* and *people's private data.* Concept clarification is a complex and effort-consuming task, in particular because one must address the multiple ways that instances of each concept can be observed in the organization.

The selection of questions of each interaction is also a matter that requires some attention. Starting the project with a list of questions as the one presented above might be appropriated if the project is motivated by the administration, thus making sure all communities are involved in the project and at the end of the first interaction one could provide a layered vision of the organization, from strategy to technology.

However, if the project is motivated by a given community, then the questions should involve mostly the concepts of that community. The other communities would be waiting for the results and to be convinced before engaging in the project.

For example, if the project is motivated within the IT community, one could focus on the application and consider the following list of key questions:

- What applications support each business process?
- What technologies support each application?
- What services are provided and requested by each application?
- What applications are being supported (infrastructured, support, licensed) and not used?
- What applications are becoming obsolescent the next years due to unsupported or obsolete technology?
- What applications are structurally dependent of each other?

These questions seem trivial, but the reality is that they might undertake some organization changes before the organization is able to provide an answer in a systematic matter. Quite often it is not clear who, in a company, decides on the existence of a new application in the enterprise or how the application's onboarding process is defined. An even more frequent situation is the lack of consensus on fundamental concepts, such as the concept of application. This is all normal if you consider that the concept of application is not clear at all, not even among IT engineers.

11.1.2   Phase 2: Concept Clarification

After having identified the concepts one needs to clarify the meaning of each concept. In Sect. 11.2 we propose a systematic method for concept clarification. The purpose is to reach a consensus between the different stakeholders with minimum effort.

Clarification often reveals new concepts to add to the meta-model. This can be an entirely straightforward exercise in which one starts with a standard meta-model (e.g., the TOGAF content model or the ArchiMate list of concepts, among others) and extends it as required. A simple situation is when on each interaction one adds more concepts to the previous iteration. Thus, the meta-model must be structured in such a way that it can easily be extended by areas, as the TOGAF content model allows it, foreseeing enrichment in different areas [1].

However, in some cases, one may have to deal with the actual change/evolution of concepts between interactions. The problem arises when there is already information collected in previous interactions, as well as with the information collection procedures already in place. In this respect, it is important that the *KB* allows a class definition to change without the need to change manually its existing instances (objects) in the *KB*.

For example, assume one has changed a class property *protocol* from a simple value into a reference, pointing to instances of class protocol. This change must be supported without the need to invalidate neither the artifacts already kept persistent in the KB nor the work done in the previous interaction.

To allow the evolution in the meta-model in a KB holding information (models), one should define a *meta-model evolution primitive catalog*, with primitives such as *Flatten Hierarchy, Merge Class, Split Class, Property to Class*, and *Class to Property*, among others[2, 3]. Using such a catalog along with the top-down and bottom-up design primitives presented in Chap. 9, one can automate the propagation of meta-model changes to the existing information in the KB [4–6].

A final remark on the topic of concept clarification: in most cases, information concepts are defined for general facts, where people tend to reach a consensus very easily. A simple and trivial definition is usually a good starting point to identify something, but one never knows if it is enough to handle the different manifestations of that concept in the enterprise. In our experience a concept is only defined when one also considers the beginning and end of its life cycle. Even if a concept is well defined in some standard in terms of "being", it is also necessary to define the "becomes" and the "cease to be".

For example, for us humans, the concept of a person should be among the simplest ones to agree upon, and we do not need to discuss and write down what a person is. However, if you are in a room full of people with one corpse on the floor and a pregnant woman in the audience, and ask to the audience how many people there are in the room, you will get different answers regarding the corpse and the person yet to be born.

An even simpler and more common example occurs between different stakeholders in a company. Consider the simple question to different stakeholders in a railway company: how many locomotives does the company have? As is, this question will also lead to different answers from different parties. For the corporate image department, the locomotive that is in the company main hall entrance counts as a locomotive because it must be painted according to the company image, but it does not count as a locomotive for the operational and financial departments. Likewise for the financial department, the locomotives that are being paid but did not arrive yet are likely to count as locomotives, whereas for the operational and image department, such locomotives are not counted as such. Finally, for the operational department only the locomotives that are available to pull train carriages count as such. A dictionary definition of a locomotive is not enough to present proper models for these different stakeholders.

So we need some indicator to tell us whether the definition we have is good enough or needs to be more detailed. We propose the adoption of a simple rule of thumb.

> The level of consensus of a given concept is easily established by asking the stakeholders to enumerate the number of instances of the concept in question. If different stakeholders count different number of instances, then the concept is not clearly defined.

11.1.3 Phase 3: Identify the Best Sources of Information

Once the artifact types and their inter-dependencies are established, one needs to identify the sources of information about the artifacts as effortless as possible. For each artifact type, we identify the best information sources to capture state changes in the artifact's lifecycle: from the moment it is conceived up to the moment it is discarded. Depending on the artifacts, one might consider a broad set of information sources.

In Fig. 11.1, on the left side, one classified the information sources being in different categories according to the time frame of the information they can provide.

- Project management tools provide information about the progress of projects and their milestones. They provide information about the beginning and end of projects, and therefore they can be used to pinpoint in time the models and artifacts associated with such projects or milestones.
- Modeling tools provide models of artifacts about the company's past or future, depending on the projects these models/artifacts are associated with. The models and artifacts associated with a given project will have their life cycle according to project's start and end dates.

  Despite the relevance that models associated with transformation initiatives have for viewing enterprise future states, they are just promises and cannot be taken for granted. Nevertheless, if no other information is available, these models are the best available forecast about enterprise future states.
- DevOps tools are sources of information about what is being built and tested, and therefore are also sources of information about the emerging *AS-IS*. If an artifact is being tested and is associated with a given project, it is likely that it will exist in the enterprise when that project ends.

  Much like the models and artifacts associated with transformation initiatives, artifacts being developed or tested in DevOps tools are just promessis. However, since they refer to a much shorter time frame they are much more likely to become a reality than the artifacts in the previous item.

  Thus, while the plans of the projects give an idea of what the organization will be in the more distant future, the DevOps tools and environments give an idea of the future closer, and probably with greater assertiveness.
- Production Environments, the infrastructure where productive artifacts run, provide information about the current state of the IT infrastructure. They usually say nothing about the organization's past or future states.
- Registration systems and operational catalogs usually provide information about the current artifacts of the enterprise, from organizational units, actors, products, services, contracts, processes, applications, among many others. The future state of these artifacts are likely to exist in models associated with projects that are planned or ongoing.

In all the above cases, the information referred to may also be in simple spreadsheets or office files, rather than in tools or information systems.

In the above sources of information there will most likely be contradictory and omitted information. The general rule is that the closer in time the information refers to the more probability it will have to be true. Thus, whenever an artifact that is planned to be delivered by some project is not seen in systems representing the *AS-IS* after the project completion, one must inquire the responsible of the project about these artifacts.

Another issue one has to consider when processing information from different sources is the possible fact that information coming from different sources might have a different meta-model.

Thus, it is necessary to define the mapping rules to use during importation and exportation. As an example consider the case where the *KB* has the *platform* and *system software* artifact types. However, if the models were produced in ArchiMate, artifacts of both *platform* and *system software* types are likely modeled as instances of *system software*, being distinguished by the fact that *platform* artifacts always aggregate more than one *system software* artifact, and the latter does not aggregate other system software. Thus, one can load them as *platforms* or as *system software* depending on the defined rule outcome.

In general, one must conciliate models that were:

- Written in different notations, with different underlying meta-models.
- Described in different levels of detail.
- Written in different tools. This yields the problem of artifact naming and identification, as presented in the next Sect. 11.1.6.2.

Of course, one cannot build an enterprise architecture without a common set of concepts and ways to visualize them. Thus, one needs an approach to capture information from multiple sources and consolidate it into a single knowledge base, minimizing the changes imposed to each *TO-BE* model produced, as described in the next sections.

The notebooks of the architects involved in a transformation initiative are also sources of information about the future of the enterprise. However, such information is most likely unstructured and difficult to access and process, and so we do not consider them in the context of this book.

11.1.4 Phase 4: Structure the Processes and Tools to Capture Information

EC projects are usually conducted by the enterprise architecture team with the participation of other units or roles, such as project managers, technical leaders, project architects, or solution architects, acting both as a consumer (stakeholders) and a producer of information. In fact, they will likely need information existing in some architectural views and produce information to construct other architectural views.

The participating teams expect the architectural information that exists in the systems they use is captured by the *EC* processes and be used to generate architectural views. Any information that has to be inserted manually will likely be a project point of failure because it means an additional effort has to be made to keep the generated views up to date.

Our approach is, firstly, to look at the tools the teams use to produce and register architecture relevant information and propose the necessary changes so that it can be automatically loaded into the *KB*. This approach allows the loading of information and the production of maps for the teams to use with a minimum negative impact on them. For example, in an enterprise that uses MS Office documents for internal project presentation and description, we can include the tables in those documents to be automatically loaded with the information (the architectural statements) about such project.

Later, after the remaining teams are using the maps generated with the information collected, we can propose more structured ways of obtaining the required information, through either the models or direct introduction in the *KB*.

11.1.5   Phase 5: Define and Configure the Architectural Views

Defining and configuring architectural views to the needs of different stakeholders is a key aspect of *EC*'s success. Stakeholders often prefer views that are combinations of views presented in Sect. 5.2.10, but each with a different level of detail [7].

A very important aspect is that the meta model is too complex for some stakeholders, and so the views they require must be generated under a simpler meta-model, defined per profile. This is very much like the view definition in relational databases, where one can define a query based table that is generated on-the-fly over on the actual tables.

A typical situation is to reduce the number of entities one needs to cross to find the dependency between two concepts, showing only the derived relations instead of the existing ones in the meta-model. For example, on a *KB* with the ArchiMate meta-model, a given user profile might want to explore and navigate the architecture through views where business processes are directly related to applications components without going through application services and application functions in between, whereas other stakeholders demand the full detail.

Because the content presented in architectural views is relative to a moment in time, their generation must take into account the lifecycle of the artifacts and their references. In the previous example, if the services between the business process and the application component are at different stages of their life cycle, what is the criterion for presenting a dependency between the process and the application: when all services are productive or will it be enough one service to be productive for the direct relationship between the business process and the application component to be presented in the simplified architectural view?

In this case it seems easy to agree that one productive service is enough for the relationship between the process and the application to be presented. However, when the relationship is "realization" or "cooperation", one needs to carefully decide the rule to follow so that the stakeholder who asked for a simple architectural view does not have to go into detail to understand it.

11.1.6 Phase 6: Populate the KB with an Initial Baseline

The initial loading of the *KB* is usually done by importing from other systems or from existing spreadsheets with relevant information. This load phase is often run in parallel with phase 5, but always after phase 4 where meta-model-related issues are addressed.

We highlight two aspects worth noting:

- The full vs. incremental loading of the *KB*
- The artifact naming policy

11.1.6.1 Incremental Loading of the KB

Initial *KB* loading is an issue that always gives rise to different opinions. The question is not so much whether the loading of the sources of information is automated or not, but more whether it is complete and correct or not. The will of the architecture team to present a mostly complete and correct architecture before disclosing the views to all the stakeholders of the company is always a point of discussion in EC projects.

On the one hand, if the views disclosed are very incomplete and with wrong facts, then the other stakeholders will simply ignore and discredit the whole project. On the other hand, if one expects to have complete and correct information to then disseminate the architectural views, then one never discloses any view ever.

Our proposal is to load the *KB* and disclose the architectural views project by project. The higher the pace of transformation, the more projects exist and the faster the *KB* becomes populated.

Another aspect is whether you start loading the *AS-IS* or the TO-BE as well. The project by project loading allows the loading of both the *AS-IS* that is necessary to know for the realization of the project, as well as the TO-BE that is intended to reach with the project. Since both views are useful for project execution, they will naturally be viewed and validated by the project team, which is a guarantee of its completeness and correctness.

11.1.6.2 Naming Enterprise Artifacts

The problem of naming in enterprise architecture has not been an issue, due to the narrow context where observation is performed.

It is commonly expected artifacts to be registered in the KB with a name and an identifier. The name is in human readable form and the ID assures the uniqueness of that artifact [8], in case different artifacts have the same name.

The use of 128-bit object identifiers (OIDs, also known as UUIDs) ensures uniqueness for most practical purposes even when generated by different and independent tools.

However, in the scenario where one gathers information from different sources of information, the same artifact may exist in different tools, each with its own generated OID. So, when consolidating models from multiple modeling tools, one needs to know and manage the correspondence of artifact OIDs between the different systems or tools.

Change is also a factor against the use of OIDs. Consider that a process modeling tool holds a model of the *sales process* in which the *CRM* application is used to inquire the status of client payments. Later, the process changes, and instead of using the *CRM* application, it now uses the *ERP* application for the same purpose. This change can be done simply by changing the application name, from *CRM* to *ERP*. However, in this case, the name has changed but the OID in the process modeling tool is the same, although the enterprise artifact has changed. This leads to a situation where the same object now refers to a different enterprise artifact, breaking the existing binding between OIDs and enterprise artifacts even in the context of a single tool.

User-defined object names can make the task of matching objects between sources easy, if object names correspond to the names of the artifacts in the enterprise. However, in most cases, object names used are not unique, since uniqueness has been assured by OIDs.

We propose a different approach where identification and denotation are established by user-defined object names, and OIDs are left for specific purposes such as audit traces. This approach implies that, from the user perspective, artifacts (objects) of the same type (class) cannot have the same name.

In practice this can be a strong restriction in large enterprises where one could expect to have multiple teams generating names for their artifacts.

This issue was resolved decades ago in the relational model, where identity is ensured by concatenation of properties with meaningful user defined names. From an *EC* perspective, the most common solution is to concatenate the structural object chain transparently to the user. For example, a component X of application Y of a Z-company might have the name Z/Y/X. This name will have to be managed whenever any of its components (X, Y, or Z) change its name. This implies that users can edit objects' names, regardless of the fact they are also unique names. For example, in the case of a *National Health System*, one could expect to have *actors* with the same name in different hospitals.

We recommend artifacts to be names in a hierarchical name space, as URLs in the web:

OrganizationName/ClassName/ArtifactNameField_N. ... .ArtifactNameField_0.

The concatenation of the fields *ArtifactNameField_N* to *ArtifactNameField_0* must be unique within the objects of the same *ClassName*. All fields are optional (i.e., can be *null*), except the last one (*ArtifactNameField_0*) that cannot be null.

The presentation of names should be adjusted automatically to the context in which objects appear. Following the previous example, the presentation of the Z/Y/X component, in the structure view of the Y application, you can omit the name hierarchy (Z/Y/), presenting the component only with the name X.

11.2 A Method for Concept Clarification

One could argue that it is enough to choose a modeling notation or enterprise architecture framework to have a complete set of concepts, each clearly explained and clarified. In fact, ArchiMate 3 defines 58 concepts (not counting relation types) and TOGAF content model presents 35 concepts (also not counting relationship types).

However, the definitions in these frameworks are often not detailed to represent the multiple manifestations of a particular concept that can be observed in the actual organization, as we saw in Sect. 11.1.2.

Thus, it is appropriate to have a systematic way of clarifying the concepts of the meta-model. The method we present below is based on the following analyses:

- Identification of relevant properties. In this first stage one identifies the properties that should be addressed in the definition of the concept, including identification and lifecycle.
- Identification of relevant perspectives. In this second stage one identifies the different stakeholders and their perspectives that need to be considered to capture the multiple manifestations of the concept that can be observed in the enterprise.
- Concept representation. Finally, in this third stage one defines the fundamental views to apply for the representation and communication of instances of that concept.

We now detail each step of the approach in the following sections.

11.2.1 Identification of Relevant Properties

The following properties and the following aspects are relevant in the definition of a concept:

- **Life cycle**. The life cycle of the artifact, from the moment it is conceived until it is discontinued, as well as the identification of intermediate states.
- **Related Concepts**. The clarification of concepts that are directly related to the concept being discussed is essential to clarify the concept itself, because it avoids possible overlaps between concepts and clarifies the function and the context of its existence.
- The **Structure**. The clarification of the elements that compose the concept is also an important issue in the definition of the concept and in the systematization of its representation.
- The **Integration**. The possible integration between the concept's instances is the last considered aspect.

These are the aspects one considers relevant in order to clearly define a concept. Again, each of these aspects should be addressed up to the point where it becomes evident that different people can count the same number of concept instances.

11.2.2   Identification of Relevant Perspectives

The perspectives to consider are those of the different stakeholders who somehow interact with the concept. A simple way to identify the different perspectives is to consider the architectural layers in which your stakeholders are included. Thus, for the artifacts of the application layer, we consider three perspectives:

- Business. The business perspective is the perspective of the end users, the ones that use IT to execute the inherent functions of their activities in the context of processes and the tasks defined in the organization.

  This perspective pursues functional logic, and is independent of how IT is implemented and operationalized.
- Information Systems. This perspective is focused on the problems of construction and maintenance of information systems, being independent of the infrastructure. Consequently, this perspective pursues a constructional logic and should address the engineering aspects related with the construction and maintenance of information systems.
- Technology. This perspective captures the issues related to the execution and operation of the information systems. This perspective pursues an operational logic, enhancing the necessary operational aspects for the execution of information systems. Issues such as capacity (cpu, ram, disk, communications) business continuity and operating costs are just examples of the concerns addressed in this perspective.

11.2.3   Concept Representation

After discussing the relevant properties and perspectives of stakeholders, we recommend discussing the appropriate architectural views to represent the concepts. This step is a validation of the above because, to adjust the views of each interested party, one must use the results of previous discussions.

The choice of views to use in the visualization of concepts should start with the fundamental architectural views (Organic, Context, Structure, and Integration) seen in Sect. 5.2.10. These can be combined into more complex views, such as the layer view. In this view, the layers above the concept under analysis indicate what it supports and the layers below the concept under analysis indicate what it requires to operate.

The approach described in this section may also be applied to enrich the meta-model with additional concepts.

We present in Sect. 11.2.4 its application to enrich the application concept in the EA meta-model.

11.2.4 An Example: Clarifying the Application Concept

Many organizations lack a clear definition of applications and different actors count different number of applications. A simple mapping of all the information systems in an application catalog is a challenge.

In many medium-sized companies, the application catalog can include many disparate entries, ranging from small software programs to large banking solutions. However, without considering the effort of an adequate clarification and definition of the notion of application, the catalog is far from having the expected benefits, driven by the lack of consensual interpretation of what is an "application" inside the enterprise.

It is a well-known fact that concept clarification is a complex endeavor. Clarification may encompass both a functional and a constructional description, and in most situations both descriptions are needed. However, the clarification of such key concepts in the IT domain rarely occurs in a systematic manner, simply because professionals of the IT community assume the concept is clear enough. This assumption is further reinforced by the fact that many modeling languages define very precise symbols and rules to represent and relate ill-defined concepts, as happens in some of the most prominent frameworks and modeling languages.

The TOGAF Technical Reference Model [1] considers two types of applications: infrastructure and business applications. However, this is a very simple classification schema that does not address fundamental issues in IT management. From an IT and business alignment point of view, a spreadsheet holding data and business rules is a business application, as SAP ERP or any other software package. But from a management and day-to-day IT operations, they have little in common.

ArchiMate [9] refers to the concept of application component as a self-contained part of a system that encapsulates its contents and exposes its functionality through a set of interfaces. This is true within a large range of scenarios; however, it does not help to establish a good enough application concept in order to simplify the communication and the actual work within the IT communities.

We start by stating that the concept of application exists and is relevant between the business units. In fact, business communities use the names of applications in many contexts (e.g., procedure manuals, risk management, and so on). However, quite often, they are not referring to any specific software components, but only to their perception of them. Moreover, from the point of view of *EC*, if one observes the phrase "to register a new employee, go to application X and choose menu Y...", in a "Human Resource" procedure manual can we assume that there is an application, even if with a name other than X? This is a problem because it hard-wires a given software element to a set of functionalities and interfaces, removing a degree of freedom from IT to choose the best implementation solutions.

For example, consider the case where the IT decides to provide access to applications via an intranet portal, that just forwards the requests to the proper application, forcing the business to revise documents and procedures. This kind of decisions should not be made more difficult by naming conventions. The situation is even worse if the application is named after the platform or software package used to develop the application.

Furthermore, we cannot expect the business to stop referring to applications and refer only to services and interfaces, as the most purists of Archimate advocate. In fact, we claim that being able to represent an "Application Component" at the business level without this representation bringing the inconveniences that we saw earlier is fundamental for the independence between IT and the Business.

There are many more examples where it is fundamental to decouple decisions at the functional level, from the decisions at the IT system level and also from the IT operation level. The decoupling of such decisions starts with a taxonomy of concepts that must be wide enough to classify a Microsoft Excel program and the Microsoft Excel data file the users create and use, but also the large software packages and software developed in-house.

The proposal for the clarification of the application concept is founded on the different needs of the business, information system, and infrastructure perspectives. The concept is desegregated into different ones, each addressing specific logic and purposes:

- The business solution concept, in the business perspective
- The solution, application, component, and release concepts, in the information system perspective
- The application release and system software concepts, in the infrastructure perspective

In Fig. 11.3 we represent the concepts we considered fundamental for the clarification and understanding of an information system, commonly modeled as "application component" in ArchiMate.

In the business layer, the information system concept is represented by a single concept, the *business solution*, which provides functions to the end users, the participants of the business processes. The business solutions are also associated with business actors and information entities.

As stated before, in ArchiMate there is no representation of software at the business layer. While this might make perfect sense in engineering terms (of how it works), we claim that having such a proxy for software at the business layer is a very practical solution to concrete problems that actual organization has as discussed in Sect. 11.2.4.1. The corresponding concepts in ArchiMate to the business solution would be the application services and the application interfaces that are visible and accessible to the business.

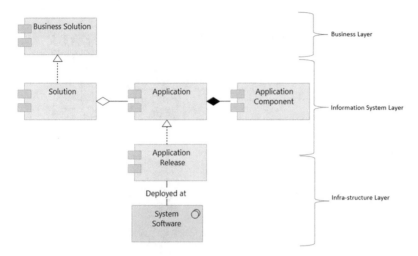

Fig. 11.3 The concept of "Application" that resulted from the proposed method for the clarification of concepts

As presented in Fig. 11.3, we consider four concepts to cover the architectural issues that information system engineers must deal in the construction of IT that realizes the business solutions:

- Solution, which represents an aggregation of deployable elements of the solution being constructed. It is the highest abstraction software artifact that implements and provides the application functions available to the business.
- Application, which represents a single deployable element. A "program" would be the most appropriate word, since it matches with the notion of a minimal unit of deployment, execution and failure. However it would be hardly accepted in most enterprises. An application can have a release that in turn can be deployed and executed in some environment.
- Application Component, which represents the constructive elements of an application. Application components cannot be deployed standalone. They are linked together to form an application. So, an application is composed of application components.
- Application release, which represents the executable manifestation of the application.

  In ArchiMate, an application release should be more properly modeled as an artifact rather than as an application component. However, this option would lead to the use of the artifact concept where people expect to see an application. The reason is the fact that one can only observe running or deployed applications in the organization and only a deployable application realizes services. In fact an application component is hardly an observable element within an enterprise.

In Fig. 11.4 we present an example of the previous concepts. At the top, there are three business solutions, the first two realized by a single solution and the third one realized by both a solution and an application. HR and Security are classified

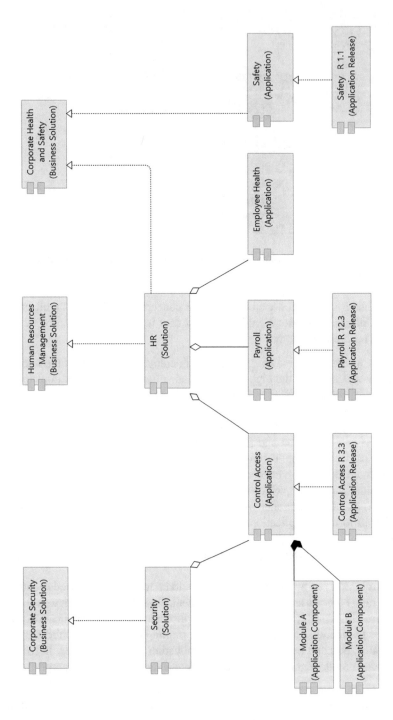

Fig. 11.4 An instantiation of the concepts presented in Fig. 11.3

as a solution because they aggregate elements realized by releases. One expects this classification to be done automatically (on-the-fly) by the tool when generating the architectural views, since this scenario may evolve with time.

The application control access is part of two solutions, the security and the HR, and has two application components, Module A and Module B. This means that neither Module A or B are deployable and able to be executed on their own. They are used to build an executable image of control access application. If one fails the other also fails because they are executed as one. Finally, one can see three application releases, the executable image of applications.

Next, we present the step by step execution of the method presented in Sect. 11.2.

11.2.4.1 Concepts at Business Layer

A business solution is a logical aggregation of functions provided by the IT. A business solution has a business actor that governs and decides how the functions will evolve, and thus decides the overall lifecycle from a business perspective. A business solution also manages business information that we refer to as information entities. The business solution concept does not express any constraint regarding the IS perspective (construction) or infrastructure (operation), the reason being the fact that there is an N to N mapping between business solutions and solutions. For example, one may decide to discontinue a business solution but the IT may decide to keep the solution up and running because it also supports other business solutions.

- Business Solution Lifecycle and Enumeration.

    The proposed lifecycle for a business solution has four major stages: conception, development, production, and decommissioned.

    The production stage can assume any sub-stage (investment, maintenance, and deprecated) in any order. The investment expresses a phase when the organization is investing in the business solution. The maintenance dictates that the organization is maintaining the functional and operational level of the business solution. The decommissioning expresses that the organization is reducing the effort associated with the business solution and consequently reducing the level of operation. As said before, the lifecycle of a business solution does not determine the lifecycle of the underlying solution.

    The lifecycle stages were considered as the basis for the establishment of the enumeration of the concept, allowing the following different counts:

    - Number of business solutions in conception
    - Number of business solutions in development
    - Number of business solutions in production

- Business Solution Related Concepts.
  As implied in the model presented in Fig. 11.3, there are a few premises inherent to the solution concept:

  – A business solution has at least one association with a business process.
  – A business solution provides at least a business function.
  – A business solution has at least one association with an information entity.
  – A business solution has someone that is responsible for its functionality.

- Business Solution Structure. A business solution is composed of sub-solutions. The decomposition criterion is majorly influenced by functional complexity, even though it may be reasonable to account for other influences such as security, where one would group the business function by access level. A business solution hierarchy is an instrument of structuring the business functions and of the way the IT provides services to the business. We also identify the following premises surrounding the business sub-solution notion:

  – A business sub-solution is not subject to solution enumerations.
  – A business sub-solution has the same lifecycle as the solution; however, it may be in a different phase.
  – A business sub-solution belongs to one and only one business solution.

  A business sub-solution can be mapped to business processes, even though it is counted individually when inquiring about the amount of solutions. From an organic point of view, the solutions should be placed in a functional hierarchy.
- Business Solution Integration. From a business perspective we can consider the possibility that two business solutions trade information between themselves and are, by consequence, integrated. However, the integration of business solutions did not come about as a useful constructor and was deemed irrelevant.

The advantages of considering the representation of software in the business layer as a business solution concept are many, including:

- Business people can name an information system independently of how it is named by the IT community. This seems an irrelevant argument, but it is in fact a very relevant one, since it is a name that appears in many business documents and activity description.
  This means that when one finds a sentence as "... *to register a new employee one must open the menu X on application Y* ..." the term "*application Y*" refers to a business solution and not to a solution or application.
  When the IT decides to rebuild the solutions and applications that support the business solution designated as "*application Y*" by the business, one does not need to update the many business documents where the term "*application Y*" appears.
- Business people are able to manage solutions independently of how they are supported by the underlying applications. For example, if different subsets of functionalities of a given solution need to be managed differently, by different

persons, then the solution can be split into two solutions, each with its own budget and responsible person. This decision is independent of how both subsets of functionalities are supported at the information system level, whether under the same application or if in different ones.

11.2.4.2   Concepts at Information System Layer

An application is an artifact in the information system perspective which implements and/or provides the business functions.

However, as presented in Fig. 11.3, the above concept needs to be further detailed because it is too generic to match the complexity of the observed reality.

All business functions provided to the end user by business solutions are provided by applications. For each business solution there is at least one solution or application that provides the respective business functions. The functions can be implemented by the application or solution itself, or by another application with which the application is integrated with. Applications may be integrated with other applications and with repositories through the application's components. The components are referenced in the structure view.

- Application Lifecycle and Enumeration. The application lifecycle is equal to the business solution lifecycle. However, coherence rules between the stages and phases of the concept's lifecycles should be considered. Regarding enumeration, the ways identified to count the applications are equal to the ones of the business solution enumeration.
- Application-Related Concepts. We identified the following premises that are inherent to the application concept (also applies to the solution concept):

  - An application is executed on at least one platform.
  - An application should have at least one associated solution. The association can be direct or indirect through another application that provides business functions implemented by the former. If the solution has sub-solutions, the association is established by the sub-solutions.
  - An application implements at least one business function.
  - An application supports information persistence, either directly through an internal repository or via integration with an external repository.
  - Applications trade information between themselves and between external repositories and thus are integrated with other application and repositories. Each integration is a relationship between integrated entities and matches an instance of the integration concept.

- Application Structure.
  An application is composed of four types of components:

  - Presentation components, which provide the business functions to the human users. The detail of these components is typically determined by technology issues. Consider, for example, an application that provides an interface view through SMS and another via web. In this scenario one should consider two presentation components.

– Core components implement the business functions. Thus, different components are mostly justified by functional aspects, although technological considerations may arise, for example, when components require different execution environments.
– Connectors that are required to establish the integrations. These connectors are represented whenever a specific parameterization is required for the integration.

The integration concept expresses a dependency between two entities and it is materialized in the information flows that those entities exchange. Therefore, the integration does not just cover the active elements that establish the communication but the flows through these elements. Various information flows can be assigned to a single integration. Integration implies that a pair of connectors exists. If there are different ways of communication between two applications that require various pairs, for example, an information transfer via web services and another via file transfer, then there are two integrations between the entities. The sole existence of connectors between applications does not imply the existence of integration because such would suggest that there was information transfer between them. Take, for example, three applications A, B and C, which have connectors to a certain communication platform, but A only exchanges information with B, and B only has trades with C. In this case there is no integration between applications A and C, because there are no flows between them.

– Repositories are components that ensure the persistence of the information managed by the application; they can relate to databases, system folders, or any other way of persistence. An application can also access information maintained in external repositories through the connectors.

From the standpoint of its structure a repository may be as complex as an application, taking all kinds of components that an application may have: presentation components, core components, connectors, and internal repositories. A repository with a back office that allows visual access to the database tables has a presentation component. Besides the business information, a repository can also store information of database accesses, logs, for example. Finally, the integration components allow integration of various applications with different technologies and protocols. Therefore, what characterizes a repository is not only its structure but the fact that its main function is to store information.

Notice that a component hardly has only one of the previous four functions. In fact most components have two or more of the functions. But this is not a structure-based classification but rather a functional one. For example, a message middleware component can have a database to store and replay message flows. This does not make a message middleware a database. However, if for any reason, one uses a message middleware fundamentally as a way to store and retrieve data, much as in a database, then the message middleware component should be classified as a persistent component, regardless of whether it was designed and marketed as a communication component.

A final comment between the fundamental difference between a communication and a persistent components: in a persistent component one expects to be able to select the order of retrieval of the information regardless of the order of arrival to the database. One can write A and then B, and later read B and then A. In a communication system the reading order is not independent of the writing order.

- Application Integration. Application integration expresses how the application components are integrated with the remaining applications and repositories.

  A connector can support more than one integration, if its configuration is common to those integrations. Nevertheless, a connector is associated with an endpoint and therefore two connectors exist for each integration, one for each integrated entity.

The advantages of this proposal of application concept are:

- IT staff can manage applications mostly driven by a constructive rationale, since constructive elements are kept hidden from business areas and from the functional aspects that drive them. For example, changing the applications or platforms that support a given solution does not require changes in the way business refers to it.
- IT staff knows that applications, integrations, and repositories have organization-specific knowledge (code and data) that must be protected and maintained. On the contrary, system software is off-the-shelf software. We claim that acquired technology should always be modeled as system software, and not as applications, regardless of the functions and services provided. The advantages are many:

  (i) The applications are unique entities (a singleton), as they instantiate the company's requirements, while the system software is always an acquired replica.
  (ii) Companies have to manage the knowledge of the construction and behavior of the applications, because no one else can do it for them, whereas the knowledge management of the system software is done by the manufacturer.
  (iii) When companies need experts in some system software, they go to the market, but when they need experts in their applications, they must do the training themselves.
  (iv) Companies have to make backups and protect their applications, but not the system software.
  (v) Normally the cost structure of the applications is associated with the effort (of construction), whereas in system software it is associated with its use and operation.

(vi) Regardless the existing dependencies, companies decide the life-cycle and evolution of their applications, whereas they have no saying regarding the life-cycle of system software.

For example, one employee spends hours developing formulas and feeding data into an MS-Excel spreadsheet, the MS-Excel spreadsheet (.xls file) should be modeled as an application (not as data), whereas the MS-Excel.exe should be modeled as system software. Likewise, when effort is spent developing ABAP scripts and configuration tables into the SAP business solution, the ABAP and the configured tables should be modeled as an application whereas the SAP business solution should be modeled as a system software.

11.2.4.2.1   Determining the Composition of an Application

As we have already mentioned, there are situations where it is not obvious to identify the structural elements of an application. It should be noted that by elements of an application we are not just talking about instances of the concept "application components". In fact, even in ArchiMate, interfaces are also structural elements of an application. By structural elements of an application we understand all the parts that make the whole of the application.

When we have to decide whether or not a certain artifact is part of an application, many of us are often influenced both by the technology it uses to interact with the remaining artifacts of the application as well as by the different execution contexts of each artifact.

Consider the example of an ABAP script that executes in SAP (running on Windows Server) and returns some data to a CRM application (or solution when considering the concepts of Fig. 11.3) that runs in linux in a remote node. The CRM application calls ABAP script via some REST services API. In this case, the ABAP script has a specific execution environment and is structurally decoupled from the CRM application.

In this scenario, most architects would consider the ABAP script as an element of the SAP application that serves the CRM application. However, this may not be the best decision.

In what conditions can the ABAP script be considered an element of the CRM application, rather than an element of the SAP application? Consider the scenario where ABAP script and REST service:

- were developed and are maintained by the same project/team that has developed and maintains the CRM application.
- behave as defined by the manager responsible for the CRM application
- serve no other purpose than serving the CRM application.

In this case, it is clear that the purpose and sole benefits of the ABAP script is to enable the execution of the CRM application. If the SAP is discarded, a replacement of the SCRIPT must be provided. Should the CRM application be discarded, the SCRIPT should also be discarded.

Rather than claiming that in the above scenario the ABAP SCRIPT and the REST service must be considered as structural elements of the CRM solution, we claim that companies must establish the criteria that allows one to decide when collaborating elements are parts of the same application or not, being just an integration between distinctive applications. A simple rule of thumb is:

A is an element of B if its sole purpose is to serve B, and therefore it can be discarded whenever B is discarded.

We claim the benefits of such a criteria overcomes its drawbacks, since structure is aligned with purposefulness. The drawback is that architectural structure must be computed and is no longer static.[2]

11.2.4.3   Concepts at the Infrastructure Layer

With regard to the concept of application as perceived by the infrastructure, we consider it to be data and code that execute in one or a set of system software, which we call platform.

A platform is an execution environment of applications and that may include different forms of technologies. One can consider various types of platforms; such classification is influenced by the type/function of applications that are executed on each platform. For example, integration platforms support the execution of connectors by which applications and repositories support their integrations.

Quite often, it corresponds to technology or a system software in ArchiMate parlance. Thus, we use the following platform concepts:

- Platform lifecycle and enumeration. The platform lifecycle is equal to the solution and application lifecycles. However, coherence rules between the stages and phases of the concept's lifecycles should be considered. Regarding enumeration, the ways identified to count the platforms are equal to the ones of the applications.
- Platform-Related Concepts. In terms of relationships with other identified concepts, a platform has the following premises:

  - The execution of a platform may be supported by another platform.
  - A platform supports the execution of at least one application, whether it belongs to an application or a repository. Such support can be direct or indirect. The latter implies that the platform supports the execution of another platform that supports the execution of one or more applications.
  - A platform aggregates at least one technology.

---

[2] In the Atlas tool by www.linkconsulting.com this computation is performed on-the-fly not only when an architectural view is displayed, but also when the time bar moves back and forward in time.

- Platform Structure. As stated before, from the standpoint of its structure, a platform may be as complex as an application, taking all kinds of components that an application may have: presentation components, core components, connectors, and internal repositories. Therefore, it is possible to consider that the structure view of the platform structure is identical to the application structure. However, that approach was not perceived to be the most useful to IT from the infrastructure perspective. A preferable way to express the structure of a platform is in terms of the technologies and modules it encompasses. The notion of technologies included in a platform concerned with the ability to support the operation of such technology, for example, operating systems, programing languages, communication protocols, etc. The notion of a module of a platform is more of a functional and licensing-related concept than a technological one.
- Platform Integration. As in the solution concept, the notion of platform integration was not considered useful at this level, and therefore no view is defined.

11.3   Exercises

This section presents enterprise cartography exercises.

Exercise 11.1

A credit bureau company (hereafter designated by *SeaExp*) provides digital services for their customers, with several information about companies, people, and general financial information. Acting as a general business information provider, they are mostly dependent on how they can gather and process information from their partners to process and correlate. With a strong transformation strategic plan, *SeaExp* needed tools to monitor the progress of its strategic roadmap.

SeaExp had a strategic plan for the entire IT that is embodied in roadmaps for the key business and technologic units of the company. These roadmaps set the targets to achieve for each area over the next 5 years. These targets are defined regarding their maturity level measured on a five-level scale. At the end of each year, each area submits a plan with the initiatives proposed for the coming year. If approved, these initiatives become real projects. Then, 1 year after, each area evaluates the progress achieved and updates the roadmap accordingly.

Roadmaps were manually maintained in many Microsoft Excel sheets, requiring a significant effort to update the roadmaps according to the results of the projects.

Your task is to design, plan, and implement an instrument that enables the integrated management of architectural views, project results, and the roadmap progress. More specifically, this tool should allow *SeaExp* to:

- Have an integrated and up-to-date view of the *AS-IS* of business and IT architecture, by consolidation of information from different sources
- Have a view of the emerging *AS-IS* state of the business and IT architecture based on the foreseen results of ongoing and planned projects

- Have the ability to identify the progress of each roadmap updated according to the projects' progression

The immediate result of the project should be to provide to the various areas of IT consolidated and updated views of the architecture of *SeaExp*: consolidated, because it results from the information provided from different areas, and updated, because it results from information sources maintained by the various areas with transparent processes in an automated manner.

Since each group shared its information with other areas, the project entails a substantial transformation in the enterprise, as it homogenized languages and tools. In this regard, the *KB* meta-model is a valuable asset because it identifies the concepts familiar to the various areas.

Following the project approach presented in this chapter, the different areas had identified 82 relevant questions, leading to a meta-model with 32 concepts. Each of the areas provided the information to be loaded in the knowledge base (KB), both regarding the roadmaps and the reality of the enterprise at different levels: processes, skills, application, and technologies. The architectural maps were defined in sessions with each of the areas.

Among the 82 relevant questions, we state a few:

- What are the current technological platforms and how will they evolve over time?
- What are the applications affected by each technological platform?
- What are the IT technological drivers?
- What technologies affect the *SeaExp* operations in the next years?
- What is the role of each department in the development of IT?

Given the above context, answer the following questions:

1. Considering the relevant questions stated above, what are the key concepts that need to be clarified?
2. How are they related with ArchiMate 3.0 concepts?
3. Could you suggest possible sources of information for each concept, both for *AS-IS* and *TO-BE*?

Exercise 11.2

The IT department of an organization (here in referred as *GlobalIT*) provides IT services and support to several national defense organizations. *GlobalIT* adopted ITIL [10] processes to improve the quality of its support services. Although the processes were defined, there was still much to improve in the description of information and concepts among the different teams involved in the execution of these operations.

Each technical area managed information relating to their respective functions and technical competencies. This information was not integrated or even shared, as each technical area had its own database with related information. One example was the lack of a coherent service catalog, since each technical service area had identified their services at different levels of granularity and fails to integrate them into a single one.

The purpose of the project is to provide the *GlobalIT* with a *KB* that is common to the various technical teams, homogenizing terms and concepts and ensuring the coherence of information used in the execution of ITIL processes. To structure the information sources, *GlobalIT* had to clarify the semantics of each concept and their relationships. They identified the information sources from each technical area in the meta-model. From the identified information, *GlobalIT* developed the architectural layers: infrastructure architecture involving the servers and networking views, data architecture with databases and instances, and application architecture.

Given the above context, answer the following questions:

1. What are the key concepts that should be in the GlobalIT meta-model?
2. How are these concepts related with ArchiMate 3.0 concepts?

Exercise 11.3

The client referred in this case study is a retail bank that operates in the Iberian Peninsula and serves almost two million customers (individuals, companies, and institutions) through its multi-channel distribution network comprising around 650 retail branches.

The bank already had an *EA* portal on their intranet to support the registration of information regarding application and technology architectures. The intranet portal included a large number of features such as a wiki, with a considerable amount of articles that described the processes and system architecture and which established an entry point for all documentation deemed more technical.

With this project, the bank was addressing several challenges. The first one was to develop the bank's *EA* practice, by improving the *EA* intranet portal to support the communication and awareness of the architecture between all stakeholders, from infrastructure teams to business areas.

The second challenge was the need to effortlessly maintain architectural representations. The bank had an experience in EA, since it went through the process of using a modeling tool to produce representations and models of its IT architecture. The approach followed was based on a central repository holding all models, each designed manually with an *EA* tool. This approach required a substantial effort to keep them up to date, in particular if one considers the consolidation of the models produced in different projects into a single and enterprise-wide view of the IT landscape. So, the maintenance effort to keep the *EA* representations was a key concern of this project. and the bank stated that "if an architectural view cannot be generated automatically with up-to-date information, then it cannot be presented in the *EA* portal." The third challenge was the need to keep audience's learning curve regarding the usage of the architecture intranet portal as lean as possible. The fourth challenge was the integration of the SOA initiative in the enterprise architecture initiative.

The project aimed at the implementation and deployment of an *EA* solution fully integrated into the existing intranet, so that all back-office housekeeping activities could be done in a seamless manner on the bank's intranet. The bank also wanted to address other architectures in domains they considered relevant, even though they did not have much information to start with, namely, business, information, user experience, and normative architectures. Both information and business architectures were domains that the bank planned to address in this project, starting with the definition in the meta-model, where the level of detail needed and how the relations with the remaining architectures are established became clear.

The user experience architecture concerns with the definition of patterns to allow the same concept (client, address, account, and so on) to appear to the user with the same paradigms, regardless of the interface and application where such experience occurs. Finally, the normative architecture structures all information regarding architectural principles, rules, best practices, and technical articles among other information. Articles represent a real knowledge base, and a wiki platform allows live interaction with end users.

The architecture views were generated on the fly and embedded in a seamless manner with the bank's intranet portal. Architectural views are the entry point to access any IT documentation, and knowledge kept in wikis. The information necessary to generate the architectural maps had to be harvested from various sources, such as Microsoft SharePoint[3] and Oracle Enterprise Repository,[4] among others.

This approach enables not only the role of the architecture views in understanding the complexities of the business and the IT underneath, but also a better and more efficient collaboration between the different stakeholders. This is expected to have a positive feedback on the use of the *EA* Internet portal as a cooperation and communication platform and in people communication and collaboration.

Given the above context, answer the following questions:

1. Explain your approach to ensure reduced maintenance effort to keep the EA representations up to date.
2. How do you propose to ensure that the EC repository supports architectures in domains that the bank does not have yet much information? How do you propose to define the concepts of meta-model for these unknown domains?

References

1. The Open Group, Togaf version 9.1 (2011)
2. G. Wachsmuth, Metamodel adaptation and model co-adaptation, in *The European Conference on Object-Oriented Programming*, vol. 4609 (ECOOP, 2007), pp. 600–624

---

[3] https://www.microsoft.com/pt-pt/microsoft-365/sharepoint/.

[4] https://www.oracle.com/middleware/technologies/enterprise-repository.html.

3. A. Cicchetti, D. Di Ruscio, R. Eramo, A. Pierantonio, Automating co-evolution in model-driven engineering, in *Proceedings of the 12th IEEE International Enterprise Distributed Object Computing Conference* (IEEE Computer Society, Washington, 2008), pp. 222–231
4. N. Silva, F. Ferreira, P. Sousa, M. Mira Da Silva, Automating the migration of enterprise architecture models. Int. J. Inf. Syst. Model. Design (IJISMD), **7**(2), 72–90 (2016). https://doi.org/10.4018/IJISMD.2016040104
5. N. Silva, M. Mira Da Silva, P. Sousa, A tool for supporting the co-evolution of enterprise architecture meta-models and models, in *27th International Conference on Information Systems Development*, Lund (2018)
6. N. Silva, P. Sousa, M. Mira Da Silva, Co-evoc: an enterprise architecture model co-evolution operations catalog, in *24th Americas Conference on Information Systems*, New Orleans (2018)
7. The Open Group, *ArchiMate® 2.1 Specification* (Van Haren Publishing, Zaltbommel, 2015)
8. P. Sousa, A. Rito, J. Alves Marques, Object identifiers and identity: a naming issue, in *IEEE Proceedings of the 4th International Workshop on Object Orientation in Operating Systems*, Lund (1995)
9. The Open Group, Archimate 3.0.1 specification 2017 (2017)
10. K. Tambralli, Configuration management database (CMDB) (2021)

Part IV
Practice: Sample Projects

Chapter 12
Enterprise Architecture Case Projects

André Vasconcelos and Pedro Sousa

Abstract This chapter presents three case studies where enterprise architecture (EA) approaches and design principles are applied. The case studies described are based on real-world projects and challenges. However, some data and information may have been changed for academic, scientific, or confidentiality reasons. For each case study the current business, information, application, and technology architectures are described; afterward several challenges are raised. The goal is to apply the EA and EC techniques introduced in the previous chapters to support the discussion and the decision making regarding the challenges presented. The first case study refers to the EA of the Urban Hygiene Unit of the Lisbon City Hall. The second case study addresses Técnico Lisboa faculty EA. Finally, the third EA case study deals with the public procurement process.

12.1 Case 1: Lisbon Smart City Enterprise Architecture[1]

The Municipal Unit of Urban Hygiene of Lisbon hired you to propose an enterprise architecture to transform Lisbon into a smart city. You will start by characterizing the current (AS-IS) enterprise architecture (EA) in order to set a common ground for defining the future path (TO-BE).

12.1.1 Introduction

The Municipal Unit of Urban Hygiene (Direção Municipal de Higiene Urbana, in Portuguese, DMHU) of the Lisbon City Council (CM-Lisboa) identified in its operation a set of opportunities that justify the definition of a strategic information systems plan, which should identify the current situation (scenario AS-IS) and

---

[1] Developed with the contribution of Professor Alberto Silva, Professor Joao Matos, and Lisbon City Hall (DMHU).

also propose improvements to be implemented in the medium term (TO-BE). The limitations provide an opportunity to review the entire circuit management system, as well as to point out measures at the level of the deposition systems, removal fleet, human resources, and management tools, namely, procedures, databases, and IT support infrastructures.

DMHU has a strong relationship with the areas of Human Resources and Finance of the City Council regarding HR (including the recruitment of prospective employees) and financial processes. The contractors and service suppliers and the Parish Councils assist DMHU in the pursuit of its mission, namely, when reporting events and requesting information from the Municipality. Reporting to the regulatory authority is also supported, and cooperation with external entities is developed.

12.1.2 Strategy

The strategy for the Urban Hygiene Unit is part of the Lisbon City Council strategy defined in [1].

The goals and results of DMHU in 2015 are described in the document [2].

12.1.3 Organization

DMHU is divided into two departments supported by seven structures. The Department of Urban Hygiene is, in turn, realized by four support centers and one division. The Repair and Maintenance Department consists of two divisions and a shared structure (Fig. 12.1).

The services provided by DMHU to the outside are structured around six topics:

- Urban hygiene
- Urban cleaning
- Urban hygiene projects
- Transport
- Environmental awareness
- Management of garages and repair shop

Please see document [3] for further details.

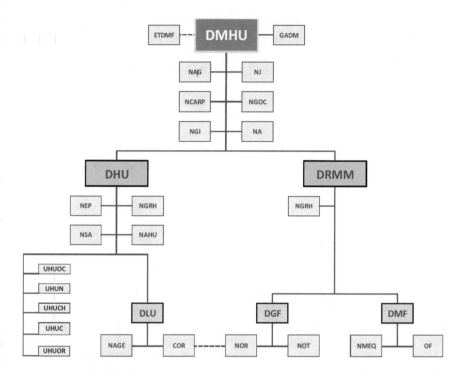

Fig. 12.1 DMHU structure

12.1.4   *Business Processes*

DMHU's core business is accomplished by five top business processes. Processes with external impact to the Municipality are Waste Collection Management and Relationship Management with the Citizen. HR Management and Warehouse Management are processes internal to DMHU. Fleet Management is another process with interaction with stakeholders external to DMHU (other municipal organic units).

The Waste Management process is structured into four subprocesses: i) planning and management of circuits, ii) management of deposition equipment and container sites, iii) execution of circuit collection, and iv) data registration and conference.

HR Management is developed through six level 1 processes. i) The Registration Management process ensures the creation and management of data of DMHU employees. ii) The HR incident management process includes the absences, attendance, overtime, and consequent payments to employees. iii) The Uniform Management, and Safety and Hygiene at Work process ensures uniform management and safety. iv) The Training Management ensures the definition of training programs and its management. v) The Vacation Management computes the vacations of each employee and updates the vacation information. Finally, vi) the performance management ensures the assessment of the employees' performance.

The Citizen Relationship Management process consists of three subprocesses. The process of interaction with Occurrence, Order, and Intervention Management (GOPI) ensures the creation of occurrences and requests for intervention at DMHU, as well as the passing of information between the GOPI and the application "Na Minha Rua Lx" ("In my street Lisbon"). The level 1 process that ensures the assessment of the citizen's requests includes the analysis of the request, requests for pests and pigeons, deposition equipment, events, requests for collection, inspection, complaints and suggestions, other types of requests, and also the management, parametrization, and monitoring.

12.1.5   Information

DMHU defines circuits for collecting garbage in Selective Collection Points (PRS). On the other hand, there are work orders, which address assistance requests (which add one or more occurrences of citizens), assigned to employees and inquiry sheets that list equipment (such as machines and vehicles). DMHU employees may also make requests to the warehouse for additional stocks (movable inventory assets).

Occurrences (complaints or suggestions) may have an associated response (and service response, internal to the DMHU), and are created by the citizens. Work orders, which may be the result of requests for assistance, have associated occurrences. Work orders aggregate operations (internal or external) and are assigned to employees.

Regarding Human Resources, the DMHU employee information is composed of his or her attendance information, accidents at work, overtime, incidents, medical aptitude record, and performance evaluation. The employee also attends training actions (integrated into the training course that forms the training plan). Uniforms are also given to the workers (including personal protective equipment). The circuits and work orders are assigned to employees.

Selective Collection Point (SCP, or PRS, in Portuguese) is also an important information, specialized in eight types (selective door-to-door, non-selective door-to-door, container fixing support, underground compactors, surface ecopoint, underground ecoisland, surface ecopoint, and door-to door SCP entity). It has a container location and deposition equipment. The circuits add several Selective Collection Points, freights, support areas, and unloading locations.

Regarding uniform management, the uniforms are given to employees, along with personal protective equipment. The equipment (which is subject to periodic inspection) can also be machines and vehicles (from which movements are recorded). Machines and vehicles can be assigned to garages. The machines are further classified into small and large machines (such as compactor and auto-compactor). On the other hand, the warehouse holds stocks (which are movable goods and inventory), which employees can request.

12.1.6   Current Applications

DMHU has used numerous computer applications over the years. Several of these applications have been developed and maintained internally by its support services (referred to as Internal Applications), while others are provided and maintained by third parties or by the central IT Department of the Lisbon City Council.

The main applications that support the DMHU processes are next described.

12.1.6.1   Relationship Management with the Citizen

The following applications are used to support and manage the relationship between the Lisbon City Council and the outside:

- Na Minha Rua Lx (Application_Web, CML-DSI Development). The events portal of the Lisbon City Council (CM-Lisboa), available at https://naminharualx. cm-lisboa.pt/, where a citizen reports problems in public spaces about municipal equipment and urban hygiene that require the intervention of CM-Lisboa or the Parish Councils
- LxRequests (Application_Desktop, Internal Development). Control of requests, complaints, compliments, and requests for information; complaint management in complaint book; interconnection with LU in handling containers by request; interconnection with urban cleaning application (LU) in handling PRS; management of joint surveys; timing and management of specific collections (monsters, greens, debris, and paper); management to support events; management of participation for administrative offenses; record of pest and pigeon control activity

12.1.6.2   Human Resource Management

Support applications for internal HR management at DMHU:

- RH2011 (Human Resources at DMHU) (Application_Desktop, Internal Development). It allows the administrative management of Human Resources with the following functions: employee registration, automation of the creation of evaluation files, postings of daily occurrences (vacations, absences, leave, and work), vacation management; provision of overtime work, elaboration of payment maps, training management, uniform management and EPIS, and social balance.
- RelgioPonto (Application_Desktop, Actuasys Development). Attendance control based on time clock system.
- SST (Workplace Safety System) (Application_Desktop, Internal Development). It includes the entire area of preventive medicine (occupational medicine consultations and issuance of aptitude sheets), professional diseases, accidents, treatments, costs, appointments, calls, etc. Notice that the Medicine at Work

component will be assumed by a new application that is in the acquisition phase; the Workplace Accident Management Component is being migrated to an application developed on Oracle.

12.1.6.3 Urban Cleaning Management

The applications that support the circuit management and urban cleaning management are:

- LU (Urban Clean) (Application_Desktop, Internal Development). Allows Urban Collection Management with the following functions: (i) management of tasks and circuits, (ii) collection point management (PRS), (iii) management of request locations and bag addresses, (iv) producer management, (v) management of container handling, (vi) management of bag delivery, (vii) management of the placement and maintenance of paper bins, (viii) parameterization of vehicles assigned to DHU, (ix) management of mechanical equipment, (x) management of the scales, and (xi) management of freight, weights, transported waste, etc.

  The LU application provides a set of interfaces (using views from the AMOS database), which allow it to be used by third-party applications (maintained by the CM-Lisbon IT), namely, through the Open Data platform of Lisbon. These interfaces provide the following information: collective collection points, community composters, domestic composters, paper receiving centers, ecoislands, underground ecoislands, ecopoints, collection of used food oils, billions, WEEE collection, container fixing support, and glass recycling container.

- Scale (Scale in Operations Management) (Application_Desktop, Internal Development). Application responsible for managing the Service Scales. Its main functionalities are related to the planning of circuits and the allocation of human resources to these circuits. The assignment of employees to their tasks is automatic as long as they are assigned to a circuit and the employee presence is recorded in the biometric system. Subsequently, HTML files are generated that are projected on the televisions of the Operation Center (COR).

- LU_SIG (LU GIS Toolbar) (Application_Desktop, Internal Development). Plugin developed for ArcGIS originally by ESRI, which allows the management of circuits under maps in ArcGIS and interacts directly with circuit management (LU). It was migrated internally from VBA to VB.NET to work on ArcGIS 10.

- Bee2Waste (Dynamic Circuits) (Application_Web, Compta Development). This application is used to plan, optimize, execute, and monitor the usage, maintenance, and other activities of the assets. This application is used to plan dynamic circuits based on the equipment's level of filling.

- Pigeons (Pigeon Management) (Application_Mobile, Internal Development). It allows to register and manage the habits and catches of pigeons.

- Paper Bins (Paper Bins Management) (Application_Mobile, Internal Development). It allows the registration in the field of the movements and maintenance of the paper bins.

12.1.6.4 Fleet Management

Applications that support fleet and vehicle management:

- GIF (Integrated Fleet Management) (Application_Desktop, Quidgest Development). GIF is an asset management application, assets being understood as everything that needs to be managed within an organization including fixed assets, movable assets, vehicles, etc., which is particularly relevant, in this case, for the management of municipal vehicles. This application is used to plan, optimize, execute, and monitor the use, maintenance, and other activities of the managed assets, covering the date of their acquisition, operation, maintenance, and disposal, that is, the entire lifecycle of the asset. It involves the components of asset management (mobile and real estate), fleet management, maintenance management, claims management, and stock and supply management. GIF provides an interface (GIF database link) that allows to consult about vehicle availability, vehicle data that are in the workshop, data related to work orders, and vehicle registration data.
- Municipal Fleet (Application_Desktop, Internal Development). It allows to consult requests made in GIF in a more intelligible and aggregated way.
- Cartrack (Cartrack—GPS System) (Application_Web, Cartrack Development). Vehicle geolocation system. Cartrack provides the Cartrack API interface.

12.1.6.5 Equipment, Uniforms, and Consumables Management

The applications that support equipment management, uniforms, and consumables are:

- Stocks (Stock Management) (Application_Desktop, Internal Development). Management of material requisitions and uniforms. It only contemplates the mechanism for issuing requisitions and delivery notes in order to highlight equipment deliveries. Contrary to what its name suggests, it does not perform stock management. It also allows to control the duration periods of the different uniforms as the forecast of future consumption.
- SAP_SRM (SAP Supplier Relationship Management) (Application_Web, SAP Development). Management of consumable orders to CML Central Warehouse.

12.1.6.6 Other Applications

Other applications that support the actions carried out by the DMHU are:

- Projects (Management of Awareness Actions) (Application_Desktop, Internal Development). Registration of awareness-raising activity, namely, in terms of recording interactions with partners and in accounting for the public present in the actions.

- ProcIndemin (Administrative Processes, Management of Insurance Processes) (Application_Desktop, Internal Development). Monitoring of administrative proceedings (i.e., requests for compensation), namely, in terms of controlling legal deadlines.
- POIs (Points of Interest Management) (Application_Desktop, Internal Development). It allows the creation and characterization of places of interest. It has been used intermittently to register places of interest to keep them under surveillance. It allows assigning coordinates and other characteristics to points; in addition to having a structured register, it allows to create configurable maps.
- GML (External Inspection) (Application_Desktop, Internal Development). It allows the registration of joint inspection actions with the Municipal Police (PM), Hospital Waste, and Photographic Archive of the Inspection Action.
- Vehicle (Vehicle Park Management) (Application_Desktop, Internal Development). Management of the CML car park: When vehicles are collected by the Municipal Police (PM), they are parked in facilities located in Vale do Forno. Through this application, DMHU can track the movements that the vehicle makes in the park and record information relevant to the process of destroying or returning the vehicle.
- SF-PM (PM Inspection Services) (Application_Mobile, Internal Development). Update information on previously loaded requests; collect evidence for transgression; register joint inspection activity with the PM; register inspection actions by hospital producers.
- TNC (Treatment of Non-Conformities (Quality)) (Application_Desktop, Internal Development). Treatment of non-conformities within the scope of the quality management process supporting the monitoring of the result of audits.
- GESCOR (Correspondence Management) (Application_Web, GFI Development). It allows the registration of incoming files, enabling the tracking of processes within the organization. It also allows the production of documents that support the processes.
- SAPFINANCAS (SAP-Finanças) (Application_Desktop, SAP Development). Financial Management Program used by CML.
- GIC (Integrated Management of Offenses) (Application_Web, SYSNO-VARE Development). Application of integrated management of offense processes.

Other applications (developed internally at DMHU) used by other entities:

- GestPet (Animal Management) (Application_Desktop, Internal Development). Management of the Lisbon house of animals (entrances and exits of animals). Note: It is exclusively used by the Green Spaces Management Business Unit.

12.1.6.7 Transverse Support Applications

Support applications that are of transversal internal use:

- GestSis (Application Management and DMHU Systems) (Application_Desktop, Internal Development). The DMHU's application and system management system, including the management of apps, users, and access.
- MeiosRec (Means and Resources Management) (Application_Desktop, Internal Development). Management of entities, employees, and contacts (internal and external). A collaborator can only exist in a system associated with an entity.
- Documents (Application_Desktop, Internal Development). Document management—production and monitoring of document circuit at the DMHU.
- CCustos (Cost Center) (Application_Desktop, Internal Development). It allows the management of cost centers.
- SendMessages (Sending messages via Email and SMS) (Application_Server, Internal Development). Application components that support the remaining internal applications for sending email messages (SendMail interface) and SMS (smsdb interface).

12.1.7 Current Infrastructure

12.1.7.1 Technological Infrastructure

The technological infrastructure that supports the applications is made of a set of physical machines (hardware), virtual machines, and other servers (e.g., operating systems, database servers). In general, internal applications, as mentioned above, are desktop applications installed in desktop machines or laptops with Windows operating system. There are also some mobile applications installed in smartphones with Android operating system. The machines/servers are maintained by the central information system department (DSI) of the Lisbon City Council (CM-Lisbon).

12.1.7.2 Support Artifacts

The internal applications consist of (i) desktop applications for Windows, developed on the Microsoft Windows Forms environment and (ii) mobile applications for Android developed on these technologies, and with common access to the AMOS database. In addition, the following frameworks and software libraries are used in the development of desktop applications:

- Framework internal to DMHU (DHURS—Framework.dll, internal). Application library with most of the objects used in the construction of applications; this library simplifies the maintenance of objects used across applications.
- Microsoft App Interop (ADODB.dll, Interop.ADODB.dll, Interop.ADOX.dll; Microsoft). Framework that supports data transfer between applications.
- MapWindows GIS OpenSource (AxInterop.MapWinGIS.dll, Interop.MapWin GIS.dll; https://www.mapwindow.org/). Framework for viewing georeferenced data.
- Microsoft Office Interop (Interop.Excel.dll, Interop.Word.dll, Interop.Office.dll, Interop. Microsoft.Office.Core.dll, Microsoft.Vbe.Interop.dll, Office.dll; Microsoft). Framework that supports the management, reading, and writing of office files.
- Oracle Instant Client (stdole.dll, oci.dll, ocijdbc11.dll, ociw32.dll, Oracle.DataAccess.dll, oran-nzsbb11.dll, oraocci11.dll, oraociei11.dll, orasql11.dll, ojdbc5.jar, ojdbc6.jar; Oracle). Framework installed on desktop clients to access Oracle databases.
- iTextSharp (itextsharp.dll; Opensource https://github.com/itext/itextsharp). Opensource library for interacting with PDF files.
- NetSpell—spell checker for .NET (NetSpell.SpellChecker.dll; Opensource www. codeproject.com). Library with spell checker.

12.1.8   Project Goals

DMHU Director has just hired your enterprise architecture services. He requested that you recommend him the enterprise architecture that DMHU should implement in the next 5 years; in order to do that, you need answers to the following questions:

1. Context

   a. What is the context of DMHU? Who are DMHU stakeholders and what concerns do they have?
   b. Which business units are involved in managing the flows between DMHU and its context?

2. Products and Services

   a. Which products and services are provided by DMHU? To which stakeholders?

3. Big Picture

   a. What is DMHU's big picture?

4. Strategy (Means and Ends)

   a. What are the drivers, goals, principles, and requirements for DMHU?

    b. Are there any goals, principles, or requirements that are contradictory among themselves?

    c. Are there any goals, principles, or requirements that are misaligned or not considered in the remaining enterprise architecture?

    d. What are the gaps among the DMHU drivers and goals of 2015 activity plan and the results achieved?

5. Organization Structure

    a. What is the organization structure (and roles) of DMHU?

6. Business Process

    a. What are the core DMHU processes (Levels 0, 1, 2)?

      i. Inputs/outputs: Information entities
      ii. Roles/actors
      iii. For the Waste Collection Management process (AS-IS), it is requested that you describe and characterize using ArchiMate (present your assumptions for describing this process), including:

        A. The flow
        B. The inputs and outputs
        C. The critical points
        D. The break points

7. Information Entities

    a. What information entities support the business processes?

      i. Major attributes
      ii. (Business) Identifier
      iii. Inmon classification for the attributes

    b. What are the structural relations among the information entities?

    c. In which business processes are the information entities created, updated, read, or deleted?

8. Application Architecture

    a. AS-IS

      i. What are the current applications that support DMHU processes?
      ii. What processes and information does each application support?
      iii. What approach do you recommend to classify each application as keep, discontinue, and don't know? Explain in detail your approach.

    b. TO-BE

      i. Ideally, what applications should be available at DMHU considering its business processes and information management (just considering the AS-IS business processes and information)? Or stated differently, if DMHU had no applications whatsoever, what applications would you recommend to support the current business and information?

ii. Considering the ideal application landscape computed above, review your answer to 8.a.iii, and propose a roadmap for each application. Typical roadmap guidelines are maintain, discard, replace, consolidate (with another), improve functionalities, or upgrade technology.

iii. Do you recommend the usage of any application patterns?

iv. What application architecture do you recommend? Model the proposed application architecture, including the application functions and services provided or consumed by the business and by other applications.

v. Besides the application structure, present the application usage, the application cooperation, and the application behavior viewpoints.

9. IT Architecture

a. What are the different technological options for implementing the applications?

b. Do you recommend any existing software package? Which are available? How do you compare them?

c. Do you recommend a custom development for all the applications? Or an off-the-shelf software package? Explain your analysis.

d. What is the processing infrastructure that you recommend? What about storage? And communication?

e. What is your recommendation for the IT architecture?

f. What are the dependencies between the IT infrastructure and the applications? Where does each application will run?

g. How did you implement each guideline or pattern in the EA of DMHU? Do you recommend considering some other guidelines?

10. Roadmap

a. What project roadmap do you recommend? Which solutions/applications should be implemented first? Where would you start?

b. Considering existing applications (AS-IS), propose a global roadmap for the change.

The report should answer the questions above using views in ArchiMate, BPMN, UML, matrix, graphs, and supporting text. This will involve choosing the most appropriate viewpoint to support your answers.

12.2   Case 2: Instituto Superior Técnico Enterprise Architecture

You have been hired to propose a new enterprise architecture for Instituto Superior Técnico (IST) faculty.

12.2.1   Introduction

Instituto Superior Técnico aims to contribute to the development of the society, promoting and sharing excellence in higher education in the fields of architecture, engineering, and science and technology. Técnico offers bachelor, master, and PhD programs and lifelong training and develops research, development, and innovation (RD&I) activities, which are essential to provide an education based on the top international standards—see Fig. 12.2.

Técnico is part of Lisbon University, the largest and the most competitive university in Portugal, and is recognized as a prestigious school at national and international level, namely, in the fields of engineering and science and technology. It comprises Portugalś most prestigious laboratories and RD&I centers.

Técnico offers a wide variety of courses to study, both at the undergraduate and graduate levels, and it is actively involved in several international mobility programs. IST has significantly contributed to creating cutting-edge science and technology, which is the main goal of the school.

12.2.2   Location

Técnico operation is located in three campuses: Alameda, Taguspark, and Tecnológico e Nuclear—see Fig. 12.3.

12.2.3   Organization

Técnico is managed through:[2]

- School bodies
- Other bodies
- Academic units
- Cross-cutting platforms
- Research units of IST
- IST associated research units
- Specialized units
- Administrative and technical support services

---

[2] Técnico organization is described here: https://tecnico.ulisboa.pt/en/about-tecnico/institutional/organisation/.

Facts and figures

1911

Instituto Superior Técnico was founded on 23rd May 1911 by Alfredo Bensaude.

42%

Of students get a job before graduation.

86%

Of graduates get a job within six months after graduation.

77%

Of 2nd Cycle graduates are employed in their field of study.

11.412

Técnico students enrolled.

2.237

Scientific publications in ISI Web of Science, of which 14 highly cited papers, 1 hot paper and 1 highly cited researchers.

53

Spin-off companies created at Técnico since 2009.

3

Técnico has 3 campuses (Alameda, Taguspark and CTN).

3

Técnico provides accommodation in 3 student residences.

31%

Of international students attend a PhD programme.

Fig. 12.2 Técnico facts and figures (source: https://tecnico.ulisboa.pt/)

Alameda

Located in one of Lisbon's most central areas, Alameda campus is surrounded by a wide range of public transportation network, allowing easy access to all points of the city. There are a wide range of cultural, leisure and sports activities around the campus.

> More information about Alameda Campus

Taguspark

Located in Oeiras, this modern campus was inaugurated in 2000, and it's part of Taguspark – Science and Technology Park, one of the most important technological parks across the country, namely in the area of information and communication technologies.

> More information about Taguspark Campus

Tecnológico e Nuclear

Located in Loures, CTN – Tecnológico e Nuclear Campus is one of the most important technology parks across the country, namely in areas related to nuclear sciences, as well as in the field of radiological protection and nuclear safety.

> More information about CTN - Tecnológico e Nuclear Campus

Fig. 12.3 Técnico campuses (source: https://tecnico.ulisboa.pt/)

12.2.4   Strategy

The strategic plan of IST[3] is materialized in a series of initiatives at the management and the operational levels, which have been grouped together into 11 focus areas; see Fig. 12.4.

The focus areas of the EA cover the three components of the core missions of IST (higher education, research, development & innovation and technology transfer) but also include the support and the cross-cutting areas. The three cross-cutting focus areas are shared by all the core activities of IST, closely associated with the needs of a global organization (internationalization and communication) and the need to consider a new aspect of the school organization, its multipolar operation across three distinct campuses. The core activities of IST depend mainly on its Human

---

[3] In terms of strategy, Técnico strategy is described here: https://tecnico.ulisboa.pt/files/2015/07/plano-estrategico-2015.pdf.

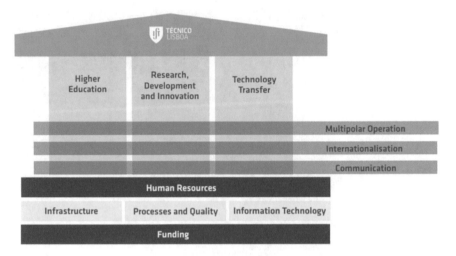

Fig. 12.4 Técnico strategic focus areas (source: https://tecnico.ulisboa.pt/files/2015/07/plano-estrategico-2015.pdf)

Resources, which themselves depend on the support of a number of different areas whose development is addressed in this plan: infrastructure, processes and quality, and information technology. Finally, all the development strategy rests on adequate and flexible funding resources, which have to be further developed in order to make IST as independent as possible from the fluctuations that are inherent to public funding. Please also consider Técnico activity plan described in https://aepq.tecnico. ulisboa.pt/files/sites/22/plano-de-atividades-ist-2017.pdf and the results achieved described in https://aepq.tecnico.ulisboa.pt/files/sites/22/ra-ist-2017_vfinal.pdf.

12.2.5   Business Process and Information

For the purpose of this case study, assume that Técnico business processes are described by the Charles Sturt University (CSU) models.[4] For further detail on the process architecture, please consider that Técnico follows the APQC Process Classification Framework for Education.[5]

Regardless of the above models, assume that Técnico information architecture is based on the following concepts:

---

[4] http://www.csu.edu.au/__data/assets/pdf_file/0003/51924/process-model-wpp.pdf.

[5] https://www.apqc.org/knowledge-base/documents/apqc-process-classification-framework-pcf-education-excel-version-721.

- Students, teachers, nonteaching staff, Erasmus students, enrollment, enrollment fees, diplomas
- Departments, BA, MA, PhD, curriculum programs, courses, classes, schedules
- Academic exams, course exams
- Accounting, property, wages, real contracts, service contracts, shopping
- Campus, buildings, rooms, equipment, laboratories
- Control point, training, vacations, career and faults of staff and teachers
- Research projects, research institutes, non-faculty researchers, scientific publications
- Library, books, book loans, canteen
- Travel, sabbatical
- Faculty reviews, disciplines reviews, and staff reviews

In addition to these entities, you should also consider those that are implicit (as required) to implement the adopted models of CSU.

12.2.6   EA Guidelines

Consider that Técnico has defined the following principles and guidelines:

- Components are centralized.
- Front-office processes are separated from back-office processes.
- Data is provided by the source.
- Data is captured once.
- IT systems communicate through services.
- Business units are autonomous.
- Management layers are minimized.
- IT systems adhere to open standards.
- IT systems are preferably open source.
- All messages are exchanged through the enterprise service bus.
- Software components are multi-platform.

12.2.7   Project Goals

Técnico's President has just hired your enterprise architecture services. He requested that you recommend him the enterprise architecture that Técnico should implement in the next 5 years' in order to do that, you need answers to the following questions:

1. Context
    a. What is the context of Técnico? Who are Técnico stakeholders and what concerns do they have?

    b. Which business units are involved in managing the flows between Técnico and its context?

2. Products and Services

    a. Which products and services are provided by Técnico? To which stakeholders?

3. Big Picture

    a. What is Técnico's big picture?

4. Strategy (Means and Ends)

    a. What are the drivers, goals, principles, and requirements for Técnico?
    b. Are there any goals, principles, or requirements that are contradictory among themselves?
    c. Are there any goals, principles, or requirements that are misaligned or not considered in the remaining enterprise architecture?
    d. What are the gaps among the Técnico drivers and goals of 2017 activity plan and the results achieved?

5. Business Process
    What are the core Técnico processes?

    a. Inputs/outputs: Information entities
    b. Roles/actors

6. Organization Structure

    a. What is the organization structure (and roles) of Técnico?

7. Information Entities

    a. What information entities support the business processes?

       i. Major attributes
      ii. (Business) Identifier
     iii. Inmon classification for the attributes

    b. What are the structural relations among the information entities?
    c. In which business processes are the information entities created, updated, read, or deleted?

8. Application Architecture.
    You are requested to propose the application architecture to Técnico, including:

    a. What applications should be available at Técnico considering its business processes and information management?
    b. Do you recommend the usage of any application patterns?

     c. What application architecture do you recommend? Model the proposed application architecture, including the application functions and services provided or consumed by the business and by other applications.

     d. Besides the application structure, please also present the application usage, the application cooperation, and the application behavior viewpoints.

9. IT Architecture

     a. What are the different technological options for implementing the applications?

     b. Do you recommend any existing software package? Which are available? How do you compare them?

     c. Do you recommend a custom development for all the applications? Or an off-the-shelf software package? Explain your analysis.

     d. What is the processing infrastructure that you recommend? What about storage? And communications?

     e. What is your recommendation for the IT architecture?

     f. What are the dependencies between the IT infrastructure and the applications? Where does each application will run?

     g. How did you implement each guideline or pattern in the EA of Técnico? Do you recommend considering some other guidelines?

10. Roadmap

     a. What project roadmap do you recommend? Which solutions/applications should be implemented first? Where would you start?

The report should answer the questions above using views in ArchiMate, BPMN, UML, matrix, graphs, and supporting text. This will involve choosing the most appropriate viewpoint to support your answers.

12.3   Case 3: Public Procurement Enterprise Architecture

12.3.1   Introduction

Procurement is a central process for any public or private organization. Procurement for government (or public administration) organizations has very well-defined rules and processes which must be applicable, when a public agency buys goods or services such as cars, builds a bridge or a road, buys consulting services, and acquires hardware or software or any product or service that is provided by the market. Government procurement processes look for robustness and transparency while permitting innovative solutions that reflect the scale, scope, and risk of the desired outcome. In the beginning of this millennium, Portugal was a pioneer country moving to an electronic procurement process within public administration. This case study is focused on modeling the current (AS-IS) Portuguese Public

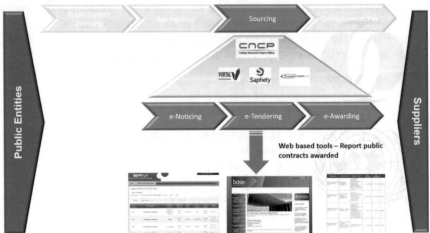

Fig. 12.5 Public Procurement in Portugal overview

Procurement Enterprise Architecture and assessing the impact of different scenarios for evolution.

12.3.1.1   AS-IS

At a high level the Public Procurement in Portugal is described according to Fig. 12.5.

12.3.1.2   Motivation

The major motivations for public procurement are:

1. Value for money
2. Encouraging competition
3. Efficient, effective, and ethical procurement
4. Accountability and transparency in procurement
5. Reducing the risk

12.3.1.3   Business Components

For the purpose of this case study, consider that the business processes that support procurement are described in [4].

Some of the stakeholders involved in the Portuguese Public Procurement process are:

1. IMPIC—http://www.impic.pt/
2. eSPap—https://www.espap.gov.pt/
3. AMA—https://www.ama.gov.pt/web/english
4. GNS—https://www.gns.gov.pt/
5. Tribunal de Contas—https://www.tcontas.pt/
6. INCM—https://www.incm.pt/
7. Public platforms (see updated list at http://www.base.gov.pt/Base/pt/Plataformas Eletronicas/EntidadesCertificadas)
8. European Commission
9. Public administration agencies and departments (buyers)
10. Suppliers

The role of each organization within the public procurement process is described, for example, at Law 96/2015, Art. 34 (see https://www.anacom.pt/render.jsp? contentId=1379112.)

12.3.1.4   Information Architecture

Some of the information assets used in the procurement process are:

1. Tender
2. Organization
3. Identifier
4. Address
5. Contact point
6. Item
7. Classification
8. Unit
9. Document
10. Lot
11. Bid
12. Parameter
13. Lot value
14. Award
15. Question
16. Complaint
17. Contract
18. Period
19. Date
20. Value
21. Revision
22. Cancellation
23. Feature

Notice that you may identify other information entities and attributes.[6]

12.3.1.5   Information System Components

Currently public procurement process is supported (from the perspective of any Portuguese public agency) in three major system components:

1. All the financial aspects of the acquisition process are supported by GERFIP, a SAP Finance Module implementation for the Portuguese public administration (see https://www.espap.pt/spfin/Paginas/spfin.aspx).
   The following SAP modules are implemented in GERFIP:

   a. AA: Asset accounting
   b. MM: Material management expenditure process
   c. SD: Sales and distribution sales process
   d. FI-TR: Treasury solutions and POCP accounting
   e. CO: Analytics accounting
   f. EAPS: Budget accounting

   GERFIP is provided to public organizations in a software-as-a-service approach by another public agency: eSPap.
2. The approach to the market, and the evaluation, submissions, and tender conclusion and contract signature processes are supported by public procurement platforms.
3. All the remaining activities within the procurement process are done without a support of a specific system, including the planning of the procurement, the procurement scope, the determination of the procurement method, and the preparation of the market approach. Most organizations support these activities using email systems and paper-based workflows.

12.3.1.6   Technological Components

From a technological perspective assume the following:

1. GERFIP is a central system shared by all public agencies supported in the following technological platforms:

   a. Presentation layer. The presentation layer is provided through Java Server Pages (JSP) and Business Server Pages (BSP).
   b. Business layer. The business layer consists of a J2EE 5 run-time environment that processes the requests passed from the Internet Communication Manager

---

[6] Please see open procurement project for further details: http://api-docs.openprocurement.org/en/latest/standard/index.html.

(ICM) and dynamically generates the responses. The business logic is written in Java (J2EE).

c. Integration layer. The local integration engine is an integral part of SAP Web AS and allows instant connection to SAP. The local integration engine provides messaging services that exchange messages between the components that are connected in SAP.

d. Connectivity layer. The Internet Communication Manager (ICM) dispatches user interface requests to the presentation layer and provides a single framework for connectivity using various communication protocols (e.g., HTTP, HTTPS, SMTP, SOAP, CGI).

e. Persistence layer. The persistence layer is supported in an Oracle 11g Enterprise Edition implemented on a Linux Red Hat Enterprise operating system in a cluster with four physical servers.

f. The connectivity, integration, business, and presentation layers are implemented in virtual machines (two VMs for each layer) that are supported in a six-blade server and a shared EMC storage (also used for the persistence layer).

2. From an infrastructure point of view, assume that the public procurement platform is supported on a Microsoft Windows server 2012 infrastructure with:

a. Database: Microsoft SQL Server 2012.
b. Active directory.
c. Microsoft SharePoint 2013 that supports the business logic.
d. IIS web server.
e. Search and document indexing is done through Microsoft FAST engine.
f. All components are redundant and there are three different security network zones for the database, web, and business logic.
g. All servers are virtual and are supported on a farm of four physical servers and an HP storage.

3. The email server used by most public agencies is a Microsoft Exchange 2019, and the client uses laptops with Windows, Outlook 2019, and Firefox browsers.

12.3.2   *Public Procurement Interoperability Initiative (TO-BE)*

In order to move the Portuguese Public Procurement to the "next level," an interoperability initiative is being implemented (see Portuguese law 96/2015). Currently, each buyer has access to a single public procurement platform, and only the suppliers enrolled in that specific platform are able to receive information or present proposals. Therefore, suppliers are required to be enrolled in several (or even all) procurement platforms (e.g., acinGov, anoGov, comprasPT, gatewit, saphetyGov, and vortalGov) to be able to present proposals to different public agencies. The major goal of the public procurement interoperability initiative is to allow each supplier (and buyer) to use a single platform and be able to interact with buyers enrolled in other platforms. The business services that platforms are expected to provide among each other are:

1. Pronounce in preliminary hearing
2. Access to procedures and published requests for proposals
3. Complaints and disputes
4. Participation in electronic auction
5. Award decision
6. Messaging
7. Qualification document delivery
8. Submission of proposals
9. Complaints on the draft contract
10. Requests for clarification and lists of errors and omissions
11. View posts and warnings created by contracting authorities

Besides these services that each platform must provide, the IMPIC and other public procurement governance entities request to have monitor and control functionalities on all acquisition procedures (gathering information from procurement platforms). Additionally AMA provides an integration platform (iAP; see http://www.iap.gov.pt/) that is being considered (among other options) to be part of the solution architecture. The Portuguese Government needs your help in selecting the right approach and solution architecture to support public procurement according to law 96/2015, in order to achieve interoperability among public procurement platforms, including an orchestration versus a coordination approach.

12.3.3   The Project to Be Done

Your mission is to propose a plan for the government to achieve the goals of their interoperability initiative for public procurement and to dematerialize and optimize the public procurement process. Your deliverables will be used to guide the interoperability initiative architecture decisions and as a reference architecture for public procurement within the public administration. Namely, your team is expected to contribute for:

1. Modeling of the AS-IS enterprise architecture from a business and system perspective
2. Identification of misalignments at the AS-IS, among IT, information systems, business processes, and strategy
3. Designing and modeling the TO-BE enterprise architecture considering the interoperability initiative and the support of procurement activities within a public agency, including the impacts in the strategy, business process, information, information systems, applications, and technology (analyzing different information system scenarios and proposing one)

4. Proposing an implementation plan that ensures the elimination of the AS-IS gaps and supports the interoperability initiative implementation

References

1. C.M. de Lisboa, Grandes opções do plano para a cidade de Lisboa (2018). Available online at https://www.am-lisboa.pt/documentos/1545323718T4cDF1de1Ud05OZ5.pdf
2. C.M. de Lisboa, Direção municipal de higiene urbana – relatório de atividades 2015 (in Portuguese) (2016). Available at https://sites.google.com/view/eacbook/
3. C.M. de Lisboa, Estrutura organizacional da direção municipal de higiene urbana- reorganização dos serviços e novo organograma (in Portuguese) (2019). Available at https://sites.google.com/view/eacbook/
4. Austrian Government, Procurement Process Considerations (2016)

Printed in the United States
by Baker & Taylor Publisher Services